The Revival of Realism

The Revival of Realism

CRITICAL STUDIES
IN CONTEMPORARY PHILOSOPHY
BY
JAMES FEIBLEMAN

KENNIKAT PRESS
Port Washington, N. Y./London

THE REVIVAL OF REALISM

Copyright, 1946, by The University of North Carolina Press
Reissued in 1972 by Kennikat Press by arrangement
Library of Congress Catalog Card No: 78-159053
ISBN 0-8046-1654-X

Manufactured by Taylor Publishing Company   Dallas, Texas

ESSAY AND GENERAL LITERATURE INDEX REPRINT SERIES

Acknowledgments

CERTAIN PORTIONS OF THIS BOOK have appeared in periodical form. I wish to thank the *Journal of Higher Education* for permission to reprint "Science from the Standpoint of Realism"; the Library of Living Philosophers for permission to reprint "A Reply to Russell's Introduction to the Second Edition of *The Principles of Mathematics*," reprinted here as "Russell's Infidelity to Realism," which appeared in *The Philosophy of Bertrand Russell;* the Oxford University Press for permission to reprint certain passages from *A Study of History,* by Arnold J. Toynbee, used in "Toynbee's Theory of History," which appeared in the *T'ien Hsia Monthly* in Peking (now unhappily defunct); *Philosophy and Phenomenological Research* for permission to reprint "Pragmatism and Inverse Probability" and "How to Read a Word"; *Social Science* for permission to reprint "Have We Exhausted Greek Culture?"; the *International Journal of Psychology* for permission to reprint "The Logic of Psychoanalysis," and the *Journal of General Psychology* for permission to reprint "Individual Psychology and the Ethics of Peirce."

J. F.

New Orleans
August, 1945

Contents

PART I

INTRODUCTION: From Nominalism to Realism . . . 3

PART II
THE REVIVAL IN PHILOSOPHY

I. The Realism of Charles S. Peirce 31
II. Whitehead's Philosophy of Organism 46
III. An Estimate of Dewey 84
IV. Lovejoy's Revolt Against Realism 99
V. Pragmatism and Inverse Probability 137

PART III
THE REVIVAL IN HISTORY

VI. Have We Exhausted Greek Culture? 153
VII. Toynbee's Theory of History 164

PART IV
THE REVIVAL IN SCIENCE

VIII. Science from the Standpoint of Realism 223
IX. The Definition of Science 241
X. The Relation of Logic to Experiment 251

PART V
THE REVIVAL IN SEMANTICS

XI. How to Read a Word 257
XII. Russell's Infidelity to Realism 269
XIII. Toward the Metaphysics of Symbolic Logic . . . 288

PART VI
THE REVIVAL IN PSYCHOLOGY

XIV. The Logic of Psychoanalysis 305
XV. Individual Psychology and the Ethics of Peirce . . 320
Index 325

Part I
From Nominalism to Realism

From Nominalism to Realism

THE RECURRENCE OF realism in the modern world is a philosophical event of sufficient importance to call for some explanation. The struggle between realism—the doctrine that universals, which have their being independently both of concrete and actual things and of thoughts, are as real as concrete things, and nominalism—the opposing doctrine that actual physical particulars (i.e., concrete things) or thoughts are alone real, has furnished the occasion for much misunderstanding. Now one tradition has seemed to triumph, now another. In the ancient Greek world, philosophy was led by realism. Since the Middle Ages in Europe philosophy has been predominantly nominalistic. But, on the other hand, realism has never completely died out, having survived its leanest years by cropping up from time to time in the illogical insights of theoretical nominalists. There has always been a certain amount of realism, too, making itself felt in the implicit presuppositions behind activities.

Some years ago anyone who discovered realism for himself, the hard way, would have thought that he was a pioneer; and he would have been shocked and delighted to discover that many others had from time to time held this world-view with him, beginning with the very greatest figures, those of Plato and Socrates. He would have understood from a study of the *Dialogues* that he had not, after all, discovered an entirely new position, but he might still have thought that almost alone he had revived it.

Therefore a second, and in some ways an even greater, shock would have awaited him. For he might have been feeling terribly isolated—a realist lost in the midst of the forest of nominalism. Then to his utter surprise, he would have begun to discover other realists, and what is more, to discover them among his contemporaries. They existed, he would have found, not only among the philosophers but among workers in other fields of inquiry. Thus, glancing about him as he moved forward toward the interpretation of cultural phenomena in terms of the philosophy of realism, he would soon have been made to understand that he was progressing, but not alone; that he was indeed in the midst of a vast concerted movement, none the less a movement for not being explicitly one, which has since come to be called the revival of realism. In the following chapters, we shall try to examine some of the evidence, both positive and negative, of this revival; but before doing so several tasks must be accomplished, in order to make the complexities of the movement more comprehensible. We shall endeavor, therefore, in this introductory chapter to show (I) what realism, and its contradictory, nominalism, mean; (II) how nominalism triumphed for a while and how realism, so to speak, went underground; and finally (III) what forms realism takes in the modern world and who in general are its advocates.

I

In the miniature theatre of ideas which was the Greek world, we may discern the origins of all modern philosophers. Attic Greece survived for only a short period, but that length of time sufficed to set the problems which the next twenty-five centuries struggled over, and which, in only slightly altered form, are with us today. A survey of the history of philosophy reveals that there are only three radically different metaphysical positions which it is possible for anyone at any date and place to assume. These three philosophies are furnished us, with their respective strengths and weaknesses clearly set forth, in the writings of Plato. There we see that Plato himself wavered between two of these positions, defending one or another against his opponents, the Sophists, who maintained the third position. The Platonic positions are: realism and idealism; the Sophistic position is: nominalism.

In order to explain realism and nominalism, let us begin by assuming the existence of two metaphysical levels, as indeed they have been assumed in traditional philosophy. We shall describe the first as the level of being and the second as the level of existence. Being has had other names, such as essence, possibility, the realm of universals, or the realm of archetypes. Existence, too, has had other names, such as actuality, the realm of particulars, or the realm of facts. Being can be described in many ways; it is eternal, it remains unaffected, its parts are undivided, it is consistent, perfect, and complete. Existence can be described in many other ways; it is temporal, it suffers affection, its parts are divided, it is characterized by conflict and contradiction, illusion, and error; it is partial and imperfect and incomplete.

The Pre-Socratics had not believed in the existence of the two metaphysical levels but had chosen one or the other without knowledge of a second. Thus Parmenides opted for the One and Anaximander for the infinite (being), whereas Heraclitus had chosen conflict and Empedocles fire (existence). Socrates and Plato, in their theory of the Ideas, set up the two metaphysical levels; but they wavered as to which one was the real. Sometimes in the Platonic writings, as in the cave analogy of the *Republic,* we are told that being is alone real, whereas existence consists merely of shadows; sometimes, on the other hand, we are told that there is a distinction with regard to reality between being and existence, as in the sunlight analogy of the *Parmenides* (131).

Here, of course, we are confronted with a genuine metaphysical problem. Given the two metaphysical levels of being and existence, how is reality to be interpreted? And according to the way in which we answer this question, we find ourselves accepting some of the three basic metaphysical positions. If we say that reality belongs to being alone (or belongs chiefly to being), we are idealists in ascribing our highest value to another world than our own. If we say that reality belongs to existence alone (or belongs chiefly to existence), we are materialists or nominalists in ascribing the highest value to our own world. If we say that reality is a non-discriminatory term in that it applies with equal force to both metaphysical levels, and in this way refuse to distinguish with respect to reality between being and existence, we are realists. It is thus paradoxical that a realist is one who does not believe that the real is a cogent term in philosophy, but such nevertheless is the case. A word of caution is in order here. In modern literary usage, in modern esthetics, and in popular usage, the term realist is employed as a synonym for materialist. We shall confine its meaning in this book to that which we have already described for it: the traditional philosophical meaning. It should be possible to see now that Plato's writings waver between idealism and realism. The Neo-Platonic philosophers followed the idealistic side, so that now we tend to regard Plato as altogether an idealist and not as a realist at all.

We have been looking at the theory of realism from the point of view of ontology or the theory of being, and we shall return to this point of view, which is the one that will primarily concern us. But it is also possible to look at realism from the point of view of epistemology or the theory of knowledge. By realism in the theory of knowledge is meant the philosophy which centers in the theory, originally also Platonic, that universals or values (or both) are objective to human perception and indeed independent of things perceived. Epistemological realism, in other words, asserts that there are more relations than there are relations known; that knowing does not create truth and then seek to apprehend it; it merely seeks to apprehend it.

We are speaking here of the ontology of realism, but not of the term. It is doubtful whether Plato ever used the term in this fashion. The materialists of the post-Platonic period, of the Epicureans and Stoics, did not call themselves materialists. The second term, nominalism, was in fact not used until the sixth century A.D., although, to be sure, there were nominalists long before that time. But before illustrating the position by describing the historical occasion which gave rise to its explicit statement, it may be well to describe nominalism itself. Nominalism is the theory of the sole reality of actual physical particulars, that everything except actual physical particulars is illusory, secondary, or derived. Thus chairs and trees and stones are real, while relations and values and laws are not. Nominalism (in Latin, *nominalis,* belonging to a name) was in scholastic philosophy the theory that abstract or general terms, or universals, represent no objective real existents, but are mere words or names, mere vocal utterances, "*flatus vocis.*" Universals, on this view, are mere generalizations about real actual things or else fictions (albeit convenient ones) of the mind, existing only after actual physical things (*post res*).

The Sophists, of course, were nominalists, whereas Socrates and Plato were realists. The Greek sceptics, men like Pyrrho of Elis and Sextus Empiricus, were nominalists. The term nominalism was first employed by Porphyry of Tyre (A.D. 233-304) in his *Introduction to the Categories* (of Aristotle), in which he raised the question of whether Aristotle was to be interpreted realistically or nominalistically. This work, in a Latin translation by Boëthius, was available to the early schoolmen, and was probably the historical source for the medieval doctrine of nominalism. Boëthius decided in favor of the nominalistic interpretation of Aristotle. The doctrine did not receive any prominence until the eleventh century, when it was applied to the Sacrament of the Eucharist by Berengar. Berengar was the first scholastic to insist upon the evidence of his senses when examining the nature of the Eucharist. The intimation contained in Berengar's lectures that perhaps the symbolic claret and wafer were merely physical objects was interpreted as the boldest kind of heresy, and Berengar was forced to retract in order to save himself from being burned at the stake. It was probably the suggestion contained in his lectures, however, which gave Roscellinus his start as the first nominalist. From the assertion of the sole reality of the physical claret and wafer to the assertion of the sole reality of *all* physical particulars was not a far step, and this step was taken by Roscellinus, who is generally credited with being the father of philosophical nominalism. The Church well understood how subversive to its influence nominalism could be, and accordingly, in the year 1092, Roscellinus was forced by the Council of Soissons to recant.

Abelard saw the value of nominalism but thought it too extreme a position. So in opposition to Roscellinus, and also to the extreme realism of William of Champeaux, he enunciated the doctrine of conceptualism,[1] in the effort to recognize both the validity of universals and their non-existence apart from actual physical particulars, except as concepts in the mind. It is somewhat surprising that the medieval doctrine of conceptualism has not been more widely revived in modern times. The attempt to discover a solution to the controversy between realism and nominalism in the psychological doctrine of conceptualism should prove most popular with the modern outlook, which seeks to find an answer to every problem by referring it to psychology. The reason is that explicitly at least the problem was not solved but dropped. Implicitly it was solved in favor of nominalism, as we shall note. Conceptualism failed to gain any great headway even in Abelard's time because it represents a midway position that falls back into nominalism by not admitting to universals any real and independent position. It has hardly satisfied anyone; and the effort to prove Aristotle a conceptualist has been ill-advised. Aristotle, it is true, often sought to correct the idealism of Plato and his followers, particularly his nephew Speusippus, who was often guilty of making the level of being alone real; but Aristotle was on the whole a realist and no historical progenitor of Abelard's.

When we speak of realism we are apt to confuse the realists, who believe in the equal reality of the two levels of being and existence, with the idealists who believe in the sole reality of the level of being. But when we speak of nominalism we ordinarily do not consider that there are two kinds of nominalists. The realists and the idealists both accept the reality of the level of being, but they differ radically in their belief concerning the reality of the other level—so radically, in fact, that we must consider them to be separate philosophies. Thus there are three philosophies:

---

1. Allard Pierson, *Disquisitio Historico-Dogmatica de Realismo et Nominalismo*, Amsterdam, 1854.

idealism, realism, and nominalism; and it is nominalism that properly divides into two philosophies. These are: materialism and subjective idealism. Materialism, which we have already named in connection with nominalism, is almost a literal reading of that position. It states that reality belongs to atoms in motion and the void. The mind and all mental things are, according to materialism, epiphenomenal. Subjective idealism, or solipsism, asserts that the mind and mental things are alone real and that nothing else has independent existence. Thus the two forms of nominalism—materialism and subjective idealism—are violently opposed.

The controversy between realism and nominalism was effectively settled in the Middle Ages, though the solution came from outside the Christian tradition. When Christianity took over and adopted the idealistic philosophy of Neo-Platonism, as set forth, for instance, by Plotinus and St. Augustine, the realistic philosophy migrated to Alexandria and Byzantium, not so often in explicit and candid form but usually implicit in the assumptions and method of natural science and in the maintenance of interest in mathematics. Hence it was an Arabian philosopher, one who was both medical scientist and metaphysician, who first solved the difficulty. Neither school, he decided, had hold of the entire truth, but each was partially correct. Universals have their status ontologically *ante res,* epistemologically *in rebus,* and psychologically *post res;* or, as we should now say: universals exist ontologically before things, epistemologically in things, and conceptually after things. Universals have an *a priori* being, but are known only *a posteriori;* that is to say, universals exist prior to actual physical particulars but are perceived in them, and human knowledge of universals (i.e., concepts) are derived from the actual physical particulars by the process of knowing. Albertus Magnus, Duns Scotus, and Thomas Aquinas accepted Avicenna's solution, though in general metaphysics only Duns Scotus asserted the implications which were inherent in it. Avicenna's solution, in effect, while appearing to consist in a compromise between the positions, actually subordinates that of nominalism in admitting its limited validity; and is thus a decision in favor of realism. But the settlement of the problem had no immediate good effect, for nominalism won out most completely and realism went underground, at least for the time being.

II

We have tried to understand how realism and its contradictory, nominalism, arose both as implicit philosophies and as declared doctrines of philosophy. We shall now take a brief glance at the triumph of nominalism in the Renaissance and again later, before we come to our main topic, the revival of realism.

It is no discovery to announce that in actual affairs the truth is never established, but that social events are governed by the complete acceptance of extreme half-truths. We have said, it will be recalled, that there are three philosophies, or rather one valid philosophy and two invalid ones. The valid philosophy is that of realism, and the invalid philosophies are those of idealism and nominalism. The Church in western Europe adopted idealism as a philosophy;[2] hence the reaction to it when it did come arrived in the name of nominalism. Realism was examined, by Duns Scotus for example, but as a living force the truth of realism was overlooked. Instead, the rival philosophies of nominalism, which we have already examined under the names of materialism and subjective idealism, came to the fore. The controversy over reality, a controversy which in any culture is almost always going on, shifted from the real disjunction between the necessary and sufficient alternatives of realism and nominalism (with idealism considered to be realism in excess) to the disjunctive trap set by the rival varieties of nominalism.

The revolt against official Christian idealism could not come from outside the Church since the Church was not only omniscient in Europe but also omnipresent. It had to come, therefore, from inside the Church, and it did come in a number of separate movements. We have already taken notice of one of these in the

---

2. Some day a Western study of the philosophy of the Orthodox Christian or Eastern Church should prove illuminating.

question of the nature of the Eucharistic Sacrament. In the thirteenth century two further nominalistic currents are to be discerned; one stemming from St. Thomas Aquinas and the other bearing the new mysticism. The shift within the Church from the authority of Plato, whose belief in the reality of universals had made the early Church possible, to the authority of Aristotle, whose restated realism was interpreted as being less drastic than Plato's since it admitted the reality of universals only *in* actual physical particulars and not *before* them, was of the utmost significance. Aquinas was largely responsible for the new authority of Aristotle. Aquinas, a faithful son of the Church, used the authority of Aristotle in an attempt to stem the tide of the nominalistic revolt which was already implicit in the tone of the arguments of other scholastics, such as Abelard and his followers, as well as in the experimentation of the empiricists. The problem that Aquinas saw he was faced with was this: some concessions had to be granted to the free exercise of reason which was bent on questioning everything, and yet faith in the Church had to be preserved at all costs and revelation was not to be questioned. The dilemma was finally solved by the division of theology into "natural" and "revealed" theology, whereby the revelations of the Church were preserved by the simple device of turning nature over to the speculation of those new crypto-rationalists, the empiricists. In this way, Aquinas, who had intended to render the Church impregnable, gave it its first serious blow. He said in effect that faith in the Church must be accepted on authority and was not to be defended by reason; but the steady decline of the Church from the times of Aquinas to our own day illustrates the principle that a faith which is not defended by reason cannot continue to be held as a faith.

The other current to be discerned in the Church at that date is the development of mysticism, as exemplified in the attitude of St. Francis and of Jan van Ruysbroek, men whose sense of infinite value did not require institutional intervention. Although true mystics, these men had adopted a view which contained nominalistic implications, since in mysticism reason is denied and belief sought for its own sake. This movement led to fideism on the one hand and the Protestant Reformation on the other, both purely nominalistic in essence. Protestant Christianity has historical origins which are nominalistic, but a realistic interpretation of Protestantism is possible, though it has not yet been accomplished, and it has been colored throughout by nominalistic interpretation. Thus we see that the doctrine of nominalism which had begun in arguments over the theological dogma radiated outward and then rebounded upon the Church itself. Nominalism in every department of culture triumphed.

Philosophical nominalism as an explicit affair came late in the day. Nominalism as a doctrine was suppressed for some two hundred years after Roscellinus. Roscellinus had not proved a much better reasoner than Berengar. His arguments were forgotten because it was most expedient to forget them, and it was not until the fourteenth century that the doctrine of nominalism was incorporated into a complete metaphysics. The scholastic philosopher, William of Occam, was the author of the first system constructed on nominalistic presuppositions, the *Inceptor Omnium Nominalium Monarcha*.[3] Occam studied the Aristotelian writings and arrived at his nominalism in what has come to be the accepted manner: by taking the order of learning to be the order of being. Knowledge of universals, he thought, is acquired from physical particulars or actual things; therefore they exist only in things. Occam was the first to observe that nominalism is a dualistic doctrine and has a subjective as well as an objective aspect. If actual physical particulars have an exclusive hold upon reality, then the mind is powerless to grasp aught but its own concepts. In this notion Occam anticipated Kant, who pushed the lack of correspondence between the logic of concepts and the facts of the external world to a constitutional inability to bridge the gap.

The history of the four centuries beginning with the fourteenth is the story of the complete victory of nominalism. Nominalism began as an attack on the authority of the Church. It was next

---

3. Stephen Chak Tornay, "William of Occam's Nominalism," *Philosophical Review*, May, 1936.

taken over by technical philosophy, and from philosophy it spread rapidly until it was soon deployed upon all the fronts of man's daily existence. A culture is a philosophy in practice; and in the four centuries named, nominalism overcame all obstacles. The new and dazzling sense of unbounded possibility had made men drunk, and was already pervading all their thoughts and influencing all their actions. The East was rapidly being opened up, and this was soon followed by an expansion of trade-routes and the enthusiastic exploration of the Far West. Petty local affairs gave way to the exciting discovery of the unknown, of uninhabited continents and strange civilizations. The rediscovery of the Greek and Roman classics which had been in storage in Constantinople was an event of major importance. Led by Italy, Europe turned to an interest in art; painters, sculptors, and poets swarmed. The Renaissance had begun. Much of the new movement was financed by the nobility and clergy, but the rapid rise of the trading middle class already constituted a threat to the security of the nobility. Rich merchants rode to hounds in imitation of the gentry; bankers appeared whose power challenged all others. The middle class was the philosophical inheritor of the real, inasmuch as trade is the exchange of goods, and these goods are specified as actual physical particulars. The needs of this middle class gave additional impetus to the rise of nationalism; and the feats of Queen Elizabeth and her traders and fighters, and the rise of England to European power, became a model for the world.

The greatest event in this period is, of course, the rise of science. The experimental study of nature, once given the sanction to proceed, spread rapidly, and in some instances got very much out of hand. According to empiricism, the investigator into the nature of reality was no longer allowed to remain at his writing table and, working only with logical possibility as a basis, to record the laws of existence as he conceived them to be, which was the way the Greek philosophers had composed their scientific treatises. The pendulum had swung to the other extreme, and now under the influence of nominalism the laws of nature were discredited wherever it could not be shown as a certificate of validity that they were answerable to actual physical particulars. No preconceived theories were admitted to have any bearing upon and none were to be admitted into the examination of irrefrangible facts. This movement, which had its flowering with Francis Bacon, Kepler, Galileo, and Copernicus, was entirely nominalistic in spirit. But the greatest of these empiricists was Galileo, who may fairly be called the first modern scientist. Empiricism is not necessarily anti-rational, and would never have been so considered had it not arisen historically as a protest against the rigid idealism of Church dogma. Empiricism as an anti-rational affair, that is, as the attempt to experiment with actual physical particulars without preconceived ideas, came to an end as a practice with Galileo (at least in physical science), for Galileo turned science from a qualitative into a quantitative study. Aside from the practice, however, philosophical empiricism, which is purely nominalistic, was affirmed by Galileo when he divided sense qualities into subjective and objective groups. Thus began the contradiction between scientific theory and practice which was to have so long a life and to be the source of so much confusion outside physical science. In the history of science from Galileo's day to our own, these main tendencies of science have become accentuated but have not changed. The practice of science remains rational and realistic, always tending toward the increased use of mathematics, whereas the metaphysics of science remains that of philosophical empiricism, being every day more and more involved in the nominalistic tangle until logical positivism has finally carried one variety of the philosophy of science to absurdity.

In the realm of philosophy the triumph of nominalism was complete. Descartes was the first important nominalist in modern philosophy. He was concerned with clearing away the last vestiges of medievalism. In order to accomplish this end, he set about methodically to make a fresh start. He endeavored to begin at the very beginning of knowledge: the fact of consciousness. He thought that it would be possible to doubt everything—even facts which there was no reason to doubt. From this beginning he went on to beg back God, and, after God, everything else that he had doubted. Having started from the subjective end of the nominalistic dilemma, he begged the objective end through God, and so arrived at a parallelism of the mental and the physical. He saw, furthermore, that if one was real and the other illusory there would be no interaction between them. Turning ontology, the study of being, over to the scientists, he confined philosophy thenceforth to the study of epistemology, or the problem of how knowledge is possible. Descartes succeeded in widening the breach between the two horns of the nominalistic dilemma, first by deprecating philosophy which he held had nothing to do with the study of the real, and secondly by endowing science with an added and unnecessary nominalistic ascription.

Descartes was a thoroughgoing nominalist, and the influence of his dualistic parallelism upon Spinoza is clear. Yet Spinoza was fundamentally a realist, and the effort to reconcile the Cartesian influence with the realist position largely accounts for Spinoza's system of ideas. Descartes' mental and physical became in Spinoza thought and extension, the only two attributes that the mind is allowed to know among the posited infinite attributes of God. This is still arrant nominalism, even though extension is supposed to contain a rational structure which is apprehensible by thought. The determinism of actuality is a further nominalistic note in Spinoza; yet the fact that he called attention to the reality of actuality as being equal though not superior to the logical realm was a good antidote to the medieval excesses of idealism. Historically the effect of Spinoza's philosophy has been on the nominalistic side, though logically, perhaps, he inclined toward realism. The modern importance of his doctrine is largely nullified by his failure to see the issue between realism and nominalism and to solve it.

Less than a century after Descartes, Newton succeeded in establishing the nominalistic cosmology in such complete and systematic form that it has remained ever since the cosmology of enlightened common sense. The outlook of Galileo was taken over by Newton, refined and completed. Newton's world of atoms in motion enjoyed an exclusive reality that made its implied mechanistic materialism fulfill the nominalistic promise of the beginnings of science. Atomism is an essentially nominalistic doctrine which does not admit that a synthesis of atoms contains any other elements than are found by analysis, and analysis always yields a collection of individual parts taken separately.

The main tradition of what is known as European philosophy has always been entangled in the meshes of nominalism. The acceptance of nominalism has been with the philosophers, as with the man in the street, largely implicit and unrecognized. For nominalism by name dropped out of the writings of the times with the acceptance of the nominalistic philosophy in the form of implicit presuppositions. According to nominalism, philosophy is a controversy over words, and so the real questions of philosophy gravitated toward more important topics, toward what, according to nominalism, is really important: the objective manipulation of materials and the study of the confines of knowledge. Locke, Berkeley, Hume, and Kant, like Descartes, started from nominalism. The philosophy of Locke is almost frankly nominalistic. Locke, the father of modern epistemology, accepted the Newtonian world-presupposition of the sole reality of actual physical particulars, and tried to discover what was available to the knowing subject. Accordingly, he developed a position starting from the apodictic knowledge of sensations, and this forced him to the division of qualities into primary and secondary, the former real and the latter supplied by the mind. The mind presents a *tabula rasa* to the impressions of sensations, and reason is confined to concepts which are mind-made. Locke's philosophy offered the first philosophical authority to irrationalism; and since irrationalism is one of the inevitable implications of the nominalistic position, it not only exercised a strong influence on later philosophers but also gained great vogue in non-philosophical circles.

Berkeley was very much influenced by Locke. Berkeley was a bishop and a very religious man. He saw that the Newtonian world of mechanistic atomism did not allow God to continue omnipotent over the mechanism he had started. He saw, too, that the belief in the sole reality of actual physical particulars constitutes a materialistic philosophy which must end in atheism and the decline of revealed morality. So he set about to remove this danger to religion; but while cutting off one horn of the nominalistic dilemma, he managed to get himself impaled on the other. He accepted the subjective predicament and considered Locke's primary qualities as being as secondary as the others. All experience of an external world, he was convinced, consists of thoughts created by the individual mind, which is not competent even to receive sensations from a validly objective source. The individual mind in turn he made into thoughts in the mind of God. The extreme subjectivism of Berkeley has hardly ever been accepted by anyone; it marks the outer limits of the attempt to avoid nominalism in at least one direction.

Hume is in some ways the most important of all European philosophers. His work is largely negative and critical, and his criticism has for the most part gone unattended. To give as brief an account as possible of his views, Hume showed that if the trend of thought of his immediate predecessors was to be accepted—if, that is to say, the sensations to which Locke had limited knowledge were to be given the Berkeleian lack of reference—the result would be a succession of unrelated images. He demonstrated, moreover, that the cause-and-effect relation is nowhere observable between events; so that if radical empiricism is valid, scientific laws, which depend upon causality, would be impossible. It is because the scientists since Hume have ignored the question he raised, that science, which proceeds realistically, can continue to claim nominalism as a philosophy. Had Hume been listened to, it would not have been necessary to wait for Peirce and others today to lead us to the truth concerning science and scientific method.

Hume's empiricism was subjective. Not content with the synthetically concocted expedient of occasionalism, which seemed to satisfy the Cartesians, nor with the ingenious yet none the less preposterous hypothesis of pre-established harmony, which seemed to satisfy Christian Wolff and the other followers of Leibniz, Hume set about frankly to face the situation. For a constructive philosopher, the predicament might have proved disastrous, but for a sceptic it was made to order. Taking the subjective end of the knowledge relation as the given and all else as unreliable, Hume found himself in a locked internal world fed only by perceptions consisting of lively impressions and of weak ones called ideas.[4] In this world where causality was utterly inexplicable,[5] he found nothing dependable to which he could cling except the temporal succession of events.[6] There exists, he claimed, a succession of impressions and ideas which is the self.[7] The self, then, can only be a notion acquired from the repetition of the ideas of reflection, such as, for instance, hearing, feelings of pain, thoughts, and willing. The idea of substance is a matter literally of custom or habit.[8] There is no external world of substance, causality being a result of customary succession.[9] Mental association is a connection of a sort, but there is nothing necessary about the causal succession of contiguity.[10] That is to say, there is a psychological necessity to succession but not a logical one. Hume's theory of perception contains no evidence that the impressions and ideas resemble what they represent. We may call our perceptions by the names of substance and accidents if we choose, but they are perceptions all the same. Hume clung to the criterion of human nature and what could be comprised within it as final, so that his doctrine may accurately be described as a kind of absolute humanism. Scepticism, in one direction at least, could go no further.

To the untenability of Hume's position, there were two philosophical reactions. Kant gave one kind of answer; Thomas Reid, the Scottish philosopher, another. Kant continued the criticism when he asked, "How are synthetic judgments *a priori* pos-

---

4. David Hume, *A Treatise of Human Nature* (Oxford, 1928), Bk. I, Pt. I, sec. ii; also Bk. I, Pt. III, sec. viii.
5. *Ibid.*, Bk. I, Pt. III, sec. vi; also Bk. I, Pt. IV, sec. i.
6. *Ibid.*, Bk. I, Pt. III, sec. vi.
7. *Ibid.*, Bk. I, Pt. IV, sec. vi.
8. *Ibid.*, Bk. I, Pt. I, sec. vi.
9. *Ibid.*, Bk. I, Pt. III, sec. xiv.
10. *Ibid.*

sible?"[11] By synthetic judgments he meant assertions of positive fact; and by *a priori,* general truths independent of experience; so that the question might be framed, how can the universal principles of human reasoning refer to external fact? Accepting the sole reality of actual physical particulars as proved, Kant was concerned with the question of how this real world could be known. After a careful examination of reason, Kant came to the conclusion that the objective world is unknowable, inasmuch as space, time, and the categories interpose themselves between the individual mind and the world. Thus the mind, he concluded, is confined to concepts of its own making. This rendered absolute truth impossible, even as a goal, and made it necessary to take God on faith since there had to be some kind of moral law. The Kantian moral law, however, turns out to be an injunction to act as if you could will your action to be universal. This categorical imperative is merely the old sanction of pleasure and pain in disguised abstraction. Kant was the last great nominalist, and in some respects the greatest of them all. Indirectly, he gave rise to the revival of realism. The influence of Reid was more direct.

The turn in philosophy occurred in Kant's day; realism had already begun its revival. But there is always a lag between the discovery of ideas and the spread of ideas. After Kant, and to some extent even still today, the victory of nominalism was complete in fields other than philosophy. Nominalism became so thoroughly accepted that none any longer knew what the term meant. The word was supposed to refer to an obsolete medieval problem in metaphysics, but the import itself went unquestioned as the very basis of truth. Such a state of affairs marks the utmost in the acceptance of a philosophy. It was assumed that the two chief reals of ordinary existence were subjective feeling and objective cash; hence psychology and economics came to the fore as disciplines, and the consequences of the acceptance of nominalism rapidly worked themselves out in practice.

---

11. *Kritik der reinen Vernunft* (Leipzig, 1925), p. 19. B.

III

The remainder of our account will be devoted to the revival of realism. The revival of realism in modern philosophy, at least in the English-speaking world (and it is in this world that it has received its chief impetus as a movement of any scope), properly begins with Reid's reactions to Hume's nominalistic strictures. While Kant's influence was wide-spread and profound, it produced no thinker of the rank of Kant. Reid's influence, while longer in getting started, yet produced an effect upon philosophy that has eventually been, as we shall see, of the utmost importance.

The corrective necessary for reëstablishing a tenable theory of the relations between the human nature of the subject and the external world in which he lives and moves and has his existence could hardly be expected to come from the external world, since that world had by definition been excluded from all real authority. It must, then, come from within the subject. Hume himself had left a hint when he declared that although the senses had to be corrected by reason, we trust them by a natural instinct, for what we doubted was never the senses but only their relations and situation.[12] Reid accepted the absolute cleavage between body and mind, and, like his predecessors, Descartes and Spinoza and Leibniz, held it to be the most important in philosophy.[13] If, however, as Hume had shown, philosophy belongs to the internal world of human nature, then we must put our trust in human nature, or philosophy will break down altogether.[14]

Trusting human nature in this sense means having faith in its profoundest faculties. Not only is the common consciousness of mankind to be trusted, with all its vast store of belief, but even such relatively superficial faculties as sensation are also.[15] We do not have to depend upon the external world to demonstrate its own validity, since we have sensation. Sensation carries with it an

---

12. Hume, *op. cit.*, Bk. I, Pt. IV, sec. ii.
13. *Essays on the Intellectual Powers of Man* (London, 1941), p. 5.
14. *Ibid.*, Essay VI, Chap. III, sec. iii (8).
15. *Ibid.*, Essay II, Chap. X, secs. i, ii.

immediate belief in the reality of its object,[16] and this is our criterion of the objectivity of truth, and of the reality of the external world.[17] The group of primitive judgments which are present to the consciousness of mankind is called common sense, and it is upon common sense that all certainty rests.[18] In this faculty the philosopher does not exceed the ordinary man.[19]

Among the primitive judgments, or principles of common sense, Reid lists some which sharply mark his departure from the nominalists who preceded him. Against Hume, he maintained as a first principle that the thoughts of which we are conscious are the thoughts of an ego,[20] so that since we have thoughts, there must be an ego or mind. Against Hume he also maintained as a first principle the existence of everything of which we are conscious,[21] and went on to assert that "there is a certain regard due to human testimony in matters of fact, and even to human authority in matters of opinion."[22] It is also a first principle that "the natural faculties, by which we distinguish truth from error, are not fallacious."[23] Thus from the confines of the internal world, and despite the acceptance of the body-mind distinction of the nominalists, Reid restored the reality of the mind and of that which the mind knows, the external world, including as well as substance, all possibilities. In the same fashion, Reid substituted for Hume's representative theory of perception the doctrine of immediate perception.[24] Every feeling suggests an object felt, because we are bound to look upon all feelings as signs.[25] Thus Reid broke the ground for a realistic version of logical symbolism, as well as for a realistic ontology, epistemology, and psychology.

---

16. *Ibid.*, Essay II, Chap. IV, sec. ii; also Essay II, Chap. V, sec. iii; and Essay II, Chap. X, sec. i.
17. *Ibid.*, Essay II, Chap. XI, sec. i.
18. *Inquiry into the Human Mind on the Principles of Common Sense* (Edinburgh, 1764), p. 52.
19. *Essays on the Powers of the Human Mind* (Edinburgh, 1819), II, 316.
20. *Essays on the Intellectual Powers of Man*, p. 360.
21. *Ibid.*
22. *Ibid.*, p. 373.
23. *Ibid.*, p. 367.
24. *Ibid.*, Essay II, Chap. III, sec. iii.
25. *Essays on the Powers of the Human Mind*, II, 304 ff.

It can hardly be claimed that Reid was one of the world's great philosophers. But he was a key figure in that he opened the path toward a secular realism, which has been followed since his work by most of the great British and the greatest of American realists. The nineteenth century was a bad period for Reid's reputation, although it was in that century that his influence was felt on the most important of American realists, Charles S. Peirce. Peirce freely acknowledged the influence of Reid, and combined the Critical philosophy of Kant with Reid's Common-Sensism into what he termed Critical Common-Sensism.[26] Peirce was a metaphysical realist[27] who felt no doubt about the possibility of reconciling the critical faculty with the common-sense beliefs of the ordinary man.[28] While considering the body of common sense to be general, and hence vaguer than Reid had supposed,[29] Peirce thought that the part of it which could pass through the scrutiny of scientific examination, which would be, incidentally, the greater part, would be all the stronger for having a high probability on its side.[30]

The epistemological realism of the early twentieth century specifically repudiated Reid as its influence, and sought rather to go on from where Kant had left off, attempting to transfer his critical attitude from its subjectivist-idealist basis to an objectivist-realist one. This gave rise to a kind of objective idealism which is equivalent to realism. But it accounted also for realists who preferred to take their start from opposition to the Kantian position. Peirce, in fact, acknowledged his obligation to Reid and to Kant.[31] But in England G. Dawes Hicks specifically repudiated the influence of Reid, whom he accused of having "disposed of the 'way of ideas' in far too rough and ready a fashion to satisfy the demands of exact and methodical inquiry."[32] Hicks, however, arrived at substantially the

---

26. *Collected Papers of Charles Sanders Peirce*, eds. Hartshorne and Weiss (6 vols., Cambridge, 1934), Vol. 5.
27. *Ibid.*, 1.20, 5.432.
28. *Ibid.*, 5.505.
29. *Ibid.*, 5.446.
30. *Ibid.*, 5.451.
31. *Ibid.*, 1.522.
32. *Critical Realism* (London, 1938), p. xiv.

same conclusions, at least with respect to the broad outlines of realism. The point of view of Reid is best carried on by the teaching of Cook Wilson, who expressed Reid's realistic position by attacking the coherence theory of truth, the subjectivist theory of knowledge, and the influence of psychology on logic; and who, moreover, sought to show the correctness of common sense in his method of inquiry by preferring to express himself in the speech of ordinary men and by avoiding all parade of learning and high-sounding terminology.[33]

Cook Wilson's realism is similar to the doctrines of the American neo-realists in that he and his followers denied the objectivity of qualities and values, which were held to be added by the subject to the process of perception. With the later British realists, the theory of realism with respect to values as well as universals returns to the fore, and the influence of Reid is once more explicitly felt. In what proved tactically the most important book defending the position of axiological realism, G. E. Moore gave credit to the work of Reid for having pointed out that perception requires that the thoughts and feelings of other persons, as well as mere material objects, have an existence objective to and independent of the perceiving subject.[34] He has held strongly to the same status for value.[35] Moore is the product of Cook Wilson multiplied by Reid. Like Wilson, he is devoted to careful and incisive analysis, and very hesitant about reaching conclusions. Of late, the influence of Wilson has predominated over that of Reid, and he has become almost exclusively a philosophical analyst. But his earlier work is marked by the adherence to Reid's position, and, indeed, by the candid defense of Reid's Common-Sensism. In one essay, written some years ago, Moore adopted the Scottish philosophy, declaring for a body of original knowledge, common to philosopher and plain man, from which all special philosophical knowledge must take its start.[36] Like Reid, he went so far as to draw up a list of

---

33. R. Metz, *Hundred Years of British Philosophy* (New York, 1938), p. 523.
34. *Philosophical Studies* (London, 1922), p. 57.
35. *Ibid.*, Chap. VIII.
36. "A Defense of Common Sense," in *Contemporary British Philosophy* (ed. J. H. Muirhead), Vol. II.

commonplace principles, and attempted to show their inescapability.

Moore's greatest pupil is Bertrand Russell, who readily acknowledged the teacher.[37] Moore, of course, made his pupil over into a realist; and Russell came heavily into debt to the Scottish school. He named his philosophy "logical atomism"[38] but pointed out that the theories of American neo-realism were close to what he intended.[39] Gradually, however, other eighteenth-century influences were brought to bear upon him, especially that of Hume, and nominalism overcame for a while the realism of Reid. It won by means of the analytical method, when Hume, so to speak, disguised as Cook Wilson, vanquished Reid. We can see the transition taking place clearly, with Russell clinging desperately to certain of the realistic presuppositions, but gradually going over to nominalism in the course of his many volumes.[40] The way was open for the logical positivists to have their day with him. There are recent signs, however, of a return to realism on the part of Russell, albeit disguised by the language and peculiar interests of the logical positivists.[41] Reid is undoubtedly once more reasserting his influence, if only implicitly and in the form of early prejudices.

Of Moore's influence on others we may cite three examples from the work of G. F. Stout, S. Alexander, and John Laird. Stout's realistic epistemology acknowledges great respect for the opinions of the ordinary man, and the ascendancy of Reid and Moore is most apparent in his appeal to common sense. As for S. Alexander, in a recent Preface to his metaphysical system, he recounts how a reading of Moore's essay on "The Refutation of Idealism"[42] was clarified for him by his own conclusion that since the cause of a thing cannot be the mental state which apprehends it, the presentation of the object must be not a mental picture but the thing itself or a

---

37. *The Principles of Mathematics* (London, 1937), p. viii.
38. *Our Knowledge of the External World* (New York, 1929), p. 4.
39. *Ibid.*
40. E.g., *Mysticism and Logic* (New York, 1929), p. 123.
41. *An Inquiry into Meaning and Truth* (New York, 1940), especially Chap. XXV.
42. Reprinted as Chapter I of *Philosophical Studies.*

selection from it.⁴³ John Laird's realism was due to the combined forces of Reid and Moore,⁴⁴ both of whom were instrumental in teaching him that the reality of the external world involves its independence of the process of knowing. Laird's work is more comprehensive, if not more systematic, than that of any of the other English realists I have mentioned, in explicitly setting forth the reality of value, a position for which he gives due acknowledgement to both Reid⁴⁵ and Moore.⁴⁶

We can hardly close the historical account of modern realism without devoting a few words to the philosophy in which Reid's tradition has been brought up to date. I mean the organic philosophy of Whitehead. Whitehead is a systematic philosopher who has acknowledged the realistic basis of his system.⁴⁷ Realism is implicit in his system in the distinction between "actual entities" and "eternal objects,"⁴⁸ and in the earlier attack upon nominalism, under the guise of "the bifurcation of nature into two systems of reality"⁴⁹ which he castigates as "vicious."⁵⁰ There are many influences on the realism of Whitehead, chiefly, perhaps, that of Plato and modern physics. But we must recall that the development of Whitehead's philosophy of organism followed his writing of the *Principia Mathematica* with Russell, and that this book was an outgrowth of *The Principles of Mathematics,* in which, as we have already noted, Russell freely acknowledged his great obligation to Moore. We may safely surmise that Reid's effect has been felt on Whitehead indirectly through Russell, and, even more indirectly, through Moore's effect on Russell. But in spite of this indirection the effect is plain enough. Whitehead's own refutation of Hume is often reminiscent of Reid, as for example in Whitehead's refutation of the sensationalist theory of perception.⁵¹ In general, White-

---

43. Samuel Alexander, *Space, Time and Deity* (London, 1934), I, xiv f.
44. *A Study in Realism* (Cambridge, 1920), pp. 2 ff., 13 ff.
45. *The Idea of Value* (Cambridge, 1929), p. 221 ff.
46. *Ibid.,* pp. 362, 365.
47. *Science and the Modern World* (New York, 1931), p. 132.
48. *Process and Reality* (New York, 1930), p. 32 et passim.
49. *The Concept of Nature* (Cambridge, 1926), p. 30.
50. *Ibid.,* p. 185.
51. *Process and Reality,* e.g., pp. viii, 220-23.

head takes his start from opposition to Descartes and the nominalistic English philosophers; may we not suppose that in thus going over ground already familiar to Reid, that the Scottish tradition of realism is showing not only its vitality, but also validity and truth?

Among contemporary philosophers, there are a number of realists outside those which we have listed in the British school. In the United States, we have E. Jordan[52] and F. S. Haserot.[53] In Germany there has been Nicolai Hartmann,[54] and there have been many others. The Catholic philosophy, which is led in the modern world by the writings of Jacques Maritain,[55] while more idealistic than realistic, contains some realistic elements. The Spanish-American Catholic philosopher, George Santayana, in his system of philosophy verges on the realist position,[56] though Montague rightly insists that this is an illusion of language, the situation itself being one better described as nominalism.[57]

The conclusion of this chapter, then, is that the theory of metaphysical realism obtained its start in modern times through Reid's objections to Hume, and through his own subsequent affirmative philosophical speculations, and has been carried down in an unbroken tradition, in both Great Britain and America, from the publication of Reid's *Inquiry* in 1764 to the present day, having included on its way the most painstaking of philosophical critics as well as the most comprehensive of system-makers. Philosophy now is but one of the many studies contributing to the ascendency of realism. Others include such diverse fields as relativity physics and quantum mechanics,[58] pure[59] and applied[60] mathematics, and mathe-

---

52. *The Esthetic Object*, Bloomington, 1937.
53. *Essays on the Logic of Being*, New York, 1932.
54. *Ethics*, trans. S. Coit, 3 vols.; London, 1932. *Zur Grundlegung der Ontologie*, Berlin, 1935.
55. *The Degrees of Knowledge*, New York, 1938.
56. *The Realms of Being*, New York, 1945.
57. W. P. Montague, *The Ways of Things* (New York, 1940), p. 257.
58. See e.g., Max Planck, *The Philosophy of Physics*, London, 1936.
59. See e.g., G. H. Hardy, *A Mathematician's Apology* (Cambridge, 1940), especially pp. 63 f.
60. See e.g., R. A. Fisher, *Statistical Method for Research Workers* (London, 1938), Chap. I.

matical logic.[61] Convincing evidence could be brought forth that even the course of actual events is directed toward realism; but we have reached the end of our particular argument.

Scholars are fond of pointing out that the traditions of philosophy alive today are as old as recorded history, that there always have been the realists, the idealists, and the two varieties of nominalists. The scholars argue from this that to take sides is to be limited with respect to knowledge; how can the truth be confined to one or another of these traditions when both are so old and so time-honored? A synthesis seems called for which would resolve the various conflicting half-truths. How can such a synthesis be reached? Not on the basis of nominalism, for nominalism has no place for the realist. Not on the basis of idealism, for idealism makes no allowance for the nominalist. Realism seems the only hope, since realism does contain something of the idealist position in admitting that there is a real and independent status for universals, and at the same time realism does have a place for both sorts of limited nominalism, since it can endorse *universalia post res,* the psychological derivation of universals as concepts in the mind from actual physical particulars.

The argument of the scholars against the desirability of resolving the conflict rests upon two fallacies, one of which is linguistic and one historical. The linguistic fallacy consists in supposing that metaphysics, being conducted by means of words, must be limited to words; and the scholars would confine metaphysical matters in one way or another to the enunciated or written propositions of metaphysics. But metaphysics is not about words, it only uses words; the words themselves have an objective reference. Events in the actual world follow one implicit philosophy or another, and it is of great concern to the future of the actual world which one it is that is followed. The historical fallacy consists in supposing that things equal in age are equal in truth; this fallacy is known in logic as the fallacy of historicism, and it rests upon the

---

61. All texts in logic written from the standpoint of the *Principia* are realistic in their presuppositions. See e.g., Morris R. Cohen and Ernest Nagel, *An Introduction to Logic and Scientific Method,* New York, 1934.

false notion that history pronounces a judgment upon value: whatever lasts the longest is the most valuable, a proposition which is emphatically untrue.

The truth always has being and thus is always possible, but to exist it requires advantages. Some advantages may be offered in the enunciation of true propositions. Needless to add, there need be no illusions as to the practical effect which this book will have in the immediate affairs of the world. The effect of written philosophy, if indeed it have any effect, lies in the future. The future of these chapters is fortuitous and problematical. On the other hand, there is the probability that there may be many errors in the argument, though it is not likely that the whole argument is wrong. Certainly, if no truth is involved, nothing good has been accomplished. On this score there is nothing more to be said.

Not all of the following chapters concern the work of realists. The aim chiefly has been the exposition, development, and defense of realism as a living and vital philosophy. Sometimes, as in the case of Toynbee, it has been necessary to separate the realistic elements. Often, as in the case of Dewey, it has been necessary to go over to the attack, in order to defend realism against its new opponents. There has certainly been no attempt to be exhaustive, however, not even so far as concerns modern movements in philosophy. For instance, little has been said about the new and frankly nominalistic movement known as logical positivism and led by Carnap and the other members of the Vienna Circle.

Part II
The Revival in Philosophy

I

The Realism of Charles S. Peirce

IT HAS BEEN THE FATE of American men of letters to come but slowly into their own. The works of Poe, Melville, Whitman, and many others were not recognized until years after these writers had died. What has been true of American literature has also been true of the greatest of American philosophers. Charles Peirce died, an old and broken man, at the beginning of the first World War, and his widow survived him for some years in the direst poverty. Until recently Peirce has been known to very few, and his name is mentioned rarely even among scholars. Although it has been recognized for some time that he gave pragmatism its philosophic meaning and contributed to the origins of symbolic logic, it has always been assumed that James was the greater pragmatist and Frege and Boole more systematic logicians. The tendency is widespread to regard Peirce merely as an ancestor, a "seminal thinker" to whom one owes much but whose work taken by itself is negligible. In 1923 Professor Morris Cohen edited a selected edition of his essays, of which scant notice was taken, and more recently the Harvard University Press undertook to publish an edition of his *Collected Papers* in ten volumes. Only six of these have appeared. The widespread attention given to these volumes as they were published, and the growing popularity of Peirce, call for a closer study of his thought. First, however, it would be well to record a few words concerning his life.

I

Charles Sanders Peirce was born in 1839, the son of Benjamin Peirce, for many years professor of mathematics at Harvard. Peirce has related how his father taught him mathematics, a subject with which he became so familiar that it was prophesied he would be an even greater mathematician. But the parental influence was not confined to mathematics. Two hours a day, for more than three years, Peirce sat at his father's feet and listened to lectures on Kant. As Peirce himself wryly put it, when he was "a babe in philosophy" his "bottle was filled from the udders of Kant," from whom he learned much concerning the necessity of reconciling rationalism or the supremacy of reason with empiricism or the necessity for experimentation, a task which Kant had never been able to accomplish without denying the objective validity of reason as the structure of the natural world. But Peirce, unlike most of his contemporaries, did not stop there. Later, he studied the scholastics closely, especially Duns Scotus, in order to learn the truth of realism; and Occam, in order to detect the error of nominalism; and so was able to remark the influence of nominalism upon the European philosophy while at the same time declaring himself as an unqualified realist. On his own account he also became proficient in Greek and medieval philosophy, physical science, and to some extent biology. He did some original work in physics on the theory of the pendulum, and wrote a brilliant essay on the symbolism of physiological analysis. Peirce's life was extremely erratic, however, and his academic career a failure. He taught for a little while at both Harvard and Johns Hopkins but did not succeed in remaining at either university. His efforts to make a living included a long association with the United States Coast and Geodetic Survey, and later the vicarious tutoring of mathematics to business men in New York, by the hour. He has recorded a contempt for Harvard and its students (who were "gentlemen and athletes" but not scholars). He planned a great many books and barely finished one; very little was published in his own lifetime besides scattered essays and reviews in professional journals.

We owe one illuminating story about Peirce's life to Joseph Jastrow. On the one occasion when Peirce managed to make a little money he ordered a house to be built, but the money gave out before the house was finished, and the capacious attic in which Peirce had planned to receive his disciples and pupils was never completed.

However, Peirce was never the least bit embittered by the failure of his life. He declared that he who would affect the future could not expect to "paint the ground in front of him," and he could record with equal satisfaction the spectacle of the perfect opportunity afforded the genius of Aristotle, and the fact that philosophy had "wafted little" his own way besides "occasional slabs of bread and butter." It is peculiarly ironic that an evil fate should dog Peirce after his death almost as persistently as it did while he was yet alive. For he is praised and claimed by those very thinkers he would most have denounced: the pragmatists who suppose that truth is a matter of what works, and the logical positivists for whom the truth is altogether a verbal affair. While it is a fact that there is some justification for both positions to be found in the random writings of Peirce on method, still the metaphysical portions of his work should have been seen long since to contradict the possibility of such affiliations.

II

The key to the whole philosophical position of Peirce lies in the realism-nominalism controversy. This is a topic he returns to again and again, one he never considered had been made sufficiently clear. The difficulties which arose in the Middle Ages between the Church and the new empirical scientists centered in this question, and it is in fact through a study of the medieval philosophies that Peirce first discovered its importance as the basis for the settlement of all contemporary problems in philosophy. The scientific tradition demands that all science be opposed to religion because experimentation originated through opposition to the Christian Church. Peirce emerged from a study of this medieval controversy with a decision in favour of the realists, openly avowing himself a follower of Duns Scotus. He saw the contradiction which makes nominalism untenable, that since nominalism allows no universal principles it cannot allow itself, since it too is a universal principle.

It was at this stage in his development that Peirce happened to read a contemporary work, Abbot's *Scientific Theism* (1885), in which it is demonstrated that despite the persistent claims of the scientists to a nominalistic philosophy, science itself always has been, and indeed must be, realistic in practice, scientific method itself implying an essential realism. Science starts with inductions to erect hypotheses, which are then tested by observations and, if found valid, used as a basis for deductions. Thus the existence of universal principles or laws is required; laws, independent of any person or collection of persons having knowledge of them. Furthermore, such deductions are not explorations of truisms. Laws, Peirce said, are not merely the summaries of known facts but also the finders of new ones. We are cautioned, then, not to follow the psychologistic account contained in the scientists' own version of what their procedure is, but rather to look for the metaphysical implications of the scientific procedure itself. This procedure proves to be irrevocably realistic, in the medieval sense of that term, as requiring the prior assumption of the real existence of universals or laws which are in no sense created by the mind of the scientist but are found by means of scientific procedure.

III

On the assumption of a realistic philosophy plus the understanding of science as realistic in method, Peirce next proceeded to establish three basic metaphysical categories. For Peirce, the logic of being is based upon these fundamental categories, which are held to be exhaustive and prior to all others. According to him these categories are: firstness, secondness, and thirdness.

Peirce says that firstness is feeling. Among feelings, he includes besides the color of magenta, the odor of attar, the sound of a railway whistle, and the taste of quinine, also the quality of the emotion upon contemplating a fine mathematical demonstration, and the quality of the feeling of love. Feeling is absolutely simple and therefore beyond analysis; it is not dependent in any way upon either mind or change. A feeling is a state which to be experienced as an outward sensation must be reproduced in memory, but which as a vivid affair is independent of all happenings. The idea of the first, says Peirce, must be separated from reference to anything else. The first must be present and immediate, it must be fresh and new, it must be original, initiative, spontaneous, and free. It precedes all synthesis and differentiation; it has no parts.

The category of secondness is described as that of reaction. Secondness is struggle, inertial hard fact, resistance, the fact of *otherness*. It is the level of actuality where things affect and are affected. It is what presents resistance to the individual will, the stubbornness of things as they are, and as they change from moment to moment. Both action and perception, the active and the passive aspects of participation in actuality, are modes of secondness. Secondness suffers change from the action of the first and is dependent upon it. It must be determined irrevocably by the first. We find secondness in occurrences, because an occurrence is something whose existence consists in our continually knocking up against it. In youth, the world is fresh and we seem free; but limitation, conflict, restraint, and secondness manage to make up the teaching of experience. Secondness consists in the recognition of an irreducible external world which is composed of elements of firstness, but is independent of any recognition of it or laws governing it. It is the mutual interaction of two things regardless of any law of action.

The category of thirdness is described by Peirce as the medium, or connecting bond, between the absolute first and last. Thirdness is continuity, generality, meaning, purpose, and reason. It is what connects elements of firstness with elements of secondness, and represents the generality of the connections of both. It represents all legality in the world, the purposive elements in organizations which constitute their final meanings. Thirdness is that to which all thought refers. It is the basis for predictability, and is what it is by virtue of imparting a quality to reactions in the future. The quantitative stage of science is its recognition of the reality of thirdness. The success of modern mathematics is due to the bridging over of discrete cases which encumbered ancient science. Thirdness is as real as the other categories; meaning cannot be reduced to quality and reaction but has a being participating in them while remaining entirely independent.

Each of the three categories can be distinguished in abstraction, but they are in some sense or other mutually involved. Any event must contain elements of all three. The quality of immediate consciousness, of the absolutely present, is firstness; the existence and brute compulsion of external reality is secondness; and the representation which mediates between the other two as their law, order, generality, and meaning is thirdness. The first is agent, the second patient, the third is the action by which the former influences the latter. The abstract presentation, mediating between the immediate consciousness and the external dead thing, is pre-eminently third. It is Peirce's contention that any elements found in the world of experience can be reduced to one or another of the three categories. Firstness, secondness, and thirdness are exhaustive of being, and while admitting of infinite variation in themselves do not allow for any fourth category of being. All further categories of fourthness, fifthness, etc., can be reduced to various combinations of the three primitive categories.

IV

Having established these ontological categories to his own satisfaction, Peirce attempted to translate the realistic metaphysics of science into an everyday philosophy which could be of more general service. He wanted to establish the realistic philosophy and at the same time hold down realism to what is strictly verifiable, in conformity with scientific practice.

It was to be expected that a philosopher who had exposed the error of nominalism, studied scholastic realism, and made himself familiar with the aims and methods of experimental science, would attempt to put the latter two together. The result was his doctrine of pragmatism, defined methodologically as follows. In order to learn the meaning of an intellectual conception, it is only necessary to consider the practical consequences which might conceivably result by necessity from the truth of such a conception. The sum of these conceivable consequences is the meaning of the conception, and, moreover, it is the entire meaning.[1]

There are two important points which should be noted at once about this definition. In the first place, Peirce says that the practical consequences of a conception result by necessity from the truth of such a conception. Thus while truth and practicality are indissolubly associated, and some acquaintance with practicality is essential in order to ascertain the complete meaning of truth, still it is truth which determines practicality, and not the reverse. Indeed, Peirce specifically says that the practical consequences result *by necessity* from truth. In the second place, observe that it is not the mere consequences as random affairs which constitute the meaning of a conception, but the *sum* of the consequences. Now, to ascertain the sum of the practical consequences of a conception, an infinite run of actuality is required, since anything less than an infinite actuality could not produce the *sum* of the consequences.

That the doctrine of pragmatism as designed by Peirce was intended to aid in the avoidance of the Scylla of idealism as well as the Charybdis of nominalism, is evident in many passages. Nominalism is ruled out by the contention that generals are real. But are *all* generals real? No, for this is the error opposite to nominalism: the fallacy of idealism. To assert that all generals are real, without ascertaining the degree of their self-consistency and their range of applicability, must mean, in some cases at least, to set up falsehoods as truths, which in turn implies generals to be unrelated to actuality. Not all general objects are real, says Peirce, but only some. Nobody ever said that all generals are real. The difficulty was that the scholastics asserted the reality of some generals for which they had not obtained empirical evidence. This was the trouble: the lack of evidence for generals held to be real; not the assertion of the reality of some generals.[2] Pragmatism is the device by which

---
1. *Collected Papers*, 5.79.
2. *Ibid.*, 5.430.

the reality of generals is to be ascertained. It is the doctrine according to which practical consequences are to be observed with the view to determining just what truths those consequences are following by necessity.

Peirce's logic proves to be that logic of pragmatism wherein the requirement of an infinity of practical consequences is made plainly evident. Peirce avoided the realistic fallacy by demanding the practical consequences of his truths to exemplify and illustrate them, holding as he did that any truth which could not develop into action could not be truth. He avoided the fallacy of nominalism by asserting the reality of truth which practical consequences follow from by necessity, but do not create. Thus he maintained the balance of the two orders of being: the value-logic order of firstness and thirdness, and the historical order of actuality, or secondness, by insisting upon the equal reality of both. This is realism as contained in part of the Platonic writings, and as asserted continuously throughout history in the implicit position of science as well as in the explicit positions of certain philosophers from Aristotle to Whitehead.

V

Since the realistic doctrine of pragmatism as set forth by Peirce has been altered somewhat by William James, and since it is James who deserves the credit for making the doctrine generally known, it will be helpful to the philosophy of realism to indicate the deviation. In a volume devoted to the topic, James first acknowledges Peirce as his source and then proceeds to expatiate on what his own doctrine of pragmatism implies. Pragmatism for James is a theory of truth; it is a way of discovering truths. It is anti-intellectualistic, and so looks away from abstractions, absolutes, fixed principles, and closed systems; it is practical, and so looks toward facts, concreteness, and action. According to Jamesian pragmatism, the only test of probable truth is what works best in the way of leading us. His pragmatism could discern no meaning in treating as not true a notion that was pragmatically successful. On the ethical side, we may note the same divergence. In real life when truths clash with vital benefits it is the truths which must go. If actions which seem demanded clash with principles, then, says James, he takes a "moral holiday." As for justification, the moral holidays are either just brazenly taken, or else as a philosopher James says he tries to justify them by some other principle.

Metaphysics is so fundamental that the slightest deviation in doctrine, the most infinitesimal difference in interpretation, may allow for divergent chains of implications which end by directly contradicting each other. Thus men may start from almost the same metaphysics yet in general appear to hold deeply opposed philosophies. By just the slightest shift of emphasis, James brought the Peirceian doctrine around to mean its direct opposite. James asks practical consequences to determine his truths and to determine them right now. He does not care about truths but about practice; he does not care about practice as a *theory* of practice but only as concrete and forceful action. And he thinks that a limited number of practical consequences are adequate for the determination of truths. Success is borne out by what is immediately successful, regardless of what may be its later failures. But how are we to know what "works best" if we do not allow it to work indefinitely? Workability, like success, may support a certain theory in practice today and relinquish it, if not directly disprove it, tomorrow. But James evidently took no such difficulties into account.

That Peirce himself recognizes the defection of James's pragmatism is evident in many passages, and since these make the contrast clear, we may cite several of them. Peirce says, first of all, that if pragmatism really made action into the end and purpose of life, that would mean its death. To live and act merely for the sake of action, and to exclude the ideas involved, is tantamount to the claim that there is no such thing as rational purport.[3] And, he adds elsewhere, that he was talking about meaning as intellectual purport. Acts cannot furnish intellectual purport, since they cannot constitute the proper interpretation of symbols.[4] There is this defense, however, to be made of James. He put his finger better than

---
3. *Ibid.*, 5.429.
4. *Ibid.*, 5.403.

did Peirce, who was seeking for more permanent contributions, upon the popular pulse, with the result that the leading thinkers and literary men of the day took up the term in its Jamesian meaning with great avidity and seemed to discover in it the satisfaction of some palpable need. But it was not Peirce's pragmatism that was adopted. Peirce himself recognized this state of affairs, and as a solution changed his own term to "pragmaticism." He relinquished the promoted term of pragmatism to its higher destiny, while he retained for his own precise purposes the term pragmaticism, which, he insisted, was so unattractive that nobody would wish to steal it from him.[5]

VI

On the ethical side we may apply the same arguments as those used against pragmatism. What are the vital benefits of James and how are these to be determined? Are they individual or social, temporary or permanent, hedonistic or stoical? The notion of the moral holiday with its post-rationalized justification opens the door to any kind of action, whether anti-social or whatever. One wonders why rational justification is required at all. Certainly if moral holidays are to be recommended regardless of what principles they come into conflict with, the brazen way of just taking them would seem to be the best. But we must not convict James on the findings of his theory, for James himself was, if the evidence of his other writings and of his friends is to be considered, a very sincere seeker after the truth, whose superabundant vitality carried him into excesses of philosophical approval of activity for its own sake; he did not mean the harm which his own version of the ethics of pragmatism would indicate.

There is no doubt of the great value of James's philosophical endeavors. He succeeded in instilling into a mordant and abandoned profession a new life and a new direction and purpose. He showed that philosophy was not a dull and useless discipline, confined to the classrooms and divorced from the most immanent and signifi-

---

5. *Ibid.*, 5.414.

cant of public affairs in the rough-and-tumble world. But unfortunately this contribution, the value of which it is hard to underestimate, does not free James from the charge of having perverted Peirce's pragmatism from a realistic to a nominalistic metaphysics, by elevating practice as concrete and actual, and above principles whose abstract nature he deplored.

There is one Platonic subject, however, in which Peirce was proficient, and that is the study of ethics. But where Plato's ethics required a more or less static world, Peirce's doctrine was closely connected with his evolutionary theory. Peirce rejected mechanical and mere chance evolution for a doctrine of chance which of itself evolves order and grows into love. "Tychistic agapism" he called it, with his fondness for new and obscure terms, a chance love destined to generate more and more order in the world. From an infinite past of indeterminacy where chance alone governed, the universe is moving toward an infinite future of the complete reign of law and order, because the tendency to obey laws always has been and always will be a growing thing. Peirce held that the development from chaos to cosmos was one from chance and disorder to love and order. Logic and love he held to be two ways of regarding the same thing. Chance carries with it the seeds of its own supplanting by order.

There are scattered throughout Peirce's papers the hints of a broad social theory which is capable of being of the utmost value today. Strange to say, it has been almost entirely overlooked. This is the theory of the unlimited community, which Peirce evolved from his study of probability. In the effort to elucidate the meaning of practical consequences is to be found the key to the ethics of Peirce. Peirce warns against understanding the practical in any low and sordid sense. He was sure that we are working collectively toward an end which it will require many, many generations to work out. Somehow, this social goal must consist of exemplified universals in the Platonic sense.[6] It is, then, from his essentially realistic, pragmatic maxim that Peirce derived his logical status.

---

6. *Ibid.*, 1.403.

If immediate practical action is to be ruled out, then individual self-interest cannot serve as the ethical criterion. Peirce next goes on to show that it is illogical for the individual to identify his interests with any limited thing. All persons die, and all limited social groups must sooner or later come to an end even though they survive the individual. Societies, corporations, nations—limited communities of whatever sort, although they may enjoy a comparatively long life—must perish eventually, and thus betray that trust which the individual places in them when he identifies his interests with theirs. Peirce showed that there is no person, custom, institution, or even civilization, which cannot be depended upon to perish within a finite, and usually within a comparatively brief, time. Whatever it is of a limited nature that we work for, and in which we place our faith and hope, we may be sure that the time will come when it will betray us by coming to an end. It is not always given to human beings to witness this defection, as Peirce demonstrates in a dramatic passage, for in place of this death is substituted.

But we may be sure that what outlives us will not outlive our trust. Logicality, Peirce then concludes, leads us to this: that we cannot be logical and yet put our trust in any affair of a limited nature. In the typical textbook of the period Peirce noted three kinds of motives for human action: love of self, of a limited class having common interests and feelings with one's self, and love of mankind. But love, which is logical, must be directed from the self through the limited class toward mankind and even beyond to the whole universe. To be thoroughly logical our interests must extend to our neighbors and past them to their neighbors, and beyond even them in an unending series, until it passes all geologic epochs and indeed all boundaries. In short, it must embrace an unlimited community.

It is not necessary, continues Peirce, that all men should be severally capable of self-sacrifice. It is sufficient that all recognize the possibility of it and perceive that only the inferences of those men who have it are really logical, considering their own inferences valid only in so far as these would be accepted by the hero.

This makes logicality attainable enough; we cannot be strictly logical and identify our interests with anything short of an unlimited community. The soldier who runs to scale a wall knows that he will probably be shot, but that is not all he cares for. He also knows that if all individuals in the regiment, with whom in feeling he identifies himself, rush forward at once, the fort will be taken. Sometimes we can personally attain to heroism, but this is rare; in other cases we can only imitate the virtue, which is often enough. But all this requires a conceived identification of one's narrow, personal interests with those of an unlimited community. The goal of the individual must be understood to lie through society, though it is not bound by any limited society, for if it were he would serve nothing who only imitated the virtue, because then there would be nothing to serve. But given the unlimited community, actions and even passive attitudes which were of no immediate service might prove eventually serviceable.

This doctrine of the unlimited community is explained and defended in the most realistic manner possible; and it represents a logical rather than revealed version of the doctrine of immanence, that the things of this world are worthy. It paves the way for the acceptance of a religion based on immanence rather than transcendence, a religion based on the doctrine of this worldliness, as being more consonant with the Fourth Gospel of which Peirce was so fond. It contains, besides the germ of a most important social theory, the possibility of a valid social science.

VII

In some ways, then, we may safely say that the vast importance of Peirce's teaching has not yet been detected even by those who wish to be his followers. The understanding of Peirce waits for the renaissance of medieval realism minus its theological excesses, signs of which are aready here and there detectable. But above all, Peirce's work is of vast importance for a generation destined to witness the failure of nominalism which has given rise to chaos in the social field. For the development of Peirce's ideas is capable of bringing harmony where differences and opposition continue.

Peirce sought to reconcile science and religion by showing them to be based on a common metaphysics; to eliminate conflict in philosophy by showing that where nominalistic philosophies are opposed not only to realistic philosophies but to each other as well, realistic philosophies contain possibilities of agreement based on a common rationality; and finally he sought to offer a social theory based on love and the direct pursuit of the good rather than on hate and the use or avoidance of evil. Truth is an eternal value, and Peirce's philosophy, which is not without its flaws, but which contains a large measure of truth, is of especial worth to a world whose beliefs are in a process of abnormal flux and change.

The recent history of Peirce's influence is even more misleading than that of pragmatism. Among the many followers of Peirce there have been few who have understood and accepted his realism. James, Royce, and Dewey—among others—may be mentioned. We have already noted how James's version of pragmatism went astray. Dewey acknowledges Peirce as one from whom he learned much, but the Deweian version of pragmatism, known as instrumentalism, requires an even more immediate demonstration of the truth. The truth for Dewey is what works now; and truth is thus made dependent upon current practice as exemplified in an extremely limited number of instances. The American Marxist, Sidney Hook, hints that Marx is logically if not historically an American pragmatist in the understanding of pragmatism according to Dewey, and he tries to show that Peirce and Marx are not irreconcilable. But since Marx is a materialist, and hence a nominalist, while Peirce is a realist, this is not so easy. Superficially, of course, there is some resemblance, as, for instance, when Marx unwittingly commits himself to realistic assumptions, and when Peirce slips by error into nominalistic implications, but this is not sufficient to demonstrate a common ground. Where Peirce and Marx are most logical they are most contradictory.

There remains yet another and very misleading attempt to claim Peirce for nominalism—that of the modern logical positivists. This effort is corollary to the position which the logical positivists assume when they wish to defend the logistic side of the controversy over the foundations of mathematics. The logical positivists are frank and obvious nominalists in denying that logic has any non-mental reference, and it is difficult to see how they could be consistent (i.e., logical) and at the same time claim as their own the realistic attempt of Peirce to lay the foundations of mathematics in an independent logic. The logical positivists are under an obligation to Peirce because he was one of the important pioneers of symbolic logic, but their frank statement of the meaninglessness of metaphysics precludes them from any sympathy with Peirce's philosophy. That the full effect of Peirce's metaphysical discoveries has been delayed may be partially explained by his own failure to set forth in an organized book his completed metaphysical system. It is indeed a great misfortune that Peirce did not write a single comprehensive work on any topic except logic. There is scattered throughout the innumerable essays, articles, and papers—both published and unpublished—which he has left behind him, a unified metaphysical position. But had he launched an attack upon nominalism in the form of a completed work, the refutation of nominalism would not have had to wait upon the proper understanding of the philosophical implications of modern physical science.

We have tried within the brief compass of this chapter to see that the history of Peirce's reputation is the account of a series of misunderstandings. Peirce is not a pragmatist like James, nor an instrumentalist like Dewey, nor a Marxist like Hook, nor, lastly, a nominalist like the logical positivists. Peirce explicitly asserts that his metaphysical position lies closer to that of Duns Scotus than to any other philosophy. This makes him a kind of Platonist. But Peirce does not often mention Plato. A blindness on the subject of esthetics, which Peirce readily confessed, perhaps led to his indifference to the philosopher whom he should most have acknowledged. Peirce apparently had no feeling for beauty, and consequently no interest in esthetics; and this topic which is so much of a preoccuption with the Platonists may have estranged him from the tradition to which he is most certainly committed by his metaphysical writings.

II

Whitehead's Philosophy of Organism

THE APPEARANCE OF Whitehead's philosophy of organism, as set forth in his *Process and Reality*, is an event of vast importance in the world. There is no substitute for a direct acquaintance with it. It is not the purpose of this chapter to present a complete analysis and criticism; such an undertaking would require many volumes. The intention is to examine the philosophy of organism only in some of those phases in which it touches upon the fundamental metaphysical question of realism. Thus neither a brief exposition nor an exhaustive summary is offered here, but simply some observations on those aspects of Whitehead's system which, from one point of view, appear most important at the present time.

Whitehead's philosophy is the first great realistic system of modern western philosophy to be systematically expressed. By "realistic" here is meant that it is based upon the being of universals independent of the mind, and indeed of all actuality, and possessing a reality of universals equal to that of actual physical things. It is the first to be systematically expressed, because the system of Peirce, which is dated earlier, was not so expressed, except in a kind of implicit fashion. But Whitehead has presented us with an explicit realistic system, and this is one of its chief virtues. He has seen that realism in philosophy is demanded by the developments of modern physics, particularly by the theory of relativity. It is this connection which has caused one critic to observe, rather wryly, that for some reason philosophy always seems to agree with the physics of the day. Of course, it would be a poor philosophy which did not. It would be a poor philosophy which did not also agree with the chemistry, the biology, the psychology of the day. For the task of philosophy is to draw a circle which will be large enough to include all known facts and to suggest others. Whitehead has had the courage of his metaphysical convictions, for only those who make daring hypotheses can even hope to be very inclusive. And only those can hope to be very right who have taken the risk of being very wrong.

The overwhelming importance of Whitehead's philosophy, apart from the realistic metaphysics which it contains, is that it ushers in a new era in which ontology is held to be central to philosophy. The end of the nineteenth century and the early part of the twentieth witnessed the emphasis on epistemology carried to absurd degrees. Philosophy as a whole, except for a little ethics, was devoted to the analysis of the knowledge process, an analysis which was encouraged to verge on the psychological. It was assumed that ontology is equivalent to dogmatism and ontology was studiously avoided for that reason. Actually, the metaphysics which was implicit in the analysis of knowledge was the metaphysics which considers the knowledge problem central: that of nominalism. Nominalism is no less ontological for considering ontology as of little account, and no less dogmatic. The man who loudly proclaims his low opinion of the whole business of holding opinions is certainly holding a very strong one. The tendency of the nominalistic tradition was to consider metaphysics in general and epistemology in particular an affair for the classroom and private study. It is fortunate for philosophy that its scope is broader than that; as broad, in fact, and often as alien, as the world. Ontology applies to everything, and in so far as it is true, it is true of everything; and no amount of denying the proposition will alter it in any way. It is Whitehead's achievement that he has understood this fact and has proclaimed it in the form of an elaborate cosmology.

Before embarking upon an examination of the realistic implications of the philosophy of organism, it may be well to review briefly its main points.

Whitehead begins with opposition to the current philosophy of static substance having qualities which he holds to be based on the simply located material bodies of Newtonian physics and the "pure sensations" of Hume. The seventeenth-century philosophy depends upon a "bifurcation of nature" into two unequal systems of reality, on the Cartesian model of mind and matter. The high abstractions of science must not be mistaken for concrete realities. Instead, Whitehead argues that there is only one reality; what appears, whatever is given in perception, is real. There is nothing existing beyond what is present in the experience of subjects, understanding by subject any actual entity. There are neither static concepts nor substances in the world, only a network of events. All events are actual extensions or spatiotemporal unities. The philosophy of organism, as Whitehead terms his work, is based upon the patterned process of events. All things or events are sensitive to the existence of all others, the relation between them consisting in a kind of feeling. Every actual entity is then a "prehensive occasion"; that is, it consists in all those active relations with other things into which it enters. An actual entity is further determined by "negative prehension," the exclusion of all that which it is not. Thus every feeling is a positive prehension; every abstraction a negative one. Every actual entity is lost as an individual when it perishes, but is preserved through its relations with other entities in the framework of the world. Also, whatever has happened must remain an absolute fact. In this sense past events have achieved "objective immortality." Except for this, the actual entities are involved in flux, into which there is the ingression of eternal objects from possibility. The selection of universals is necessary to the actual entities. Thus the actual world is a selection from the realm of possibilities. The actual entities are certain selections from among eternal objects. God is the principle of concretion which determines the selection. "Creativity" is the primal cause whereby possibilities are selected in the advance of actuality toward novelty. This movement is termed the consequent nature of God. The pure possibility of the eternal objects themselves is termed His primordial nature.

First of all, it may be observed that the terminology is significant. Readers of *Process and Reality* will recall, too, that it is impossible to overlook Whitehead's turn of phrase. Whitehead's sense of humor appears most clearly in his literary style. Someone has observed that the ideal of style is that it shall be unobtrusive, the meaning and the manner in which that meaning is conveyed being so inextricably intertwined that no distinction is possible. In a sense Whitehead has achieved this ideal and in another sense he has not.

The sense in which he has achieved it is of dubious value. All metaphysics, as Whitehead clearly sees (20),[1] endeavors to get beyond detailed denotation and relies upon the connotative values which only imagination can limn. In metaphysics meaning is always forced somewhat beyond the confines of language; and to represent this there are elements of turgidity and obscurity in Whitehead's writing. It is not always entirely clear just what he does mean. Not only does the import of many sentences depend heavily upon context, but also the import of the context is regressive, so that an understanding of the entire work is requisite for the understanding of a particular part of it. This is what is meant by obscurity; the whole of meaning cannot be assumed in the parts, or at least this presence of the whole in the parts cannot be relied on when the work is first approached. Whitehead himself has the whole in mind in dealing with the parts, so that he frequently begins a sentence with the word "also" (197), where the connection is not readily evident but has been taken for granted. The good side of this sense of similarity between content and expression is contained in the fact that in endeavoring to reach beyond denotation in expression, Whitehead is correspondingly endeavoring to reach beyond language in metaphysics. The turgidity frequently produces a far-reaching suggestiveness.

The sense in which he has not achieved a unity of style and content has its drawbacks, but in a work of this sort it has undoubted value. To the extent to which we are able to distinguish between style and content we can penetrate beneath the style to the content,

---

1. All numbers in parentheses in the text refer to the pages of *Process and Reality*, New York, 1930.

dismiss the vehicle, so to speak, and get at the inner essence of the meaning which it carries, isolated from everything else. Whitehead inverts expressions so often, for instance, that we know it cannot correspond to meaning. He refers to the substitution of the forms of process for the procession of forms, and to so many other pairs in like fashion that it begins to appear as a favorite trick, and we cease to analyze its meaning, having met the same sleight of hand so many times before in the same pages. There are other familiar literary tricks—juxtaposition of incongruent elements, the sublime and the ridiculous is a common one, frequently not ineffective. We learn in the same sentence that the fairies dance and that Christ was (expressed as "is") nailed to the cross. We learn that the reason we see an elephant is that he is sometimes absent, i.e., that we do not always see him. In other words, the object is indicated as important when present *and* (in the sense of *because*) it is sometimes absent. And so on.

Meaning, particularly the abstract and universal meaning intended in speculative metaphysics, is an elusive affair. The danger always has been to identify the metaphysical component of meaning with its accompanying furniture. Metaphysics is in the mind, or it is in the material world, or it is in activity, or it is in operations conducted by the subject upon the object, or it is in the language whereby it is communicated and conveyed. It is frantically identified with anything and everything, in short, except with itself. The universal, or as Whitehead prefers to call it, the eternal object, "tree" let us say, is not in my head, or in *that* tree, or in the activity of growing as a tree or of being climbed or otherwise used as a tree, or in the four letters, t-r-e-e. It simply is not that easy. The tree is the name for a certain universal function and value, which we have labelled "tree," and which has a constant nature however much it may vary from actual tree to actual tree. Now, the particular danger of current metaphysical interpretation is its tendency to identify metaphysics with the metaphysics which is in books; with the language in which it is written and with the words whereby it is expressed. For according to our contemporary nominalistic empiricism, where else can we place it, with what other actual physical thing can we identify it? Whitehead has taken precautions to see that this modern bit of subjectivism, however much he may abstractly subscribe to subjectivism, shall not be committed in his case. He understands and has endeavored to explain that metaphysics is not confined to language, although language must be employed to express it, and he offers as evidence of this fact the further fact that not all metaphysics can be expressed in language; that metaphysics, in other words, always strains to get beyond language. To express the inexpressible might be taken as a good description of the labors of metaphysicians.

Whitehead's style, then, has its good and its bad points. At first it will always be a surprise. But the understanding of the philosophy of organism depends to some extent upon the elimination of this element of surprise, and the achievement of a familiarity with the method of presentation that will enable the reader to forget it and to concentrate exclusively upon the meaning which it is intended to convey in so far as such meaning can be conveyed, and to suggest further meaning to the imagination where it cannot. Always behind the style, however, is the reliance upon the distinction between the seen and the unseen world, the order of actuality and its prehensive actual entities upon the one hand, and of possible but not actual eternal objects upon the other.

The origins of Whitehead's philosophy are to be found, as he acknowledges, in Plato and Aristotle. Whitehead is a Platonist in that he is a realist in the medieval sense of the term; that is, he believes in the reality of universals. He is also a realist in the Greek sense, in that he believes in the reality of values as well. But he wishes to trace his philosophy to the nominalistic school of European empiricists, as he says, from Descartes to Hume. There does not seem to be any good philosophical reason for so doing. Whitehead has to twist himself into many strange shapes in order to credit his nominalistic predecessors with his realistic philosophy. It has elsewhere been shown that he is closer to Peirce in his philosophical thought; yet he mentions James—James the radical empiricist, rather than Peirce the realist—as the American philosopher for whom he has the most respect. He does not mention Peirce at all, even though he was anticipated by Peirce not only in many of his leading ideas but also in the conception of the system itself. He wishes to acknowledge Descartes, Newton, Locke, Hume, and Kant, because they left out of their systematic philosophies just those elements which he considered important enough to put at the base of his philosophy of organism (vi). A curious obligation indeed, unless he has brought himself to believe that these men ate the skins of truth and threw away the fruit. Elsewhere he indicates that he is particularly interested in the ideas which the same group of thinkers, plus a few others, repudiated (16). What is the particular advantage of claiming to stem indirectly from thinkers with whom one disagrees, when one could so easily show the logical derivation from thinkers with whom one agrees? Historically, it may be argued, the actual derivation took place in the former manner; certainly it is true that one can often learn more from detecting the errors committed by others than from memorizing the truths discovered by others. But it is necessary to show the tradition in which one *logically* belongs, as well as that from which one has *historically* derived. He seems to be obsessed with the desire to read himself into the modern European tradition of philosophy, and particularly into the English empirical tradition, from the seventeenth century onward, although his own viewpoint, determined in large measure by metaphysical realism, puts him in violent opposition to it. His philosophy is negatively determined by the English empiricists only as an afterthought: it is unlikely that Whitehead arrived at his own position by rejecting the conclusions of the English empirical school.

Another curious feature of Whitehead's avowals is his intention to rescue Bergson, James, and Dewey from the charge of anti-intellectualism, which "rightly or wrongly" (vii) has been associated with them. It is not possible to think of any philosopher with whom the author of the philosophy of organism has less in common than Dewey. But that is not the chief issue; if Whitehead thinks it is, he is entitled to his opinion. But if the charge of anti-intellectualism has been levelled against these philosophers "rightly," why would Whitehead wish to rescue them from it? That would not be defending philosophy so much as it would be cheating justice. No one could conscientiously wish to rescue anyone else from a charge of which the latter is guilty. And Bergson, Dewey, and James are guilty. Bergson's philosophy has many of the features of Whitehead's, but it lacks just those elements which render the philosophy of organism metaphysically realistic, such elements as the eternal objects, the realm of possibility and the primordial nature of God. James was hardly a philosopher, he was more of a genial literary speculator and psychologist; but in so far as we can discern the outlines of his metaphysics, they are deeply opposed to Whitehead's. James would never have countenanced raising logic and reason, the negative judgment, negative prehension, and the like, to the ontological eminence to which Whitehead raises them. Experience meant more to James than rationality. Finally, Dewey, the Dewey who proclaimed at a meeting at Harvard in honor of Whitehead, that he could not understand the abstract-mathematical method; is this the same Dewey Whitehead wishes to rescue from the charge of anti-intellectualism?

Whitehead goes on to insist that although he often differs from Bradley, the outcome of their work is much the same. Bradley, the Kantian who repudiated Kant but who distinguished ontologically between appearance and reality, and who limited human knowledge to appearance, finds an outcome to his philosophy which is proclaimed by Whitehead to be the same as his own even while he denounces the Kantian doctrine that the world is a "theoretical construct from subjective experience" (viii). A fantastic outcome indeed.

Of course, no philosopher could be said to be great who did not learn something from everyone. Whitehead is right in acknowledging the influence of even those thinkers with whom his system is in the sharpest disagreement. What makes it strange is that he does not anywhere acknowledge also the influence of those European philosophers with whom the philosophy of organism is the most in agreement. Can it be that there was no such influence? He does not seem to know that there have been any other realists prior to the English and American realists of his own day. He does not seem to remember the English realistic tradition that started before Thomas Reid and continued uninterruptedly to G. E. Moore. He does not mention Duns Scotus, the first English philosophic realist; he does not admit any large indebtedness to Augustine or Nicholas of Cusa, both European realists. Realism, in the chain of Whitehead's acknowledgments, skips from Aristotle to Whitehead, and is spotted in between by nominalists from whom Whitehead found he could conveniently take off by disagreement. Now, this may have been the true situation; but if so it is an odd one. It is odd that having seen this himself, Whitehead would not have gone back to recover the classic realists he had overlooked. Particularly is this true in the case of Duns Scotus, who was both a realist and an Englishman, or at least a Scotchman.

The influence of Descartes and of the nominalistic traditions of the seventeenth century have not left Whitehead's philosophy unmarked. The categories of the mental and the physical play a relatively important part in the scheme of things envisaged in the philosophy of organism. There they appear under the guise of prehensions and poles: mental prehensions and mental poles, physical prehensions and physical poles. These are dangerous words for a realist. The Cartesian *res cogitans* and *res extensa* carry with them nominalistic errors in both the epistemological and ontological fields.

Epistemologically, it is an error to suppose that the processes of knowledge are analyzable in terms of the mental and the physical. Whitehead is perilously near the nominalism of the mental and the physical when he identifies the former with the proposition and the latter with actual occasions (290), which he does in his analysis of judgment as subsuming both by what he calls the intellectual prehension. Not all knowing is mental; much more, in fact, is psychic, and remains below the high level of the mental. The psychic and subconscious processes of knowing are complex and elaborate, and the mental is merely that division of the knowing process whereby knowledge is first received into the psyche: conscious processes of ratiocination. Similarly, not all that is known is physical.

The physical in this division is confused with the actual. Not all that is actual is physical; and not all that is physical is actual. The physical consists in the functions of the spatiotemporal world. The actual is that which affects or is affected. What about the forms in things, the triangularity, for instance, of a shadow upon the floor? It is actual but hardly physical. And what about the possibility of there being an automobile with thirty-two cylinders? It is physical but hardly actual. Thought and extension have their categorical place in philosophy, but it is not that of the foundations of epistemology.

Ontologically, therefore, it is an error to suppose that being is composed of the mental and the physical, as exhaustive and mutually exclusive categories. Whitehead is playing with the premises of a philosophy to which his own is opposed when he sets up the mental and the physical poles (40, 49). We have noted that there is more in the world than the mental and the physical. Whitehead himself has seen this, for his cosmology is divided into the two worlds of possibility (46) and the actual world (34), which are peopled with eternal objects and actual entities respectively. These are ontological categories, and they must render any attempt to crowd the mental and the physical into the same cosmology with them confusing and contradictory. Older and more confining ontological schemes often have to be eliminated in setting up broader ones. It is not always possible to subordinate the more limited simply because it is more limited, after the fashion of the smoother dialectic which marks the progress of the science of physics. Frequently in philosophy the earlier conception carries with it connotations which defeat the efforts to trim them down and which therefore hamper the later conception. The distinction between the mental and the physical is of this nature. They may be fitted in, perhaps, as common sense notions, but they simply will not permit themselves to be used as either epistemological or ontological categories in a realistic cosmological scheme.

The old nominalistic metaphysics of mind and matter, inherited from Aristotle and enshrined by the radical empiricists of the English empirical tradition from Locke to Hume, has been retained, then, by Whitehead and fitted into his new terminology. It does not belong there; it is not at home there; it was never needed. We find the distinction again lurking in the division of eternal objects into two kinds: the subjective and the objective species (445). The categories of subject and object have epistemological validity in a realistic system of philosophy, but whenever they are employed ontologically the implication resulting is always that of nominalism. There is no realistic ontological status of high importance for subject and object. Yet they are always given such a status in a system where mind and matter prevail as ontological terms. The two sets of terms are employed in the nominalistic conception interchangeably; the subject is always the mind and the object is always the material world.

In epistemology, it is true that everything which stands in the knowledge relation has a physical, or material, substrate. And everything which knows is at least a potential mental substrate. But that which has a physical or material substrate is not necessarily itself either physical or material. The form of an actual planet has a physical substrate but cannot be said to be physical. Mental images have the substrate of the somatic organism but are not themselves either physical or mental. Roughly, and exclusively for the purposes of epistemology, that which knows, that which is affected by the object known, is the subject; and that which is known, that which affects the subject, is the object. The knowledge relation, however, in which these terms find their validity, is only one of the relations which enjoy being. Not all things are things known. And all relations which have being are ontological relations.

Whitehead himself admits that he has been trying to fuse the cosmology of the *Timaeus* with that of the seventeenth century empiricists (ix). This is just what cannot be done. For that of the *Timaeus* is realistic (in the medieval sense of the term) and that of the seventeenth century nominalistic. There are two ways in which realism can be abandoned. Realism from one point of view means the according of an equal reality to the two orders, namely essence, or being, and existence, or becoming. The supposition that the latter is alone real yields a kind of materialistic nominalism. The supposition that the former is alone real yields a kind of mentalistic nominalism. Being is not exclusively mental any more than becoming is exclusively material. There are passages in the *Dialogues* in which Plato commits the realistic fallacy of supposing that universals, the entities of the realm of being, are either alone real or possessed of a superior grade of reality. And there are few passages in the seventeenth century men of genius in which actuality, with its mental-physical division, the name for the realm of becoming, is not either alone real or possessed of a superior grade of reality. The effort to draft a new conception of realism in terms of modern science was a gigantic one, and Whitehead's greatness is his success therein. The confusion in his work results from the attempt to reconcile the new conception with two conflicting cosmologies with which it has little in common.

Let us turn, now, to a somewhat more detailed examination of the categories in terms of which the philosophy of organism has been framed.

First in importance are the eternal objects. Eternal objects are listed among the Categories of Existence (32) and not among the Categories of the Ultimate. There is, in fact, only one Category of the Ultimate, namely Creativity, and it is described as the "universal of universals" (31). Thus creativity is ontologically superior to universals, or, in other words, universals are subject to the process of creativity. This can mean nothing that would exclude the idea of change. But if creativity applies to universals and they change, in what sense can they be said to be eternal? Presumably, nothing is eternal except the process of creativity. Eternal objects may be objects—objects of creativity; but nothing is eternal which is also subject to change. It is hard to connect logically a principle which is described as the "principle of novelty" (31) and objects which are described as eternal objects.

Another difficulty with the conception of eternal objects is that which is also applicable to universals. If they are divided, then they must exist in actual things. But they cannot be spoken of as divided and also as possible; for the realm of being is not a divided realm. In the logical order of possibility, there are no distinct things, only distinguishable things having their being as parts of a whole. We can allude to them as eternal objects in the order of possibility only in a quasi-concrete way of referring to the abstract. This second criticism leads us back to the first. If eternal objects are only plural when actual, that is, when existing in actual things as their forms, then it should be noted that it is the carrier of the forms, the vehicle, which changes and not the eternal objects. Creativity, conceived as novelty in the way in which Whitehead does conceive it, ought to be understood as applying to the actual carriers of eternal objects and not to the eternal objects themselves. For they are independent of the actuality in which they partially inhere, and thus they are independent too of all vicissitude and change. Nothing is novel about them.

There can be no doubt of the realism of Whitehead's philosophy, if we consider merely his definition of eternal objects. "An eternal object is defined as any entity whose recognition does not involve enforced reference to the actual world" (p. 70). The eternal object, we are informed on the same page, is neutral as to its ingression into the actual world. And further, that there is not a limited class of eternal objects whose components constitute the class but rather a multiplicity of them (73). The danger of realism is the tendency to confine it by supposing that the universals (or eternal objects) which are known are the sum of those that have being. This was the error of medieval realism as fostered by the Catholic Church; and it is still the error of the prescribed Aristotelian realism of the theologians. The infinite field of being has a way of breaking through the ignorances with which we limit and bound our knowledge; there is always more to the universe than was dreamed of in *any* philosophy. By replacing the class of eternal objects with the multiplicity of eternal objects, Whitehead has left their number obscure and their pursuit permanently desirable. This is the kind of unlimited realism which accords well with the spirit and method of science, and promises to avoid the restrictions which have eventually brought to an end all limited realisms of the past.

The reason for making eternal objects eternal is perfectly clear.

Like universals, they are eternal in that they are not subject to change, and they are ubiquitous, also, as is implied by Whitehead's definition, in that they are not confined anywhere and are thus applicable everywhere. But the reason for making eternal objects objects, while equally clear, has its disadvantages. The reason probably was to keep the eternal objects objective to the human mind and so to prevent them from being understood as mental, in the way in which the term, ideas, has come to be considered exclusively mental, an understanding which is far from Plato's usage of the term. This purpose is accomplished. It is difficult, however, to correct one error without falling into the danger of committing another. There is something too concrete-sounding about the term eternal objects. We are not accustomed to thinking of eternal things as actual, but objects somehow sounds not only actual but even physically actual. An eternal object has the ring of a physical object; it sounds hard, visible, and even tangible. It certainly occupies space-time, and it certainly resists all efforts to make it, or to read it as, other than it is—or at least such is the impression given by the term.

Of course, it is fair to employ a term in any way one wishes, provided one defines the term and does not use it in any way other than that authorized by the definition. These conditions Whitehead meets, at least in so far as eternal objects are concerned. Nevertheless, terms having a history of their own in the English language also have a connotation which is difficult to eliminate by decree, and this is just what we endeavor to do when we use an old term in a new way and announce our intention of so doing. Whitehead, we may say, is not using an old term in a new way so much as he is using two old terms in a new way; but the new way, as it happens, is inimical to the connotation of the old terms taken separately. The point is important because it is illustrative of the method frequently adopted by Whitehead, and of its drawbacks. The problem is, could the subjective side of universals—and perhaps also of values—have been eliminated without coining a term with the connotations of actuality still clinging to its words? We do not want to think about universals or values, or about eternal objects, for that matter, as concrete things existing outside of space-time, and perhaps dwelling in some perfect place forever in all their wholeness and perfection. There is nothing in the universe except actuality and its contents; that is, there is no-*thing,* but there is the possibility of there being things, and these possibilities are what is meant by universals and values, and presumably what is meant also by eternal objects. We can gather from context that by eternal objects Whitehead means not objects that are eternal but rather the eternal possibility of there being actual objects.

Are eternal objects values or merely universals? Do they contain the possibility of power and action or merely that of relation? It is difficult to say. It is difficult to know whether Whitehead does not finally commit the error so many neo-realists have committed of assuming that while universals are independent of actuality, values are confined to it, and thus of supposing a world whose actuality is affective but whose possibility is not. Such a conception ultimately reduces to a Lockeian system wherein the form is primary and the material is secondary, a world in which the relations are objective and the elections subjective, a world of real structure and illusory content. Strictly by the definition of eternal objects, it would seem that as entities involving no enforced reference to actuality they could include elections as well as relations, value as well as logic. Eternal objects considered as entities have altogether too concrete a ring about them. They sound very actual, which is just what a possibility is not supposed to be. Yet they do offer the advantage of seeming to include forces as well as logical relations. We shall see as we proceed that the category of prehension offers something of the same difficulty in that it seems to represent what we have termed value and yet in a sense to confine that value to actuality.

The business of philosophy, says Whitehead, is to explain abstractions, not concretions. Explanation itself is always in terms of the concretions (30). The name for concretions in the philosophy of organism is actual entities. The actual entities are the final ultimate real things, a claim which would make Whitehead a nominalist were it not for the contradictory assumptions relied on in other passages that the eternal objects are also real, as real as anything. It is a strange contrast which allows eternal objects to sound concrete and actual entities abstract when just the opposite is the case. Both eternal objects and actual entities are described as fundamental types without distinction (37). But the fact is that when Whitehead is discussing one at a time, he conveys the impression that he intends one to be taken as the most real and the other as derivative. Actual entities are prehending things (65), a statement which is derived from Descartes by the simple device of substituting *prehendens* for *cogitans,* terms which assuredly do not mean the same thing at all! They are the interactive properties of the immediate world of time and space. Space and presumably also time depend upon the actual entities (73). Existence depends upon actual entities or occasions (113), and thus whatever arises from existence by abstraction is dependent upon actual entities. It is assumed, of course, that eternal objects are not derived. The actual entities are parts of actuality considered by themselves. Now, actuality is an unstable affair characterized by flux and change, and this flux and change is therefore also attributable to the actual entities. The actual entities are asked to carry a heavy load, for they bear all the characteristics upon which their actuality depends.

The actual entities are seldom mentioned without the accompaniment of what Whitehead describes as the ontological principle. The ontological principle simply states that all explanation must be in terms of the actual entities (28). Reasons can never be given for anything except in terms of the actual entities (37). But since God is an actual entity (28), this leaves considerable latitude to explanation. The intention to hold speculation down to what is concrete and demonstrable is defeated by allowing what is speculatively inferential—God, for instance—to be part of the ground of that by which explanation is rendered demonstrable. Why call this principle the ontological principle? Names are important and something significant was obviously intended here. If the dependence of all explanation upon the actual entities is *the* ontological principle rather than just one more principle whose ontological nature can be taken for granted as being no more ontological than that of any other universal and abstract principle referring to the questions of ontology (which alone is under discussion), then actual entities are made the sole realities.

It is hard at times to believe that Whitehead does not mean the actual entities to be the superior realities, and one can be saved from this opinion only by reading about the eternal objects again. For the eternal objects are the Platonic forms (70, 73), and this *is* a Platonic philosophy we are discussing, it is well to remind ourselves. It is well to remember, too, that the ontological principle, which refers the limitation of explanatory value to the actual entities, is itself a principle and not an actual entity. A principle is, according to Whitehead's definitions, closer to what he has termed an eternal object. It is dependent upon no specific reference to any actual entity for its meaning, but instead is perfectly general. Thus the principle which saves explanation for actual entities cannot itself be explained in terms of actual entities, due to its universality and abstractness. That it still has validity in the Whiteheadian scheme can be only because of the fact that abstractions are as real and as valid as concretions, universals as real and valid as particulars, the logical order as real and valid as the historical order. But if this is true, then explanation could just as well be in terms of eternal objects as of actual entities, and the truth of the ontological principle falls down.

The validity of the ontological principle can be saved only by the postulation of a corresponding factual principle. If the ontological principle refers all explanation to actual entities where eternal objects are concerned, then the factual principle would refer all explanation to eternal objects where actual entities were concerned. The two orders of being, the logical order of eternal objects and the historical order of actual entities, cannot be knitted together properly by placing all emphasis and responsibility upon the actual entities, not, that is, without according a superior reality to the actual entities, which no metaphysical realist would wish to do.

Nevertheless, in one unfortunate passage, Whitehead declares that besides the actual entities there is nothing, nothing which comes into the world from nowhere (373). Either this statement is misleading or the remainder of his philosophy is misconceived. For if there is nothing besides the actual entities, what status can be assigned to the eternal objects? Presumably they are nothing, and made of sheer nothingness. But this is contradicted by what is written about the eternal objects. The eternal objects are said to be Forms of Definiteness and Pure Potentials for the Specific Determination of Fact (32). Are forms and potentials nothing? Again, we are told that physical prehensions involve actual entities, as distinct from conceptual prehensions which evidently do not (35). Then are conceptual prehensions also nothing? We are clearly led to believe so. The quotations and examples could be multiplied many times. It is obvious from the lengthy context of the cosmology that what Whitehead should have said is that apart from the actual entities there is nothing actual. There are metaphysical schemes in which potentials and forms are consistently held as nothing, but Whitehead's philosophy is not one of them.

Whitehead is more afraid of committing the realistic fallacy than he is of committing the nominalistic fallacy. The fallacy of extreme realism, in which universals are accorded a sole or superior reality and actual things deemed shadowy, is the bane of every Platonist, for it is certainly representative of one of the two philosophies which are to be found in the Platonic writings. Whitehead evidently does not wish to be thought a believer in the supreme universals with their concomitant derogation of the actual world, when the truth lies with more moderate realism.

But in the effort to escape from one pitfall, it is possible that Whitehead comes near to being a victim of the other. Too often he insists that the eternal objects are only abstractions from the actual entities (30). But abstractions have a reality which depends upon the concretions from which they were abstracted, thus putting the eternal objects under obligation for their reality to the actual entities. This defeats the realistic caution of an equality with respect to reality between the orders of being. Then, too, the eternal objects are described as potentials, pure potentials (32, 34).

But, as many a metaphysician has pointed out, possibility and potentiality are hardly the same. Whitehead uses the term, potentiality, advisedly, in the sense that potentiality means possibility in the thing, in the actual thing. But this, also, is a way of pinning reality down to actuality. So that we see in the two explanations a prejudice in favor of the actual which savors of nominalism.

The tightrope of realism is difficult to walk. On one side there is the danger of extreme realism, with its corollary threat of subjective idealism, of believing that universals dwell in the mind. On the other hand there is the danger of nominalism, of believing that only the flux of existence is real. The former is the fallacy which the Renaissance came to correct. The latter is the corrective excess which the Renaissance committed. Can not the philosophers at least learn to cut down the width of the dialectic swath which the alteration of extreme error carves? Does Whitehead, the Whitehead who acknowledges that Plato and Aristotle are the two founders of all Western thought, and who insists that European philosophy has only written footnotes to Plato, honestly believe that becoming constitutes being so far as actual entities are concerned? Is he willing to set up the fallacy of historicism as the principle of process (34-5)? It is a position impossible to accept, and can only be counted an excess of caution, if we are to save the consistency of the philosophy of organism.

That Whitehead has other intentions is clear from the status of independence elsewhere accorded the eternal objects. The very term, eternal, indicates that the eternal objects do not suffer the same fate of the actual entities which are involved in change, becoming, and other actual forms of creativity. Thus they cannot be said to be abstractions merely. They are discovered by abstraction, perhaps, and they can only be discussed, as Whitehead says, in terms of their potentiality for ingression into actual entities; but their being does not hang upon their potentiality for existence. They are always possible, and potential only when participating in the interaction of actual entities. Eternal objects have eternal being and become actual only because of their accidents. Later on in Whitehead's exposition, they are shown to participate in being by the nature of the primordial side of God. So we must think of them as universals rather than concepts, as essences rather than abstractions from existence.

The ideas which particularly mark the philosophy of organism from all previous philosophies are, in Whitehead's opinion, actual entity, prehension, nexus, and ontological principle (27). We have already discussed actual entities and the ontological principle. The former are items in actuality—actual things—and the latter declares that there shall be no valid explanation except in terms of actual things. These are strange over-emphases in a realistic philosophy, for after all, nominalism only goes one step further in declaring that there is nothing else to explain except actual things. We have yet to discuss prehension and nexus. We shall consider them in that order.

It is in the analysis of the actual entity that the prehension is to be found. The prehension reproduces the characteristic of the actual entity—any characteristic (28). Thus prehensions are the most concrete kind of analysis (29); they are in effect relatednesses expressed as concrete facts (32). Prehensions are either physical, when they are prehensions *of* actual entities, or conceptual, when they are prehensions *of* eternal objects (35).

It often appears as though Whitehead has strained a point to show the derivation of his own ideas from those of the English philosophical tradition. See, for instance, his effort to compare Locke's "idea" with his own "prehension" or "feeling" (37). Locke, he says, restricted his term to conscious mentality; whereas for Whitehead, there is the prehension or feeling of anything, a stone or a planet. What has a universal, which is not restricted to conscious mentality, in common with one which is? A prehension is closer to a value than to an idea in Locke's sense of the latter term. And Whitehead's use of the notion of feeling makes it definitely not exclusively subjective to human beings: anything which can exist as a distinct entity is capable of having a feeling. Then what has a feeling to do with an idea? Nothing at all, except a remarkably clear difference. For an idea is confined to the mind of the human subject, while the feeling certainly is not. There can be no good philosophical reason for insisting in this way upon the historical relation of conceptions which are neither logically nor historically related.

Whitehead has described the philosophy of organism in general as a cell-theory of all actuality (334), and in doing so he has both aptly characterized it and also indicated its acute limitations. For it is evident that what Whitehead means by prehension is what other philosophers have meant by value—objective value such as is possessed by anything and everything actual: the value of the ground for a stone, of water for a plant, of catnip for a cat, and of a woman for a man. Too many philosophies are abstract in the sense that they leave out the effective nature of things, but almost all philosophies since Plato's have left out the possible nature of value, and even Whitehead's philosophy of organism is guilty of this omission so far as positive prehensions are concerned. For prehension is repeatedly described as a characteristic of actuality, and is to be found exclusively in the analysis of the actual entities. The eternal objects are possibilities; they are universals, but they are not intended to be possible values as well. There are no corresponding possibilities in the philosophy of organism. All possibility in the philosophy of organism is logical possibility—which would mean logically that only universals can become actualized in the future, only logical forms can take their place in the future, and the only prehensions which can exist are those which already do. This would yield a skeleton world of the future, a world in which all prehension had been exhausted by previous states of actuality and in which only the universals, the logical forms, were actual. Of course Whitehead did not intend anything so silly as this, but something equally silly is what is called for in his scheme of things—and in many others, for that matter—by failing to allow the powers, the energies, the values, to have their unlimited share in the world of essences or possibilities.

Another serious criticism to be levelled at the idea of prehensions as Whitehead has set it up, is the division into physical and conceptual types. The substance philosophy and the sensationalist doctrine of perception, against which Whitehead inveighs so vehemently time and again, still refuse to be banished from the philosophy of organism. They are implicit in the ontological distinction between the mental and the physical which returns over and over to haunt the philosophy of organism. Is it possible that only those actual entities which are capable of forming concepts can prehend eternal objects? What is the status of the forms in actual things which are not minds of human beings? The shape of the star-fish, or the moon, for example? Are human beings, who can have conceptions, the only ones who can prehend eternal objects? Presumably, in the realist philosophy any actual thing apprehends its own universal form, since everything has a form and forms are universals independent of all actuality.

On the credit side, we must concede that Whitehead in his notion of prehension has gotten rid of the static description of actuality which the substance philosophy generally entailed. Since every actual entity analyzes into prehensions, the world of actuality is a world of prehensive occasions, certainly a dynamic and interlaced affair. There is no reason to consider a bit of fluxing actuality as itself unmoved and unmoving. In the notion of prehension, we find the yearning of all actual things for all other actual things, the desire to find self-fulfillment in grasping and in being grasped. Value, perhaps, was too neutral a term and has been badly tainted with the connotation of higher value and with subjective meaning merely. The choice of the term prehension corrects some of these misconceptions.

Everything in philosophy is for our experience derived by abstraction from three primitive notions which are descriptive of the ultimate facts of experience, says Whitehead (30). These notions are: actual entities and their prehensions and nexus. We shall discuss next the meaning of the term, nexus, and then return to the implications of this claim.

A nexus, we are told, is the particular togetherness of actual entities (30). A nexus is a public matter of fact (32). The world of an actual entity is a nexus (42), and all nexus are contrasts (349).

It is difficult to see just what the idea of nexus adds to the philosophy of organism. Actual entities might have no togetherness were it not for prehensions or nexus, but since there could be no prehension without togetherness in some sense, namely the dynamic sense, why is the nexus, which seems to be a static togetherness, needed? Nexus restores the static notion of togetherness which prehension was partially designed to eliminate. Actual entities are together in that they grasp each other, and now presumably they can be together also in a sense which is distinct from their grasping.

In setting up the notions of actual entities, prehensions and nexus, as primitive for our experience, Whitehead is dangerously near the error of erecting the psychological order into the ontological one. The phrase, "for our experience," perhaps saves him from this error. Perhaps, too, it does not. Certainly it means that eternal objects are derived by abstraction. But are we then to understand that the psychological derivation of eternal objects from actual entities, prehensions and nexus, is the statement of their ontological condition? For a philosophy which is overwhelmingly Platonic, and which depends upon the distinction between the order of essences and the order of existences, the essences of the system, which in this case are the eternal objects, are repeatedly derogated almost as though on principle. To make the eternal objects dependent upon the abstractive process by which they become known as a factor in experience is to reduce their being to its existence by confining them to the actual entities in which they first become experienced. This is suggestive of Aristotelian realism rather than of Platonic realism.

In every philosophy it is necessary to decide whether the order as well as the facts of experience are to be taken as bearing the stamp of ontological authority. In general, realistic philosophies take the facts (but not their order) and reassemble them according to the requirements of ideal evaluation and of logic, on the assumption, wholly realistic, that things that happen together do not necessarily belong together. Nominalistic philosophies tend to regard experience as exhaustive of ontology, so that the latter term is discarded from philosophy, and its endorsement and credentials turned over to experience. Whitehead, in every case where this choice confronts him, wishes to keep the broad inclusiveness of his system and to rule out all exclusiveness, at least where this practice can be maintained in accordance with the demands of consistency. But it simply cannot be done completely, else there would be no need to distinguish between the two traditions. Any philosophy can be broadened so as to include what it thinks are the truths of rival views, but no philosophy is broad enough to include in the scope of its truths both truth and error; not, that is, if it hopes to retain the slightest trace of consistency.

It is interesting to observe, then, as we consider the nexus, the last of the three ultimate facts of experience, that Whitehead considers them—together with the ontological principle which cautions us to refer everything to them—to be the four novel contributions made to philosophy by the philosophy of organism. For it is obvious to the thoroughgoing realist that eternal objects are to be found in our actual experience. The relations which hold between the actual entities, entities which are described affectively as prehensions and relationally as nexus, are the eternal objects themselves. We learn from our experience that the actual world is partial and that we cannot understand it except in terms of elements not present; this lesson *of* experience is also present *in* experience. No purpose, for instance, is actually ever perceived. Thus we learn both from what is present in experience and from what is not present that experience itself requires elements which do not depend upon experience for their being. We learn this, it should be emphasized, from direct experience and not from mulling over what we have experienced. One conclusion from these considerations must be that the prehensions and nexus, despite the claims of their exclusively actual nature, are made to carry the missing values and universals respectively, without which the terms of the ontological principle could not be validated.

In some ways the most valuable, true, and suggestive contribution which Whitehead has made to philosophy is that of the negative prehension. Prehension, as we have noted, is a term for objective and independent value. Negative prehension is the abstraction from prehension, or, in other words, it is logic. That is to say, it includes logic and all abstract relations in the old meaning of the word, but it is cast in a new ontological mold. For it shows how logic derives from value and that logic is something in itself.

Long ago, Plato had asserted in the *Sophist* that non-being is not negation but rather positive difference. What exists, what has value, or in Whitehead's term, prehension, has that existence as value in virtue of the absence, the difference, the otherness, of everything else. Thus everything positively prehends everything else affectively, and negatively prehends everything else abstractly. The former is value; the latter, logic. Things are related in virtue of the force of attraction and repulsion which they exert upon each other; and they are also related in virtue of the lines of difference which exist to make their identity possible. A thing has presence in space and time *as* a thing only because of the absence from the same space and time of everything else. Negative prehension, when taken in conjunction with positive prehension, shows the inter-relatedness of all things in the unity of the actual universe.

In negative prehension, feeling is eliminated (35). The abstract nature of the negative prehension, presenting merely the universals of possibility, is expressed by Whitehead as the process of holding data inoperative (35). The negative prehension says, this other thing is no part of my internal constitution. But such a statement immediately involves the second statement which declares, my internal constitution depends upon the otherness of this thing. Both statements represent actual facts but they also express the existence of a possible world in which dwell the inoperative data. Thus negative prehension shows how being is a unity, how value is its nature, and finally, how logic derives from the nature of value. It accounts for the negative nature of logic but admits to this negative nature the performance of a necessary positive function. It produces for logic the reasons for the validity of its claim to eminent ontological status.

From the notion of negative prehension we pass to a consideration of two leading principles. The philosophy of organism is gradually unfolding, a philosophy which is nothing if not full of surprises. Consider, for example, the two principles entitled the "subjectivist" principle and the "sensationalist" principle (239). The subjectivist principle tells us that the datum of experience yields on analysis nothing except universals. The sensationalist principle tells us that the act of experience is simply and purely the entertainment of the datum. Thus experience is the entertainment of universals and the datum of experience does not contain anything except universals.

After acquiring some knowledge of the philosophy of organism with its emphasis upon actual entities, there is so much to wonder about in these two new principles that it is difficult indeed to know where to begin. Why is the term, universals, employed and not eternal objects? And what is even more significant, why universals or eternal objects rather than actual entities? Are the actual entities now to become abstractions from experience construed as the experience of universals? As soon as we are ready to abandon Whitehead to nominalism, he returns new evidence of uncompromising and even extreme forms of realism.

Everything besides the actual entities and their components, the prehensions and nexus, are to be derived by abstraction from experience, as we learned earlier. But now suddenly experience itself proves to contain nothing besides universals. Thus when we refer everything to experience we refer everything indirectly to universals. The ontological principle stated that validation involved reference to actual entities. The subjectivist principle states in effect that there is nothing truly subjective except the bare entertainment of universals which do not depend for their ontological being upon either the subject or the object (in this case the actual entities). The subjectivist bias of modern philosophy, which Whitehead insists the philosophy of organism accepts in its entirety (253), is nothing like what can be gathered from the subjectivist principle; indeed, it is the exact opposite. For where modern subjectivism insists that the datum of experience is subjective and yields much besides the universals, Whitehead's subjectivism claims that the datum is objective and yields nothing besides the universals. It is difficult, if not impossible, to reconcile the ontological principle with the subjectivist principle; each tries to save elements which, in the same philosophy, must prove hopelessly irreconcilable.

Is there any true justification for the use of subjective terms to describe objective processes and entities? The practice seems to be a common one with Whitehead. The purpose is apparently to aid in the explanation of the activity of all actual things and the aliveness of all things both animate and inanimate. Whitehead wishes to take us inside things, much in the same way that we are inside ourselves. He wishes us to view the world as it is viewed by other things. To some extent this effort is successful; but it is only possible after we have come to understand the philosophy of organism from within. The terminology is not one designed to assist us in getting inside the philosophy. Given the viewpoint which takes off from the realism of universals and values, the subjective terminology of the philosophy of organism is very understandable and even enlightening. But for those who start from some variety of nominalism, as most of us in the modern world in fact do, the subjective terminology is apt to be very misleading. It is apt to induce the reader to suppose that what is intended is the subjective human viewpoint merely. To say, as Whitehead says, that negative prehensions also have a subjective side (35) is for the unwary nominalist to suggest that all universals are equivalent to concepts in the mind, which is very far indeed from being Whitehead's belief. Whitehead is trying to say that each thing in the world has its subjective side; that is, it looks at the world from inside itself much as we ourselves do. It knows the world by its feeling, however minimal that feeling may be. This is a kind of advanced and complex animism, presupposing epistemological and ontological realism. It must not be confused with human subjectivism, which is merely a part of it.

Kant constructed the objective world out of the experience of the subject, an objective world of appearance. Whitehead explains nothing by the experience of the subject except the subject; but he goes on to show that the world is nothing but the sum total of experiencing, or feeling, subjects (135). Thus the apparent subjectivity of Whitehead's philosophy in one phase turns out to be purely objective. Paradoxically, there is nothing more objective in spirit that can be conceived to exist than a world constructed *entirely* of feeling subjects. For the feeling subject of metaphysics is for Whitehead (and for all true realists) not confined to human beings or even to organic beings. All actual entities are feeling subjects, even a stone. This generalization of subject and of feeling to extend to everything which can be called an actual entity cancels the nominalism implicit in the limitation of feeling to human subjects, and in the epistemological ontology which is usually based upon it.

The philosophy of organism is founded on an atomic theory, what Whitehead terms a cell-theory (334), in which the actual world consists of a number of separate entities or cells, each of which is a subject capable of having feelings objectively inspired. The world for each actual entity or cell is the environment of that entity, and is felt by it in a certain order. The actual entity prehends all other actual entities but only some eternal objects (335). In feeling it takes for its internal parts some elements of the universe (353). There is no objectivity to be compared with that of the world-view which is to be obtained from the interior of a feeling subject; the world is felt as out *there* and is, in fact, all that can be felt; for everything which is felt is objective—it is objectively felt out there in the world.

By embracing extreme subjectivism, a subjectivism which is universal in that every actual entity can be a subject, Whitehead has avoided metaphyical subjectivism. There can be no solipsism so long as the world is considered to be composed of subjects interconnected by means of feeling. Kant made his world a construction of subjective appearances; Whitehead makes his one of the subjects themselves. This method of approach partly answers the question, already raised: how can the objectivity of realism be explained in terms of a consistent subjective terminology? The viewpoint of subjectivism is embraced and then pushed to its logical conclusion in order to get rid of the error of subjectivism. The feat is accomplished by giving an ontological universality to an epistemological subjectivity.

Objectivity is the final and permanent condition of the actual entity. Every actual entity finally achieves what Whitehead terms its objective immortality. The over-riding conception of the philosophy of organism is that of creativity—creative advance into novelty. This presumably is the first surge of movement in which all actual entities are caught up, and the end toward which they move is the immobile state of objective immortality. Thus the notions of creativity and of objective immortality are component conceptions, to be found throughout the development of the system of the philosophy of organism.

Whitehead does not hesitate to make process ultimate (11), and so he must take the consequences of having made this step. If creativity is the ultimate category underlying all forms (30), then all is flux. Creativity, Whitehead tells us, is the universal of universals (31). It substitutes for the Aristotelian matter and the Russellian neutral stuff (46). We cannot go behind it. And since it is the principle of novelty as well (31), we are safe in assuming that it is ever-changing.

How, then, we may ask, can there be eternal objects which do not change? The topic is an elusive one, and not susceptible of being satisfactorily settled by what is already written in the philosophy of organism. But there is some help to be found, as we have noted, in the notion of objective immortality.

Actual entities perish perpetually from the subjective viewpoint, but objectively they acquire immortality (44). Indeed all actual entities are so privileged (89). They gain in objective immortality what they lose in absoluteness (94). The question arises then, are eternal objects actual entities which have found their objective immortality? Do actual entities in their forward plunge reach a frozen state in which they cease to have adventures, lose their value as novelties, and, in compensation, remain unchanged thenceforth? Certainly it is true in Whitehead's conception that out of the flux of actual entities the permanent forms come forth. The doctrine of objective immortality is explicitly held to express a further doctrine; namely, that the process of generation issues from the actual entities since it must be described entirely in terms of the latter (94). A Platonist would insist that all that could be gained from the actual entities either in novelty or in objective immortality would be a knowledge of eternal objects. The eternal objects themselves would have to have their ontological being prior to their participation in actuality, as parts of actual entities. In other passages this appears to be Whitehead's position. The conflict arises from his desire to reconcile a basic metaphysical realism of the Platonic variety with an empiricism interpreted nominalistically which recognizes the ubiquity of the flux. The conflict returns again and again to haunt the philosophy of organism; the only escape from it lies in recognizing that the ubiquity of the flux is not the universality of the flux, and hence in denying the nominalistic absolutism of empiricism.

There is a sense in which Whitehead's philosophy is a hash of all the others. It is possible that Whitehead has overdone the effort to be all-inclusive in his cosmology. He manages to get everything in, but only by the simple device of not requiring everything to be consistent. Spinoza's thought and extension, Descartes' mental and physical parallelism, the sensationalism of Locke, Berkeley, and Hume (declared out but retained), Leibniz's monads and pre-established harmony, the objectivity of realism and the subjectivity of nominalism, the substantiality of materialism and the forms of Plato—all are there and all exist in Whitehead's system unreconciled. Even modern physics, biology, and psychology have contributed more than their quota of unreconciled items. The world seems to be dominated by the geometrical properties which characterize physical spaces and times, such as dimensions, degrees, loci, etc., and also by the biological properties such as sensitivity, life, creativity, etc. The consistency of all these innately and essentially contradictory ideas lies in the irrelevant fact of their co-presence in the same system, not in their proper ordination.

Perhaps this lushness is what aids the impression that Whitehead's work is suggestive. Why is it that inconsistency so often seems to carry the suggestion of abundance? Does the explanation lie in the contention that contradictions are not meaningless but mean too much? Does it prove conclusively that Walt Whitman's contention was correct: that because he contradicted himself he contained everything? If this were so, half of the aim of philosophy would prove nugatory; for philosophy aims to be both all-inclusive and absolutely consistent. To discover a system which will omit nothing is the ambition of ontology. It is possible that the business of cosmology is simply to surround a right little, tight little ontology with some of the cosmic insolubles, the appeals to infinite reaches, to unlimited beginnings and endings. It is not every ontologist but rather every cosmologist who is a theologian in disguise.

Cosmologists are committed in the ontological department, particularly on the question of the relative reality of the two orders of being. Of the two orders of being, it appears that in Whitehead's view, for instance, actuality is the only one which is real. In certain passages, possibility has the overtone of non-being. Then, more or less *ad hoc,* the eternal objects are introduced and pronounced real—in the mind of God. As in Berkeley's system, it is frequently the mind of God which is the only salvation from mentalism or materialism. God himself is limited in vision; he cannot see, he can only envisage. He is transcended by some turns of events, and the stream of actuality is able to flow on without him, even though it is true that without him it is a poor thing at best. Actuality is interpreted according to the great tradition, in that it is construed to be God striving to complete himself. But what does it mean to say, then, that God himself is an actual entity? Can God strive through actuality, be an actual entity, be the ground of all actualization, have a primordial as well as a consequent nature, and house the eternal objects? The spectacle is as confused as the one Whitehead castigates for its theological antitheses between which there is no choice (528). It is as true to say that God strives through actual entities, as to say that he is an Actual Entity. It is, in this connection, difficult to see just what is the distinction between actuality and the consequent nature of God. The consequent nature of God is, in fact, nothing more nor less than actuality cast in theological rather than ontological terms. Cosmology is the ground where ontology and theology meet. The fate of actuality, a perfectly neutral ontological term, is typical. It becomes the consequent nature of God.

We may illustratively compare Whitehead's two ultimate cosmological categories with those of Spinoza. Whitehead's two realms, the possible and the actual, peopled respectively by eternal objects and actual entities, become in cosmological or theological terms the primordial and the consequent natures of God. These, Whitehead declares, are the two sides to the nature of God; thus they are in the philosophy of organism the ultimate distinction. Now it so happens that Spinoza, too, posited two sides to God's nature, or, to employ his terminology, two infinite attributes. These are: thought and extension. Spinoza is here continuing the *res cogitans* and *res extensa* of Descartes, the philosopher whose thought started the train of ideas which, Whitehead tells us (v), ended with the philosophy of organism. Spinoza is here, however, making ultimate categories out of an old nominalistic distinction between mind and matter. Spinoza's distinction is subjective, Whitehead's objective. It is interesting to note that both mind and matter on the one hand and possibility and actuality on the other find their source together in the metaphysics of Aristotle. But in the latter case, the distinction has led to an ontological realism, in the hands of the British school, while in the former it has led to an epistemological nominalism, in continental philosophy. Both distinctions exist in both traditions, of course; the important difference depends upon which is considered primary. There is no doubt in the distinction elevated to eminence by Spinoza a tendency to base ontology upon epistemology, and a reverse one in the distinction chosen as first by Whitehead. But nominalism invalidates the one and realism validates the other.

Despite the vast metaphysical gap which lies between these two theological conceptions, one tone of similarity pervades them. In both cases, two theological categories have been posited as two among many—two among an infinite number, in fact. While Whitehead does not explicitly say so, he cannot posit two sides to God's nature without supposing that there are other sides. In Spinoza's case, the reference is even more explicit, for he believed in an infinite number of attributes. Thus what both men have accomplished in this direction is immensely suggestive; they have set up a qualitative description for the principal unknown divisions which can be asserted for God's existence. Such substantive imaginings carry with them the threat of a future orthodoxy, but they are also wide open in the sense of offering the two realms of being of our present-day ontology merely as samples of what through God's nature is available, or may somehow become available. Contrary to supposition, some categories make known new possibilities, new vistas; while others close inquiry. The mind-matter distinction is an invidious one; but no doubt Whitehead is close to Spinoza in offering a qualitative description of aspects of being which lie beyond knowledge.

It is true that the positing of a plenitude of worlds, from the hint given us by the knowledge and experience we have of the being of at least two, furnishes a kind of abundance to philosophy which is refreshing. But the fact is that such a conception is more charming than it is necessary to the system from any logical point of view. Perhaps the conception would seem less philosophically supererogatory were it couched in less fervent terms. God is an affective description of the unity of the universes of being, the oneness of all that is or could be, the only independent. There are moods in which prayer as adoration is appropriate, but the mood in which we approach metaphysics does not contain them. Cosmology is on the borderline between ontology and theology, and Whitehead has stated that language is often inadequate to express our thoughts. All the same, it is the structure of the system of cosmology on its theological side which is being set up when Whitehead describes the primordial and the consequent natures of God. Perhaps if instead of "God" he had said "infinite unity" or "the independent," it would be better. But it so happens that Whitehead aspires to be something more than a metaphysician. Every nominalist is a practical-minded man; every realist, a dreamer. Whitehead, like Spinoza, may well be described as God-intoxicated, and his system of philosophy, his cosmology of process and reality, is bent in that direction. He would not be able to accept a more animistic system, despite his own animistic leanings; a system in which, for example, it may be said that the primordial and the consequent are two of the gods of nature. According to certain elements of his system, according to the primacy of the actual entities and the fact that there is nothing beyond them, we should expect that nature would come out better than in fact it does. But Whitehead the worshipper is unwilling to surrender to Whitehead the system-maker, even on the assumption that system-makers on the grand scale on which cosmologists can be included, are worshippers only once removed. But this criticism takes into account only the ingredients of the theology and not the mixture in which they appear as the theological aspects of a well-blended cosmology. There, perhaps, Whitehead succeeds in justifying for the whole what appears to be questionable in the parts.

Whitehead rightly insists that there is no point in paying compliments to God. To make positive statements about God's being or existence, such as that he is one or many or actual, etc., is to limit him and to express no truth which is wider than any other statement about him (528). Yet Whitehead elsewhere says that God has a primordial nature (521) and another side which is his consequent nature (523). Is God the principle of concretion any more than he is every other principle (374)? Whitehead is here faced with the dilemma of the philosopher who accepts only the negative theology and who yet wishes to elevate his ontology into a cosmology through the employment of theological terms.

In this procedure lurk many dangers. Why is it that ontology is never felt to be enough? The effort to encompass all of being in the smallest viable number of categories should, if successful, be satisfying. Beyond that lies dogmatism. Ontology is a hard discipline, and the soul which can find it sufficient is indeed that of a superman. Ontology expressed in affective terms, the affective terms of theology, is submitting itself to the lordship of those who would commit mayhem if necessary in the defense of an accepted proposition. For belief, too, can become a vested interest. But the metaphysician is one who must be willing to give up his limited truth, and this he cannot do if he has felt it too deeply. That is why those who advocate the scientific method compare the philosophic method so unfavorably with it. The scientific method almost becomes a dogma itself, in the hope that if everyone demands a dogma it is the least harmful and in itself allows for the change from limited truth to less limited truth. So also should the philosophic method lead us on; but it cannot do this when we immediately enshrine a set of reasonably broad ontological categories. Whitehead has high hopes for his followers, but he has also set limits to their achievement by showing his categories to be readily amenable to religious treatment. That way lies dogma, and the wars of religion and religious persecutions. Far better to be what Spinoza was, a God-intoxicated man, but without God-intoxicated ontological categories. There is something religious about metaphysics just as there is about science. To pursue the truth is as much to seek the nature of God as to worship him, a fact which the man of God has been loath to admit to the scientist or to the philosopher.

Whitehead affirms the closeness of his philosophy with that of Spinoza. However, by abandoning the subject-predicate form of thought he hopes to escape the substance-quality construction, and in many connections he substitutes creativity for God. Let us consider these claims. The subject-predicate form of expression may be disavowed by Whitehead, as indeed it is (viii), but concretely it is employed throughout the presentation of the cosmology. The English language in which the cosmology is expressed makes such usage necessary, despite Whitehead's denunciation of language as an inadequate expression of metaphysics. We have seen the substance-quality philosophy readmitted into the philosophy of organism through the categories of the mental and the physical, and also through the subjective and objective division of the prehensions. As to creativity, it is true that Whitehead sets it up as an ultimate, as, in fact, the only category of the ultimate. But it is also true that God and the world are discussed at length, and that the two sides of God's existence are established, corresponding to possibility and actuality. It is difficult, therefore, to see how the introduction of the leading principle of creativity has dispensed with the notion of God.

The truth is that all philosophers of the ontologically monistic variety, Whitehead and Spinoza alike, achieve their monism by uniting all knowledge under the simplest categories and then by attributing these simple categories to God, with the additional and altogether gratuitous compliment that he must have many others, too, about which we in our ignorance know nothing. There is, of course, no help for this sort of procedure. Ontological pluralism is so fundamentally antithetical to our ways of thinking —to logic, in fact—that it is not a conceivable alternative. We are then driven to ontological monism, and the danger always exists that God shall prove to be only a catch-all category wherein we unite all the random threads of our cosmology; yet it is difficult, if not impossible, to conclude otherwise. In many ways, Whitehead's system is not only the latest but also the greatest of these efforts.

It is doubtful whether philosophy, or the world of human actualities, will ever be the same once the philosophy of organism has been well assimilated by the society in which it has been produced and to which it is to be left. Whitehead himself has claimed that a new alternative is a shock from which philosophy never entirely recovers (16). This is sure to be true of the revival of realism. As soon as we have come to see the world in another way, it is not likely that our conduct toward it will remain unaffected. We are molded as much by what we know and love as by what we have done and hope to do. Philosophy is only the name for the largest element in the environment as it affects us. We live according to the dictates of fact but also within the limits of system. Whitehead has well said that all facts are elements of a system, so that what we have come to believe as well as what we encounter plays a vigorous part in our lives. With the philosophy of organism in a broad way, that is, with the philosophy of realism, we may expect to leave the extreme subjectivity of nominalism, so prevalent in our age, for the objectivity of the external and independent world upon which we depend so wholeheartedly. Philosophy, Whitehead says, is the effort of consciousness to correct its early emphasis on subjectivity (22). Subjectivity in any serious sense is only another name for mental disorder, and there is no sharp break between philosophic solipsism and psychopathic catatonia. The alternative to subjective idealism, which is materialism, is only another form of subjectivism in disguise, a subjectivism once removed which depends upon sensation for its validity. Realism supposes that the world of action and reaction, the actual world containing both subject and object, is only half the story of being, the other half of which is contained in the infinitely larger, eternal and ubiquitous order of possibility. Realism reaffirms the equal reality of these two halves of being: the value-logic order of possibility and the historical order of actuality. There is some validity to the contention that no set of categories should be allowed to stand in the way of freedom of philosophic inquiry. Whitehead seeks to escape from the enshrinement of his two orders of being in their theological fixation by constant reference to creativity and process. In these conceptions lie the exits to dogma, so that while we are free to embrace his philosophy we are not bound to accept it absolutely everywhere and forever. It is our task to separate the embracing from the limited, the true from the false, the good from the bad, and to retain what ought to be retained. This will involve some criticism but also will require understanding before criticism.

Great work must be approached in a sympathetic rather than a critical frame of mind. It is not possible to understand the idea of a comprehensive philosopher without being able to view his scheme of things from the inside; thus the paradox is presented that it is not possible to understand a philosophy without first being able to understand it. Just how this difficulty is to be overcome is not clear. It requires many weeks and months of intense study and an effort to accept *pro tem* for the benefit of a greater understanding what is not readily evident. Once on the inside and thoroughly conversant with the scheme, its shortcomings begin to make themselves evident. But then they only limit the achievement as a whole; they do not negate it. The meaning of the philosophy of organism, and the light which it is able to throw upon other topics and pursuits, is more easily available to those who approach it from realistic premises. Unfortunately, those premises are today possessed by very few. In a day when Plato is misunderstood as having intended a kind of idealistic mentalism exclusively, how can we hope that Whitehead will be properly comprehended?

Nevertheless, there are hopeful signs. Men are rarely converted to a viewpoint; more often they are replaced by generations who grow up in it. Nobody knows exactly why or how this process works. The influence of a set of ideas is far in excess of its reputation, and the most powerful ideas are those which gain general acceptance by being so taken for granted as to merit no explicit discussion. In the nineteenth century, Aristotle's static conception of substance, his notion of substance with its inalienable qualities and with its accidents, was the self-evident world even of those uneducated persons who had perhaps never even heard of the existence of such a thing as philosophy. The birthright of one philosophy makes the perception of the truth of another a matter of the extremest difficulty. It is true to an enormous degree that the self-evident truths—the common sense—of one generation consist in the influential metaphysics of some previous thinker or group of thinkers. We cannot, for instance, quickly grasp how an object can be something aimed at a subject, without assuming this to mean an absolutely passive view of the knower. Still less quickly can we understand how the subordination of the subject to the object could be known as the subjectivist principle. Such conceptions challenge our sanity; we must literally grow accustomed to them. Those who were provoked to outbursts of furious anger on first hearing Stravinsky's early music may have difficulty in explaining why it sounds so familiar and agreeable now. Whitehead's reputation, his influence, must wait, but unless gradually widening limited truths are to have no future, the day of the power of his work will come. It was in the hope of speeding this day, as well as from the necessity of pointing out certain shortcomings, that the present chapter was undertaken.

III

An Estimate of Dewey

IN ORDER TO SEE A PHILOSOPHICAL contribution steadily and as a whole it is often necessary to omit many details. We cannot hope to evaluate the power of a searchlight by counting the number of things its turning beam illuminates. Although John Dewey and his work are both close to us in time, it is probably not too early to begin to consider his chief position as briefly as possible, in an effort to place his ideas where they belong in the history of philosophy.

The tendency of certain strains of idealism to regard as unreal anything which is imperfect has impoverished philosophy. The fact that, while nothing in experience is as it ought to be, much exists, has escaped many philosophers who have fixed their gaze so determinedly upon the ideals of the future that they have failed to recognize the philosophical importance of the conditions of the present. Dewey's emphasis upon the experiential, considered as an element of the philosophical domain which whole schools of philosophy have preferred to suppose to be somewhat lacking in reality, has great value. It will recall us to the necessity for recognizing what is here and now, irrespective of what ought to be. And since we are compelled to work toward what we want through what we have, methodologically, even for the idealist, Dewey has contributed an important idea. One thesis of this chapter, however, is that his attack is directed mainly toward subjective idealism from a position in "experience" which proves to rest equally on subjective grounds. We shall see that, in addition to this, Dewey recognizes only one type of idealism, namely the subjective, deeming objective idealism to be only a slight variant; which is another way of saying that he fails to recognize the autonomy of realism as a third metaphysical position. But before we can consider the second point we must take up the first and examine the "philosophy of experience."

All philosophers are in a sense monomaniacs who interpret the general problems of philosophy in terms of their own favorite conceptions. Rare indeed is the philosopher (if he exist at all) whose writings do not have a center. The central notion or premise in terms of which Dewey's whole philosophy is constructed is that of experience. For him the world has meaning just in proportion to its connections with an experiencing subject. The subject himself, the process of experiencing and that which is experienced, all hang equally for their reality upon the act of experience. Nothing, then, is constant. The ideas of fixed forms, of order, and of being, are hypostatizations of elements lifted from experience. All changes take place in terms of experience and there is nothing outside it or apart from it. Many valid elements of experience have been overlooked in virtue of the past habits of philosophers who have selected certain other elements and raised them to an exclusive eminence. The preference has been for things static, good, beautiful, and true, and we have thus rewarded what is desirable with a superior metaphysical status, through the adroit use of the logico-abstractive method. This has removed philosophy from the concreteness of the world of experience, where the fragmentary, the incomplete, the forceful, and the chaotic must be recognized as existent. Philosophy should return to the empirical-genetic method which refuses to eliminate anything from the experiential realm.

Dewey's preoccupation with the conception of experience springs not only from his anxiety to refute idealism which is only its negative aspect. More positively, he is concerned to point out that philosophers who must take everything into account, have been more occupied with the world as it ought to be than with the world as it exists about them. He wishes to remind us that we have been overlooking in philosophy the most importunate elements in experience. Yet are we likely to miss the aspects of existence which Dewey is so anxious to stress? In life, no; but in philosophy, perhaps. We live in the actual world and we are constantly reminded of its distinguishing features. But what about that other world which the limitations and shortcomings of actuality suggest, that timeless and spaceless possible realm which is capable of becoming the actual world of a future date and place? There is good reason why philosophers have been so devoted to the ideal; it furnishes an aim to the present and a goal in the future. Yet Dewey is correct in his emphasis in that philosophers have failed to take the proper account of the obstacles which actuality offers to the reformer.

Despite the valid aspects of Dewey's conception of experience, there are, however, serious difficulties. Dewey opposes his conception of experience to the subjective conception of idealism. Experience is perhaps intended to be an objective category; if so, it does not fulfill this intention. The serious efforts which Dewey has made to keep experience objective have ended in failure. Considered just by itself, experience is epistemologically neutral: the subject and the object belong to it. Thus far, so good. But in his use of the notion, that which is experienced and the act of experience itself become equally instrumentalities of the experiencing subject. The definition of experience which he gives is sufficiently broad; he makes it almost equivalent to any instance of action-reaction. But throughout his epistemology he uses it as a subjective affair. Obviously, he did not need to do this and in a way did not mean it; the slip is revelatory of a metaphysics which stands in the way of a thorough-going objective conception. It should be kept constantly in mind that the conception of perfectly ordinary experience is no ordinary conception. The man in the street does not have the conception of the man in the street, and the pedestrian thinker does not himself have the notion of pedestrian thought. The experiencing subject shares with the object of experience the rarity of any such conception of experience as that put forth by Dewey. Such a conception could only have been the result of high abstraction.

There certainly is a confusion in the conception of experience as

Dewey employs it. The best that can be hoped is that by experience Dewey does mean an objective affair, an instance of reaction; in short, the experience of anything by anything else. There is reason to believe this, but there is equally good reason to believe that he means something less sweeping and more narrowly humanocentric. At times, for example, he writes as though experience were only the experience of organisms. At other times we are led to understand that he means only the experience of those higher organisms which are called human beings. And at still other times there can be little doubt that he plainly intends only certain higher experience of human beings; namely, that of the concious mind. Whatever broader definition Dewey may frequently intend, the fact is that experience is not seldom employed to mean conscious human experience, and the confusion is one which nobody could fairly deny.

Let us look a little further into this problem. If experience were to have the broader reference which Dewey often assumes it to have, then any instance of actuality, any act, would be an example of experience. Anything would, in short, be capable of enjoying or suffering experience. But we find that such is not the case. For when experience is revealed to own a purpose, which anything must have unless teleology is assumed to be entirely subjective, we find that this experience now becomes inquiry and is confined to the human province. Experience, then, in the grand sense becomes inquiry. Inquiry, like experience, creates its own end-terms. It is held responsible both for the inquirer and the object of inquiry. There evidently is no logic to brute experience, since logic is defined as inquiry into inquiry: self-conscious inquiry. This requires that there shall be no logic operative in the world apart from the intentions and actions of human beings. It denies that conflict can be interpreted as actual contradiction. Furthermore, it means that there can be no guide to inquiry in the sense of a valid principle lying outside of inquiry. The guide to future inquiry can be nothing but present inquiry. If logic is to be confined to the theory of inquiry, that into which we inquire will have to be assumed to be entirely logical, at least to the extent to which there is any inquiry and any logic at all.

So far as concerns the human being, credit must be given to Dewey for having made one enormous point. He has shown that the whole of human life is an inquiry, that living in the human sense means inquiring into the nature of things. He has defined the purpose, at least the central purpose so far as we seem able to know it, of human nature: men struggle for subsistence in order that by its aid they may conduct the inquiry into their own existence. But it is characteristic of philosophers that no sooner do they discover a valuable truth but they must proclaim it to be the only one. The error he commits lies in erecting this very valuable observation into a cosmology, a theory of existence. We cannot explain all being in terms of the purpose of human beings, even though we can explain a great deal about human beings and the psychological order. It is strange that the very mistake he makes in this connection constitutes the basis of his own criticism of the Greeks. He charges them with having raised human affairs into cosmic realities, the very charge that can be levelled against him, for he certainly does not hesitate to assert that the cosmos is merely a product of human inquiry. It is a fashion among modern thinkers who wish to sever all ties with the past, on the assumption that by this method past errors are sure to be avoided, to regard the classic Greeks as extraordinary children, very bright for their age, but dead too early to have developed their talents as we, for instance, are developing ours. The conception upon which modern thinkers base this conviction of superiority is that of history, or rather (since the Greeks did have some history) the conception of the historical order. Dewey is so struck by this that he drops the other necessary conception which the Greeks did have of an abstractive and static order of logical possibilities, of universals and powers.

If, as Dewey insists, the object of inquiry is a product of inquiry, then the infinity of the cosmos is inconsistent with the fact that some problems of inquiry do get solved. The key to this contradiction lies in the conflict which exists between the theory of the primacy of inquiry and the metaphysical theory which Dewey thinks it presupposes. An ontology based on inquiry is not only not needed for inquiry but is actually inconsistent with it. Dewey supposes that inquiry makes changes in the subject-matter inquired into, also in the inquirer, which is true; but it is not true that nothing remains the same. Since philosophy, too, is an inquiry, it must change from time to time. But this would mean that Dewey's philosophy is contradictory, since his idea that everything changes will itself change. But the idea of change has nothing to change into except permanence. Thus the self-application of the idea of change cancels its generality. Again, if inquiry were infinite, its problems must be infinite. But its problems do get solved occasionally. Thus an infinite inquiry is inconsistent with the finite solution of problems based ontologically upon inquiry.

We must learn to distinguish between Dewey's ostensive and cryptic ontologies. Ostensively, Dewey's hold on nominalistic materialism is unbreakable. Of the two traditional orders of being, the essential and the existential, he recognizes only one, namely the existential. In the existential, he stresses elements of change, materiality, and social reality. This leaves no dwelling place for pure being or essence except the mind, and produces a mentalistic confusion of the very kind which Dewey is so constantly railing against as he discovers it in more candid forms of subjective idealism. The cryptic philosophy which occasionally compels him could not be made more candid without some admission of the validity of ontology. This is precisely what Dewey finds that he cannot admit. He is only concerned with philosophies which have some existential bearing, and so is confined to his ostensive ontology on the unfortunate assumption that since it has existential bearing it cannot possibly be described as ontology. Yet what reason is there to suppose that ontology can have no bearing on practical living moral and social questions? Indeed there is every argument to accept the opposite contention.

The result of all this is that Dewey has blinded himself to many aspects of "experience" without which his own ideas would be worthless. He has, for example, confused being with knowledge. It may be true that the knowledge of being is gained through experience, but it is doubtful whether being depends upon our knowledge of it. Experience may be indispensable in the acquisition of knowledge. But this is quite different from the further assertion that nature is dependent upon the knowledge of nature. The continuity of experience and nature, a continuity which Dewey recognizes so well it almost leads him into realism, makes experience possible but does not make nature possible. Nature is possible only in virtue of its being. Our knowledge of the vast temporal and spatial reaches of the actual world may be due to the connections which they have with some present experience, but this does not prevent us from drawing the inference of their ontological independence. Indeed it furnishes us with the compelling conditions for such an inference. The very fact that our knowledge of the moon owes its existence to our connections with the moon ought to be enough to caution us that the moon itself does not have any such debt.

To confuse being with knowledge is sooner or later to make being dependent upon knowledge, and somehow to assign corresponding roles to the topics under which they are studied. This, in fact, is exactly what Dewey does do. For him epistemology is empirical but ontology merely speculative. Ontology, he evidently imagines, will offer nothing final and decisive so long as it has no well-defined empirical field of operations; but the same is not true of epistemology which examines the processes, undoubtedly real and actual, by which the knowledge which we have is acquired. Thus he is led to prefer the genetic to the abstractive method, to the exclusion of the latter. Abstractions become more and more wispy and tenuous, as opposed to developments which approach closer and closer to home. The abstractive method starts with the present and ends in a nebulous world of dubious fancy. The genetic method starts with a nebulous world of dubious fancy as regards origins but ends with the present. The results of the latter seem to Dewey safer somehow, despite day-to-day demonstrations of physical science that the reverse is true. Obviously, neither of the two methods is complete; they are two halves of a single whole; and to offer opposition to one half by asserting the sole validity of the other is foolishness.

The broader case of the opposition between epistemology and

ontology while not exactly similar is far more striking. Against the assertion of the sole reliability of epistemology as a guide to being may be offered two arguments. In the first place, if epistemology is more empirical than ontology, why have not its controversies been more easily settled? It is still possible to observe as many different schools of epistemology as of ontology, each, incidentally, claiming to be the only empirical one. But if epistemology were as empirical as it is asserted to be, the basic questions of the subject would by this time be more or less generally agreed on. Moreover, there is a suspicious likeness between the contentions of the warring epistemological schools and those of the ontological ones, which, though hardly conclusive, has yet to be explained away as a mere coincidence.

In the second place, it can be argued that the knowledge process is only one among many kinds of processes which are known to go on in the world. Certain strains of recent scientific knowledge have indeed gone so far as to suppose a process for every entity. Then again, the knowledge relation is only one kind of relation among all the relations which are known to exist. What reason is there to suppose, then, that it takes precedence over the others and even determines them in an ontological way? No evidence from either epistemology or ontology can be adduced to demonstrate such a contention. Broadly speaking, it may be argued that epistemology provides a method for ontology, whereas ontology constitutes the aim of epistemology. More has being than is known, but all knowledge has being.

From time to time Dewey stops to deny that he is a nominalist; and yet his reliance upon a changing materialism, a final reality of the historical order of actuality which is linked now to inquiry and now to the existence of society, prevents him from being anything else. He seems to think that there is only one kind of nominalism, that of mentalism, yet the ancient definition of nominalism relies upon another kind: the belief in the sole reality of physical particulars. Nominalism consists in holding either of the two ontological orders of being to be superior in reality to the other. The subjective idealists, who hold the mental realm alone to be real, are also nominalists. Dewey's mission, as he evidently must conceive it, is to oppose one brand of nominalism with another. His action consists in denying that there are two orders of being. He charges that the order of essence or pure being is composed of what we would like to have existent; that, in other words, reality is wishful thinking, while the remainder, the imperfections of existence, must rest content with a lesser ontological status. This is a grave charge and it rests for justification upon the subjective idealist's position.

As a matter of fact, subjective idealists seem to commit exactly the error with which Dewey charges them and are open to the very objections which he lays against them. To divide the world into two realms or orders of being (as assuredly we must) and to assume one more real than the other (as assuredly we must not) means to assume that other less real. But does this alternative, plus Dewey's alternative which consists in denying not only the reality but even the existence of the other realm, exhaust the possibilities? Dewey manages to reduce the order of being or essence to the order of existence, and in this way eliminates it so that he can consider the order of existence alone as real and valuable. If it is unfair to impugn one order for its ontological inferiority, how much worse to assume that one order is not only inferior but—that greatest degree of inferiority—non-existent. Dewey is happy over his decision simply because he has condemned a realm different from that one chosen for condemnation by the idealists.

There is, of course, a third alternative to the choices of Dewey and the idealists. This is the alternative of the realists who accept two orders of realms of being but deny that a distinction can be made between them on the basis of their reality, or lack of it. For the true realist, reality, paradoxically enough, is a non-discriminating term and one which can for all useful purposes be ruled out of technical philosophy. Existence consists in logic and conflicts, perfections and imperfections. The ideal order of being is composed of a chain of all possible perfect things, of which the order of existence is a broken and helter-skelter selection. But no distinction can be made between being and existence on the basis of a difference in reality, only on that of desirability. We desire existence for its vividity but despise it for its imperfections; we desire being for its completeness but deplore its lack of existence. The necessity for demonstrating the mediating relations between these two realms remains one of the principal tasks of metaphysics.

In defence of Dewey it must be maintained that his ostensive philosophy, which is a variety of materialistic nominalism involving an emphasis upon dynamic change without exception, and upon the inter-subjective social criterion of reality, does not always hold sway. The inconsistencies of nominalistic philosophers are perforce realistic. His insights, which do not check with his ostensive premises, are keen and unusually good and true. But they would be more consonant with Platonic realism of the objective brand. Many instances could be brought forth in support of this view of the cryptic philosophy on which from time to time Dewey allows himself to rely through his instinct for the truth. The arguments against subjective idealism are often taken from a realistic orientation. For instance, in the effort to show that thoughts do not represent an exclusively subjective subject-matter, he often assumes an objective and non-actual status for universals. He understands that values have the same status as in his argument in recognition of the importance of the incomplete and the partial, the hazardous and the imperfect, as preconditions for the enjoyment of value, which would be unified but not vivid and vital without some such condition as that which actuality presents. He comprehends the value of imagination as an organ offering not merely its own self-concocted images but also the dim perspective of possibilities toward which eventualities are now moving. Could we long for a perfect world amid imperfections were we not able to recognize our own world as imperfect and a perfect world as possible?

Every existent may be an event, but even Dewey is forced to recognize the relative fixity of changing things, that those which change slowly are stable in comparison with those which change faster. An unchanging constant is required for the relative fixity of the most slowly changing of things. And a constant between variables is constant even though it be between variables. We may fear the use of ends in connection with existential processes, but what would the processes be without them? Could we in that case even speak of them as processes? The emphasis upon instrumentalism does not overlook the significant fact which the objectivity of tools represents for human progress. The replacement of the ear by the vibrating membrane and of the eye by the spectroscope are examples taken from physics of the denial of subjectivity in scientific method. In justice to Dewey it must be admitted that, despite his ostensive philosophy, he does launch out occasionally from the basis of his cryptic philosophy against the division of the world into categories of unequivalent reality. All breaks in the continuity between man and the world which seem required in order to enable man to be what he is are arbitrary and inadmissible.

The main shortcoming of Dewey's point of view is made manifest, however, when we survey his philosophy as a whole. This has been done, in a way, by examining his major metaphysical premises. It can be done in still another way by studying the relations which it has with other studies in the perspective which Dewey offers. Consider, for example, his definition of philosophy. He asserts it to be a cultural growth and explains it as that which has come to be what it is in the social milieu. Of course, considered simply as a cultural phenomenon, philosophy is no doubt a social enterprise; however, it is only one among many. People do investigate philosophical problems, and they also give their time and energy to other kinds of investigation. In this fashion, philosophy may be assigned a subordinate role, namely, that of a function of social inquiry, as only one and not the most importunate one of a myriad human enterprises and activities in a busy world where the necessity for survival through the activities of feeding and procreating are the prime requisites.

But importunateness should not be confused with importance in quite this facile a manner. What is most importunate in a situation is seldom what is most important. Then again, the social activity of philosophy is a measure of the human interest which there is in it, but is not to be construed as a measure of the place of philosophy in the nature of things. There is a sense in which men exist for philosophy; if men had chosen not to engage in philosophical inquiries at all, that would have involved a loss to men but not to philosophy. Principles exercise a negative control over actual situations whether we happen to know about them or not. We benefit from knowing about them because then we are in a position to work with them rather than against them. Truth is not invalidated by the assertion of a falsehood, but the attempted practice of the action which seems demanded by a falsehood may prove disastrous.

However, if we temporarily accept Dewey's understanding of philosophy as a genetic-cultural development, how does that definition distinguish it from any other social enterprise? The activities of war, of the drama, of politics, and of family life may also be described as cultural phenomena which have grown up through the centuries, constantly suffering sea changes, and manifesting growth (or retrogression). The description of philosophy as a genetic-cultural phenomena fails to be sufficiently specific: what kind of genetic-cultural phenomena is it? Here we are led back to the necessity for some kind of logical and abstract definition of philosophy, the very thing against which Dewey inveighs.

The understanding of philosophy as a cultural development carries with it a further source of confusion and one which pervades all of Dewey's work. How can the criterion of social reality be made to check with the touchstone of experience? Experience is individual; social reality hinges upon the organization of individuals into a social group. From the position of the strict empiricist, experience is final and unique, whereas society is a construction put upon the aggregate of individuals. Yet Dewey alternates between these two views arbitrarily.

The final charge to be brought against Dewey's position is the error of oversimplification by single emphasis. According to Dewey, everything is to be explained quite easily by referring it to the social reality of a constantly changing existential world. This orientation produces a facile progressivism which assumes that the golden age of the future is just around the corner by presupposing the possibility of an easy victory over the very difficulties of evil, conflict, incompleteness, and strain, which his philosophy had come into the world to proclaim were irrefrangible.

Is not faith in progress and inevitable ameliorationism the same as the acceptance of an ultimate goal? Reality is that which is changing, growing, developing, as stated a theory implying that it will also change, grow and develop for the better. The progressivism of society is Dewey's absolute, introduced in order to banish all classical expressions of static absolutes. But to end with absolutes instead of beginning with them is not the way to get rid of absolutes. We may well wonder whether it is not at all possible to get along without absolutes, as Dewey tries to do.

Let us consider the proposition, "Everything changes," a proposition which Dewey would be willing to accept. If everything changes, then the proposition that everything changes is also subject to change, thus admitting the truth of the contradictory, "There is something that does not change." But if the proposition, "Everything changes," is not construed as applying to itself as well as to everything else, then it is self-contradictory for there would then be something which did not change, namely the proposition, "Everything changes." Philosophy is simply impossible upon the assumption that there are no absolutes discoverable.

Admittedly, many of the so-called absolutes in past philosophy have proved to be false, and this is the shortcoming which Dewey is seeking to avoid. But from the observation that past pretensions to absolutism have proved fallacious, it cannot be argued that nothing is absolute. We may settle upon the position that absolutes are discoverable, and that in philosophy, while we do not claim to have laid hold upon them, we can claim to be working toward them. We must assume a tentative position with respect to absolutes, but this can only be done by at least presupposing that there are absolutes to be approached. Those who, like Dewey, would banish absolutes from the world of philosophy, think that they have done enough if they destroy absolute dogmatism. But absolute scepticism is also a variety of absolute, and it must be banished as well.

The world of actuality is not the only world we experience, since its fragmentariness, its incompleteness, its partiality, and its shortcomings and limitations in general, offer pretty good evidence for the positing of a perfect world. We may say that just as we experience imperfect things we experience the necessity for perfection. But can we regard a perfect world as necessary simply because it is real and possible? Dewey, in fact, deplores its reality, as posited in the mind by subjective idealists, but approves its reality as an inevitable event in the future. Thus he commits another error he has been most anxious to avoid. The world is what it is, the empiricists are constantly reminding the idealists, but the latter maintain that it is not what it ought to be. Dewey agrees with the realists that a perfect world or golden age must be assigned to an objective reality in the future rather than to a subjective one in the mind, but he is more dogmatic and absolute than they in regarding it as inevitable.

If actuality is by its nature limited and forlorn, by what right can we assume that it will vanish suddenly, leaving us exactly the world we wish to have? There is always before us the remote prospect or vista of a golden age in the future, but can we truly believe that we shall attain it shortly? The workability of James's truth was conceived to be in a near future; that of Dewey's is if anything closer still; only Peirce among the pragmatists understood the identity of such a future with infinity. The fact is that possibility is not tantamount to necessity: a perfect world is impossible, but possibility is not a promise except in an infinitely remote date and place.

We can perhaps get a better comprehension of Dewey's singleness of outlook by comparing him with two of his contemporaries: Whitehead and Bergson. Admittedly, all philosophers endeavor to discover the key to all problems. But in the solutions of some the key hangs by a single thread. Compare Dewey in this regard with Whitehead. Whitehead carries a broad field forward in terms of a number of conceptions. Dewey carries a single conception forward by spreading it over a broad field. The comparison with Bergson would perhaps be more favorable, for Dewey, like Bergson, explains everything in the universe by means of a central idea which is held to be all-important. Of course this method is not without merit, but it also has serious limitations. Overemphasis does serve to call attention to neglected truths in such a way that they are not likely to be neglected again, but the necessity for swinging back to a more balanced position once the deficiency has been corrected is equally important.

Dewey's early philosophy of experience calls for action without understanding; his later work calls for an understanding of action. He has substituted for a desire to help make the world a desire to find out how the world is being made. Experience has given way to inquiry. Both points of view presuppose a knowledge of the unchanging principles in terms of which change is made possible; that is, the earlier outlook, as well as the later, contradicts Dewey's ostensive ontology and presupposes his cryptic one.

All of this is not to assert that Dewey has not made an important contribution. We shall not soon overlook the metaphysical character of the shortcomings of actuality; we shall remember the limited social basis of reality, the value of experience as experience, and the directive property of inquiry. We shall remember these, but we shall learn to put them in their proper perspective, and this cannot be done without ontology. It will involve also the unification of ontologies so that what is cryptic will not remain at odds with what is ostensive. It will mean that we can view inferences from ontology candidly as deductions rather than indirectly as deviations. For the work of Dewey, like that of so many modern philosophers who have chosen to emphasize activity rather than logic, the human rather than the cosmic, and temporality rather than eternal conditions, must inevitably run into difficulties which continue to cry out for a return to the problems of ontology; a return which, however, in deference to Dewey, will fortunately carry some important lessons with it.

IV

Lovejoy's Revolt Against Realism

OCCASION FOR THIS REPLY

IT IS OFTEN POSSIBLE to form some estimate of the value of a movement by considering the strength of its opposition. Despite the number of realists in contemporary philosophy, realism, defined as the being of universals independent of all actuality, has in many quarters been considered a dead issue, regarded as a philosophical position which was long ago exposed in all its fallacies and hence no longer worthy of attack. We should all be grateful to Professor Lovejoy for the correction of this attitude by the profound criticism of realism which he has launched in two of his works.[1] The negative position of such a formidable adversary must do more than the positive presentation of realism by its modern proponents ever could to call to everyone's attention the amazing vitality, and by consequence the certain validity, of the realist philosophy. In addition, the critical philosophy of Professor Lovejoy is not to be put aside without the reply which it deserves. Lovejoy has chosen as his professional mission the destruction of realism by means of the exposition of its fallacies, a mission which is, however, not entirely explicit with him. Many of his criticisms are sure to be unanswerable, and the revision of realism to that

---

1. *The Revolt Against Dualism*, Chicago, 1930, and *The Great Chain of Being*, Cambridge, 1936. In this chapter we shall be concerned solely with the latter book (hereinafter referred to as *GCB*).

extent is accordingly demanded. Hence the necessity for a careful study of his remarks.

From the examination of the arguments of this critical philosophy, there is another and far more important advantage to be expected. There is much which modern realism does not attempt to explain; any philosophy which has not been developed to the fullest is likely to be crude, and the exploration of realistic implications has hardly more than begun. Valid criticism points out shortcomings which might not have been otherwise noticed, and which it is important to catch in the early stages. The true philosophy of realism can be advanced to a greater degree of fullness by accepting the attacks of the critical philosophy as a challenge. Thus a reply to Professor Lovejoy should constitute a further development of the realist philosophy in terms which will make this philosophy more easily understandable to a modern.

PLENITUDE, CONTINUITY, GRADATION

Our interest in Lovejoy's work begins with his study of the genesis of the idea of the Idea in Greek philosophy, more specifically in the writings of Plato. This notion consists in the belief in an independent set of Ideas or essences, whose fragments or shadows form the real and actual world. Notice is taken immediately of the fact that there is more than one philosophy in the Platonic *Dialogues*.[2] Platonism as a consequence has given rise to two forms of realism: the philosophy which puts its emphasis on the reality of the essences, as contrasted with the shadow-like existence of the actual world; and the philosophy which puts its emphasis on the equal reality of both realms, resulting from the fact that this actual world is constituted of fragments of the essences which are as real even though not as complete as the essences themselves. The former is termed by Lovejoy "otherworldliness" and the latter "thisworldliness."[3] The thisworldly version is, as we shall see, never finally rejected by Lovejoy, and

---

2. *GCB*, p. 21.
3. *Ibid.*, p. 24.

the otherworldly one is made representative of Platonic realism, and as such set up as the target of continual attack.

The chain of being is characterized according to Lovejoy chiefly by three properties. These he terms plenitude, continuity, and gradation. The principle of plenitude consists in the necessity of the essences to contain everything possible, to be "full."[4] Plenitude consists not only in the thesis

> that the universe is a *plenum formarum* in which the range of conceivable diversity of *kinds* of living things is exhaustively exemplified, but also any other deductions from the assumption that no genuine potentiality can remain unfulfilled, that the extent and abundance of the creation must be as great as the possibility of existence and commensurate with the productive capacity of a 'perfect' and inexhaustible Source, and that the world is the better the more things it contains.[5]

The second property of the chain of being is continuity, and for this formulation Lovejoy accepts Aristotle's definition: "Things are said to be continuous whenever there is one and the same limit of both wherein they overlap and which they possess in common."[6] The third property of the chain is the arrangement of essences in an ascending scale of values, the criterion being the degree of perfection. This is termed by Lovejoy the principle of gradation: "All individual things may be graded according to the degree to which they are infected with potentiality."[7] It is in virtue of these three properties of plenitude, continuity, and gradation that the realm of existence as set forth by Plato and others after him came to be known as the "chain of being."

Lovejoy writes most of the time as though the three properties apply to the vivid and experienced world of actuality.[8] Much of his attack on realism is based on the proposition that actuality exhibits plenitude, continuity, and gradation. The philosophy which consists in the deductions from the opposite view, namely

---

4. *Ibid.*, p. 52.
5. *Ibid.*, p. 52.
6. *Ibid.*, p. 55, from Aristotle, *Metaphysics*, X, 1069^{a}5.
7. *Ibid.*, p. 59, quoted from W. D. Ross, *Aristotle*, p. 178.
8. *Ibid.*, pp. 63-65, 67.

that these properties apply only to possibility and not to actuality, is not considered by Lovejoy. It is one of the theses of this paper that this confusion invalidates much of Lovejoy's criticism. Any doctrine of the perfection of actuality is doomed to confusion; for actuality is in its nature incomplete, partial, and imperfect. The perfect world is the otherworld and not the thisworld at all. Another observation which may be made at the outset is that Lovejoy devotes most of his work to the history and exposition of the principle of plenitude, and comparatively little to the other two principles. There is, it must be admitted, some justification for this bias, inasmuch as continuity and gradation are deductions from plenitude, but the preference is worth noting.

PLENITUDE.—Let us, then, isolate the principle of plenitude and consider it in the light of Lovejoy's discussion. The proposition that plenitude applies to possibility in the same manner in which it applies to actuality is contained in the peculiar way in which it is asserted about actuality. It will be remembered that plenitude was defined above, as the exhaustive exemplification of the range of conceivable diversity. This means that possibility must be full, and that actuality must necessarily be so too. There is no reason to challenge the first assertion. Possibility by definition includes everything that is possible—all possibles. It is the second point that seems invalid. Why should it be assumed that because possibility is full, everything which is possible either is or must become actual? Lovejoy quotes Aristotle's denial of this assertion in his own words; they are important enough to deserve quoting again. "It is possible," says Aristotle, "for that which has a potency not to realize it," and again, "It is not necessary that everything that is possible should exist in actuality."[9]

Lovejoy seems to believe that the validity of the first point hangs upon that of the second. His hidden assumption is that if actuality does not contain or receive all possibility, possibility is not full. This assumption is more dangerous for being veiled, and deals a staggering blow to the many arguments against plenitude which

---

9. *Metaphysics*, XI, 1071^{b}13, and II, 1003^{a}2; quoted in *GCB*, p. 55.

are couched in the form of an historical exposition of its absurdity.[10] Indeed, most attacks on realism prove to be of this variety: valid attacks upon idealism. The fallacy of idealism consists in the error of regarding possibility as a realm of perfect actuals. Such crypto-materialism is implicative of the plenitude-of-actuality theory.

Possibility does not require actualization of itself. Possibility, potentiality, or power, is simply capability of actualization. But capability is *not* necessity. Lovejoy indeed quotes the seventeenth century Fénelon to this effect. "No doubt, the Archbishop of Cambrai grants, it may be said to be *'plus parfait à un être d'être fécond que de ne l'être pas'*; but it does not follow that the divine perfection requires 'an actual production.' The possession of power is sufficient without the exercise of it."[11] "A strange proposition," adds Lovejoy, although it is difficult to see why. As a matter of fact, Fénelon was right. We cannot take the omnipotent point of view but must rely upon the human perspective: it is not true that power requires its own use. The ascription to essences of a craving for existence requires the crypto-materialism of a realm of essences which are actual but differ from actuality in residing elsewhere and in being more perfect. If essences be understood not as actual things at all, perfect or imperfect, but merely as the forms which actual things are capable of assuming, the fatal error committed by the opposite position is avoided.

The clearing up of this confusion easily disposes of other errors arising from it. The formal statement of the principle of plenitude leads to an ignorant state of optimism and to the paralysis of all initiative. For if all possibles must in themselves contain the necessity of becoming actual, then everything we could wish for does and will happen, and we need do nothing to promote a better state of actual affairs. Actuality as well as possibility is, or is to become, the best of all possible worlds. Such foolish optimism and defeatism are dissipated by the fact that they are deducible from a plenitude of actuality but not from a plenitude confined to pos-

---

10. The discussion of Kant is typical. *GCB*, p. 140.
11. *Ibid.*, p. 162.

sibility. With a plenitude of actuality, of course there is no need to do anything, since all that can happen will and must happen in good time. But with plenitude confined to possibility, the need remains to strive toward their actualization and the consequent improvement of actuality. The worlds of possibility and of actuality are the best possible by definition; possibility means the best possible; actuality means the best possible under the circumstances. Actuality can never be perfect, that is to say it can never be identical with possibility, but it can be improved.

Lovejoy devotes a chapter to the survey of the optimism which was so widespread in the eighteenth century.[12] The entire description is one of a plenitude of actuality. But since contradiction more often than not leads to further contradiction, it should not be surprising to remember that Leibniz in the seventeenth century had fallen into the same error of which Spinoza had been so profoundly guilty: the belief in an absolute determinism of actuality. If everything which can happen must happen, then actuality is determined. But once again, we see that the correct understanding of plenitude, as applying solely to possibility, eliminates the error: a possible plenitude does not mean a determined actuality. Not only logical possibility determines what is to become actual and what is not, but all the forces which reside in actuality alone have some bearing on this decision: evil and ugliness, error and contradiction play their part. Thus actuality, although partly determined, is also partly open to current influences, determinism as an absolute affair being confined to the realm of possibility.

CONTINUITY.—The chief part of Lovejoy's discussion is devoted to plenitude, but there is some occasional discussion also of continuity and gradation. In discussing rationalism in connection with the Leibnizian principle of sufficient reason, Lovejoy seems to think that continuity and rationalism demand a finite world, since an infinite world presents rationality with a host of denials. He says "the real existence of a quantitative or numerical infinite ... seemed rather to make reality essentially alien to man's reason,

---

12. *Ibid.*, Chap. VII.

permeated throughout with paradoxes and contradictions. He who thus followed the principle of sufficient reason to what appeared to be its ultimate consequence, found his conclusion destructive of the assumption from which it had been derived."[13]

Since Kant, the paradoxes of the infinite have been known to deny rationality. Reason breaks down when faced with the regions designated as nothing and everything, zero and infinity. But in the vast territory between these extremes, rationality functions perfectly well, and the limits of the finite world can be pushed back indefinitely without running counter to reason. Moreover, there is a perfectly good *reason* why reason does not apply to the extremes. Since logic deals with partiality, it cannot apply to the whole universe any more than it can apply to nothing, since neither nothing nor the whole universe can in any way be construed as parts. It is in this connection that Leibniz points out with good judgment that God's freedom is not inconsistent with his determinism.[14] Lovejoy is confused again when he argues against Leibniz on the basis of selectivity for actualization; to the extent to which one of two logical alternatives is selected for actualization the other is of necessity ruled out. But this is to bring the argument down within the realm of rationality again.

Lovejoy does not trace the historical development of the notions of continuity and gradation with the same painstaking completeness with which he has sought to trace that of plenitude. Continuity in rationalism is discussed from time to time, but continuity in other historical fields is omitted. The reason is not so obvious; but there are difficulties. For instance, as Haserot has correctly indicated, "Physics has never been able to decide conclusively for one or the other hypothesis, namely, discontinuous matter and the void or continuous matter and the plenum."[15] If explicit physics, which has always presented a strikingly uniform front on most matters with which it has been concerned a sufficient length of time to reach some agreement, cannot decide the question of con-

---

13. *Ibid.*, p. 130.
14. *Ibid.*, p. 173.
15. Francis S. Haserot, *Essays on the Logic of Being* (New York, 1932), p. 253.

tinuity, what is to be expected of other fields in which agreement is at all times minimal?

GRADATION.—Gradation does not seem to be as eminently important a principle as that of plenitude. Indeed, the principle of gradation is hardly ever discussed alone, but is always considered in connection with the problem of evil. The question with all its implications resolves down to this: Is evil a necessary element in the actual world in order that the graded hierarchy of possibilities can become actual, or can this gradation become actual without the aid of evil? In the historical controversy which Lovejoy faithfully repeats, neither solution appears to be entirely satisfactory, and the reason for this failure is not far to seek. For throughout the controversy both sides accept a definition of evil which is fallacious. Evil, according to the Neo-Platonic tradition, is synonymous with negation or partiality. It is the absence of what ought to be in the actual world which is evil, or so this tradition would have it.

Now here the Neo-Platonic tradition, though wrong, is not far from the truth. Lovejoy's method frequently resorted to throughout *The Great Chain of Being* is the indirect one of denying by implication the importance of the topic under discussion by exhibiting the fallaciousness of both arguments concerning it. But this method seems to accomplish more than was perhaps even intended. It seems to deny the validity of metaphysics. What is really being called into question is whether such arguments have any significance whatsoever, one way or the other. The answer, however, is just the opposite of that implied. The ultimate problems of ontology and epistemology lie so deep at the base of all other studies that the slightest error in the former is capable of leading to gross errors in the latter. Further, the ultimate problems of ontology which Lovejoy has chosen to examine are such fundamental ones that they are capable of leading to gross errors in systematic ontology itself. This is not to deny the validity of metaphysics but rather to assert its high value, and to call for the utmost caution in asserting anything on ultimately prior problems.

Having attempted to dispose of the implied derogation of the question under discussion, let us return to the problem of evil and try to discover why the Neo-Platonic definition is unacceptable. To make evil synonymous with negation or partiality is to give it the same status with regard to possibility that is shared by the good. But if evil is as much a part of the great chain of being as is the good, there would be no reason to avoid one and to seek the other, and consequently it would no more be evil in the sense in which we have come to know it. But we do not in fact regard evil in this light; evil is rather the privation of the good, and it can only be privation of the good on one condition. This condition consists in assuming that evil is not on the same level with the good but is a property of actuality alone. Then if this is so, it is still possible for evil to be synonymous with negation. We find, however, that the graded hierarchy of possible can become actual without evil. The extent to which a cake of soap falls short of being an ideal and perfect cake of soap is not evil, yet it may become the occasion for the rise of some specific evil. The point is that partiality does not require evil. In actuality, evil may result from partiality, and often does; but partiality itself does not necessitate evil, but only occasions it. We may conclude that there is no causal connection between gradation and evil, but that the principle of gradation occasions partiality in actuality, and that partiality occasions evil.

Certain writers, as Lovejoy points out, drew the inevitable conclusions as to human action from the view that for the hierarchy of possibles to become actual, gradation requires evil. They saw that this makes evil necessary in the world. To this supposedly unavoidable truth, Voltaire and Spinoza, for example,[16] reacted differently. For Voltaire, the inevitability of evil was no comfort; for Spinoza it was. But Spinoza's optimism and Voltaire's pessimism should indicate the fact that if two contradictory conclusions can both be reached logically from the same premise, then the premise itself must contain a fallacy. That it does so easily follows from the view stated above, that evil is not identical with partiality but is

---

16. *GCB*, p. 210.

actually occasioned by it. For identities and causes are necessary, but occasions are not. Since evil is not necessary in actuality, it is not determined to be actual, and is thus at least susceptible to being abated. Whether a minimal evil is inevitable in actuality is another question; but a certain amount of evil, such as actuality has continued to experience since history has taken cognizance of it, is certainly not necessary. Therefore the necessity of evil in the Voltaire-Spinoza sense does not exist, and what is imperative for human action is rather the abatement of evil than any reconciliation with its necessity. Whether such a crusade takes the form of a more active pursuit of the good or of a more active campaign against evil is irrelevant: the only point to be remembered is that the implications to human action from the fact that evil is occasional and not necessary is that no reconciliation with its necessity is required but simply an effort to reduce its prevalent existence as much as possible. Thus a goal is set for action, an infinite goal which can be approached but never reached in finite actuality, of improving the actual world. And positive action capable of achieving some good is substituted for negative acceptance, capable only of becoming sweetly or sourly reconciled with an inevitably bad world.

REALISM AND IDEALISM

We have noted in an earlier chapter that broadly speaking there are only three philosophies, or as perhaps we should say, only three classes of philosophies. These are: realism, nominalism, and idealism, which last might be termed the realistic fallacy. Philosophies fall into one or another of these classes according as they hold the balance between possibility and actuality, make actuality superior in reality, or make possibility superior. By the canon of the philosophy of realism, whose history Lovejoy has chosen to trace and which constitutes the object direct or implied of his attack, the governing principle in the avoidance of the two errors of nominalism on the one hand and idealism on the other is the equal reality of both levels: the logical order of possibility and the historical order of actuality. To hold concrete and actual things more real than abstract universals is the position of nominalism. To hold abstract universals more real than concrete and actual things is the position of idealism (the realistic fallacy). To hold concrete and actual things and abstract universals alike with respect to reality is the position of realism.

But the main body of Lovejoy's criticism seems to relate to realism and idealism (though he does not employ these terms), for he does not enter much into the question of nominalism.

Lovejoy can indeed hardly be said to have given the philosophy of nominalism the credit which it historically deserves.[17] For nominalism has occasioned much of the Western world's philosophy, especially since the eleventh century. By the same token, idealism is given credit for too much of Western development, as we shall later see. From the point of view of realism, however, nominalism is a negative philosophy and realism is positive. These positions constitute two thoroughgoing but opposed philosophies, in the sense that they carry implications to every field of thought. But in the sense of assuming, as realism does, that nominalism is a negative error, a denial of the truth, the three positions should be said rather to be philosophy (realism), with its dogmatic excesses of idealism (the realistic fallacy), and the revolt against its dogmatic excesses (nominalism).

The rediscovery of the importance of individual man as a human being, which was an eighteenth century accomplishment, was one effect of nominalism. Lovejoy would have the chain of being partly responsible for the ideas both of man's importance and of his unimportance in the world.[18] Such a notion is to overlook altogether the historical importance of nominalism. Nominalism, by denying the reality of ideas—and hence also of the chain of being—threw the emphasis of reality back upon the actual world in two ways. It gave rise to subjective philosophies which supposed that man was the creator of his universe, or at least limited to that part of the universe which he could know (Kantism). It gave rise to ob-

---

17. Cf. Julius W. Friend and James Feibleman, *The Unlimited Community* (London, 1936), Chap. I.
18. *GCB*, p. 186.

jective philosophies which supposed that man was the helpless victim of largely unfriendly forces active in a hostile universe (mechanistic materialism).

Returning to Lovejoy's exposition of and attack upon the realistic philosophy, we may recall that Lovejoy himself discerned that there are two philosophies in the writings of Plato, which he termed "otherworldliness" and "thisworldliness." We shall see that he dismisses one of these and devotes the major part of his expository denunciation to the other. He singles out as most representative of Plato's position "otherworldliness" and derogates "thisworldliness," perhaps because the former has had the greatest historical influence. This "otherworldliness" consists in the notion of a realm of essence of divided universals which demand their own actualization, and of which this actual world is but a shadowy and reflected image. This is the philosophy which was held during the Middle Ages, an "extreme realism" which we have described as idealism, or the realistic fallacy.[19]

Realism is distinguished from idealism in that it posits universals as undivided in the logical order of possibility and divided only upon their actualization. They do not crave for actualization and act only when actualized. Realism accepts the existence of an actuality which consists in the fragmentary and incomplete but none the less real actualization of universals. To this philosophy Lovejoy gives scant heed. Although in several places he considers it, the result is always a summary dismissal without trial. The fact that true realism has not had the historical importance of idealism does not mean that it has gone without its advocates. And if history is not to be confused with logic, Lovejoy may be said to have refuted one branch of *historical* realism which stood in need of refutation; but he has not refuted *logical* and true realism at all.

---

19. "Exaggerated realism" as used by certain Catholic philosophers is a phrase to denote not what I call idealism but rather what I call true realism. Maurice de Wulf (*History of Mediaeval Philosophy*, Vol. I) means by "moderate realism" that there is nothing *praeter individuum,* or, in other words, nominalism. But this was emphatically *not* the position of Aquinas, who adopted Avicenna's view of the nominalist-realist controversy.

LOVEJOY AND REALISM

THE REJECTION OF REALISM.—Let us examine in detail the passages in which Lovejoy considers that philosophy which we have termed realism. In the first passage, Lovejoy presents a largely fair account of realism.[20] He says:

> The fundamental contention of that theory is merely that our judgments, both of fact and of value, when reached by due process of reflection, possess objective validity, and that we can therefore attain a knowledge of things as they are independently of our apprehension of them. . . . 'Ideas' are universals because *words* always designate universals; and true knowledge is *of* Ideas chiefly in the sense that "every representation as such has a universal relation, not the individual phenomenon, as its content."[21]

The summary, though incomplete, is fair enough; but what is Lovejoy's answer? He begins by warning us that according to Ritter these observations representing the Platonic position were not intended by Plato "to be taken seriously,"[22] and his consideration really rests upon two points.

The first of these is that to assume this presentation to be Plato's theory of the Ideas necessitates the further "highly improbable assumption that Aristotle's account of the Theory of Ideas is false."[23] Is this, however, the case? Lovejoy has already admitted that there are two distinct philosophies in Plato. Why do we have to assume that Aristotle was attacking one when he may just as well have been attacking the other? Against the citation of Lovejoy's authority, Professor Shorey, we have the weight of one of the best modern Aristotelians, Werner Jaeger, who emphatically maintains that Aristotle was the leading Platonist.[24] It is more likely that Aristotle was a faithful Platonist who wished to advocate true realism and to correct the excesses of the realistic fallacy of idealism, since these were found in the writings of Plato himself and in the Neo-Pythagorean excesses of the contemporaries of Aristotle

---

20. *GCB*, pp. 35-36.
21. This is part of Lovejoy's summary of and quotation from the leading German Platonist, Constantin Ritter.
22. *GCB*, p. 36.
23. *Ibid.*, pp. 36-37.
24. Werner Jaeger, *Aristotle* (Oxford, 1934), p. 3 *et seq.*

in the Academy, Speusippus and his school. Indeed, as Jaeger attempts to show, it was on account of these very differences that Aristotle and Xenocrates split off from the Academy.[25] That Aristotle did not accept his own version and refutation of the theory of the Ideas is attested by other of his writings, which reveal a tacit acceptance of the metaphysics of true realism.

Lovejoy's second argument rejects Ritter in an elaboration of the phrase already quoted; namely, that Plato did not intend his theory of Ideas to be taken seriously. This argument rests upon Plato's warning that language has its limitations, since it was formed for the conveyance of materialistic rather than relationistic philosophies. But what is not to be taken literally may yet be intended to be taken seriously. Plato's resort to parables and myths at the most crucial passages in his explanation of his theory can not be offered as evidence that Plato meant this theory to be taken only in a poetic sense.[26] In defense of this contention Lovejoy offers the word of Professor Shorey, who maintains that such a position as Plato's in this regard was held in the full knowledge that it was alien to common sense, but was not for that reason offered by Plato as a deliberate absurdity.[27]

There is another authority to pose against Ritter. Professor Whitehead takes what seems to be the more accurate view of the matter. He urges that Plato was correct in his warning that language beyond a certain point is apt to be misleading and therefore not to be trusted, and that he was justified in resorting to myth.[28] The effort to explain true realism, if made too literally, is more likely to lead to idealism. Utter reliance on denotative language as an infallible conveyer of meaning is ill-advised, and brings about such absurdities as the exaggerated views of some modern logical positivists. Often in philosophy it is yet necessary to resort to connotation to convey the highest and most abstruse meanings. But this is still very far from saying that such meanings are "not to be taken seriously."

---

25. *Ibid.*, p. 111.
26. *GCB*, pp. 37-38.
27. *Ibid.*, p. 38.
28. A. N. Whitehead, "Remarks," *The Philosophical Review*, XLVI (1937), 182-83.

The difficulty with the Platonic tradition has always been that many of its advocates as well as most of its opponents have agreed that Plato's "World of Ideas" is either "a glorified, detemporalized replica of this world" or "a blank negation of it."[29] Both phrases, however, describe the realistic fallacy of idealism, and neither describes true realism. A glorified, detemporalized replica of this world would indeed itself be a blank negation of it. But the fact is that true realism calls for an actual world which consists in a fragmentary and incomplete but real part of a real world of being. This world of being (the logical order of possibility) is a whole which is more complete but neither more nor less real than the actual and partial world.

The second passage in which Lovejoy considers true realism is one in which he discusses the practical effects of the theological contradiction between the One and the Many.[30] The coincidence of opposites in medieval theology, which is valid and rests upon the failure of finite logical distinctions to hold for the infinite, seems to Lovejoy to demonstrate that "logical difficulties, with respect to the ultimate objects of thought, did not greatly trouble the mediaeval mind."[31] The satiric criticism of medieval theology is an old game, which should be by now too easy to occupy Lovejoy's attention. Such scorn contains no truth. For in fact, the medieval theologians, as such eminent non-Catholics as Peirce have eloquently attested, greatly troubled themselves with almost nothing else, and moreover often to considerable purpose. The fact that the One desires the Many and the Many the One may be a contradiction, but it is an ultimate contradiction as all ultimate distinctions of necessity must be. And there is nothing foolish about it. True realism requires, as we shall later have occasion to discuss, that the Many could not desire the One did not the One have a place for the Many.

Lovejoy's quarrel, however, is that as practical ideals the doctrines are irreconcilable, and here for a moment he has a glimpse of the truth.

---

29. *GCB*, p. 38.
30. *Ibid.*, pp. 83-84.
31. *Ibid.*, p. 83.

There was no way in which the flight from the Many to the One, the quest of a perfection defined wholly in terms of contrast with the created world, could be effectually harmonized with the imitation of a Goodness that delights in diversity and manifests itself in the emanation of the Many out of the One.[32]

Of course not, and here true realism takes sides. That the search for the One has taken the religious turn of a denial of the Many does not negate any but the false doctrine of idealism. The way to the One lies not through a denial of the Many but rather through a long and painstaking integration of the Many toward the goal of achieving a single Unity out of them. This program is envisioned by Lovejoy, who complains that in the early Middle Ages it was never formulated. But he sees it well enough; and he says that "it would have placed the active life above the contemplative; and it would, perhaps, have conceived of the activity of the creative artist, who at once loves, imitates, and augments the 'orderly variousness' of the sensible world, as the mode of human life most like the divine."[33]

To know and to love the Unity of the universe is better done when we know (and love) the diversity (the Many) of which this Unity consists. Thus we must both love Unity (since we cannot know anything about it other than that it *is*) *and* know and love (but especially *know*) diversity. This statement of the ethics of true realism is so well put that it leads to the suspicion that Lovejoy longs to be a realist and is secretly one, but is prevented from coming out candidly and announcing himself so only because of the (to him) insuperable obstacles of its apparent contradictions. It is not long before Lovejoy is once again fearful of the contradictions of true realism, and hence scornful of it. "The ascent of the ladder of created things," he says, "is, after all, only another name for a progressive *contemptus mundi*."[34] But this is just what a few pages back was the doctrine he had been discussing with such approval, the ethical doctrine which "if it had been formulated, would have

---

32. *Ibid.*, p. 83.
33. *Ibid.*, p. 84.
34. *Ibid.*, p. 92.

summoned men to participate, in some finite measure, in the creative passion of God, to collaborate consciously in the processes by which the diversity of things, the fullness of the universe, is achieved."[35] The enviable, unformulated doctrine is now a *contemptus mundi*. Just when Lovejoy allows himself a little latitude for true realism, he runs for cover again.

True realism indeed is hardly lifted up into the light again the rest of the book. Later on it is mentioned as "one of these two conflicting Platonic conceptions"[36] and once again summarily dismissed. The realistic fallacy of idealism, however, is, after all, not the only version of Platonism which has enjoyed an historical career. Why was the history of true realism not traced, and if so desired rejected, by Lovejoy? To describe and reject the most vulnerable of two closely related philosophies both stemming from the same source seems to dispose of them both, but in fact does not. The fact that Lovejoy has chosen to trace what we have described as the realistic fallacy of idealism and has also chosen not to trace the tradition of true realism makes his entire work, in a sense at least, misleading. For his book is constituted of a series of chronologically correct episodes, with some—but only a very few—influences shown.

Perhaps the most serious fault of the work is the fact that in the chronological account Lovejoy skips from Pseudo-Dionysius to the Middle Ages. Even the unsuspecting reader must be tempted to wonder what happened in this interim of centuries. The truth is that the influence of Arabic and Moslem thought is overlooked or purposely omitted. Averroes is mentioned, but the true realism of such an important figure as the Arabian philosopher, Avicenna, who first solved the controversy over universals to the satisfaction of the medieval world, is never mentioned by Lovejoy. Such mention must have thrown a different cast upon the outcome of Lovejoy's researches into the eventual reduction to absurdity of the realistic tradition. Finally, Peirce, instead of James, might have brought the account up to date.

35. *Ibid.*, p. 84.
36. *Ibid.*, p. 156.

ATTACK ON THE REALISTIC FALLACY OF IDEALISM.—The thesis maintained here that Lovejoy's chief quarrel is not with true realism but with the realistic fallacy of idealism is evidenced throughout the book. The few mentions of true realism, always with some doubt expressed, constitute one argument in favor of this thesis. Another lies in the fact that Lovejoy frequently directs his arguments against obscure historical realists whose work, though of some contemporary importance, has never been seriously considered representative in the history of philosophy. One such example of this is William Derham.[37] Derham's position, as we should all admit, is absurd. But to refute him and others like him, as Lovejoy frequently does, is not to call into question the issue of true realism. It is only to heap forth ridicule upon the heads of men who have so well deserved their obscurity. Arguments against a school are made to seem far more cogent and forceful than they really are by being directed against its less representative members. To confuse realism with the realistic fallacy of idealism should be mistake enough. But to go further and point out the ridiculousness of the weakest of the upholders of the philosophy founded upon idealism is to do nothing toward clarifying the truth of true philosophy, which we must take to be the task of all sincere and serious philosophers.

There are several prominent occasions for confusion which should serve to throw light on the contention that realism is confused with idealism. Among these are Plato's Idea of The Good, the distinction between essence and existence, the distinction between appearance and reality, and finally, the distinction between possibility and actuality, which has been mentioned already above. Let us give some attention to these questions in the hands of Lovejoy.

The theologically prominent ontological distinction between the realm of essence and the realm of existence is one which Spinoza sought to solve by defining cause of itself as "that whose essence involves existence."[38] To admit, however, that any *causa sui* can be

---
37. *Ibid.*, pp. 133 f. Others are William King, Soame Jenyns, etc.
38. Spinoza, *Ethics*, Part I, Def. I.

in this sense, is to admit that universals demand their own actualization. And this is to admit an *actual* potency to a realm which is not supposed to be actual but only possible, and thus to fall into the realistic fallacy of positing a realm of essence containing both a power which is and a reality which is not enjoyed by the actually existent world. Spinoza did, in fact, believe in the "necessary actualization of all possibles," as Lovejoy maintains. Moreover, the division of everything in the universe between "thought" and "extension" is enough to convict Spinoza of a nominalistic philosophy which, after all, shares with idealism the fact that neither of them is realistic. They frequently do become one philosophy. Lovejoy's argument[39] is an attack upon Spinozism and as such cogent—but true realism is not involved. What Spinoza set forth was an actual plenitude, or in the terms under discussion, a plenitude applicable to extension; and this, as we have already seen,[40] is the realistic fallacy.

Lovejoy thinks that Plato's Idea of The Good leads of necessity to an otherworldly philosophy.[41] If God is the highest good, then the highest good is not of this earth. And the Idea of the good itself becomes divorced from the contexts in which it occurs in this actual world. The Good for Plato, meant, however, at least on some occasions, the highest or most good (God). But this does not lead necessarily to an otherworldly philosophy, since the good is merely extent of value or power according to Plato. Thus whosoever possesses the good in lesser extent than God, possesses, after all, some good. There is reason to suppose that Lovejoy himself is aware of this.

He who attempts a theodicy without first shutting his eyes to a large range of the facts of experience, must necessarily take for the object of his piety the God of Things as They Are; and since things as they are include the whole countless troup of natural ills, it becomes necessary so to transform the conception of good as to make it possible to argue that these ills are—not, indeed, goods, considered by themselves,

---

39. *GCB*, p. 151 f.
40. See above, p. 110.
41. *GCB*, pp. 4-5.

but implicates of some supreme good, in the realization of which the essential nature of deity is most truly manifested.⁴²

Partial good is good. The whole of the Good is simply the sum of the infinite partial goods. This latter is true realism and not the realistic fallacy. It must be perverted to the understanding that the highest Good is alone good before it is fallacious enough to be the subject of an attack upon the realistic fallacy.

The most vicious of all distinctions which have led to the confusion of realism with idealism is perhaps the familiar distinction between appearance and reality. This distinction hangs like a curtain of obscurity over all Neo-Platonic philosophy, giving it the definite cast of the realistic fallacy of idealism. To make form real but material content an appearance is to commit excessive subjectivism or mentalism.⁴³ No division of levels of real entities or objects can ever be made on the basis of a difference in reality. We can never judge as to the real status of objects in the natural world by the canon of their accessibility to human cognition. Although the forms of cognition do color our efforts to apprehend the objective and independent nature of the real world, there is on the other hand no evidence that our cognition is a necessary relation of such real objects.

POSSIBILITY AND ACTUALITY.—The distinction between possibility and actuality has been reserved for the last, because it is fundamental to realism, and indeed to metaphysics in general. We have discussed above the question of the logical order of possibility and the historical order of actuality in relation to Lovejoy's principle of plenitude. Here we shall deal with other related questions discussed by Lovejoy.

The chain of being, as set forth by Lovejoy, always understands a definite and sharp separation of possibility and actuality. But it does not presuppose a realm of possibility (or essences), some of which never becomes actualized, and an actuality which is at

---

42. *Ibid.*, p. 222.
43. To make material content real and form an appearance is to commit excessive actual objectivism, or materialism. This is the basis of the nominalistic philosophy, which, as has been noted above, is given too little historical credit in Lovejoy's survey.

least partly intractable to logic. Actuality, according to true realism is the name for a *part* of possibility, namely that part of it which has become actualized. For if possibility includes everything which is non-contradictory, as it must, and if any non-contradictions are actual, they must have been possible. The logical order is a thread running through the historical order and governing it whenever limits are exceeded; neither order, however, yields any understanding except in terms of the other. There are, of course, possibilities which may never become actual; but then on the other hand they also may; and it is this unbreakable relation between unactualized possibilities and the possibility of their actualization which preserves meaning.

Lovejoy refers to the view that possibilities have to become actualized, that they are, so to speak, motivated by this urge. He interprets the Pseudo-Dionysius in a passage on the superabundance of the good[44] as intending that the Platonic Ideas are always "aspirants for the grace of actual existence." Once again it must be repeated, this philosophy is to be found in Plato. The Platonic writings are full of passages which can only be interpreted as a realism so extreme that it can best be described as idealism. But there are other passages which demand attention and which have not had the full force of historical influence that idealism has enjoyed. It is this latter philosophy which is here termed true realism. Now in terms of true realism, the ideas have their being as possibles in an undivided, non-discrete state. They are divided and made discrete only when they become actualized. Hence they do not "aspire" to anything. It is the import of existence that it seeks to be full. To attribute aspirations to unactualized ideas is to grant them a sort of ideal, super-actual state when they are not actualized; a state in which, as we have seen, through a sort of crypto-materialism where everything is just like it is in actuality only more real and more perfect, the ideas yet are dissatisfied and yearn for the more imperfect state of our actual world.

This is obvious nonsense, and Lovejoy was right to reject it. The

---

44. *GCB*, p. 68.

determination of what ideas shall become actual and when and where is not a question for the ideas themselves to decide. As Whitehead has shown, "eternal objects tell no tales as to their ingressions."[45] The error lies in supposing that all possibility has to become actual, which is the principle of plenitude that has been historically applied by mistake to actuality as well as to possibility, when it should have been applied to possibility alone. The point is that the determination of what possibles shall become actual is neither necessary for all the ideas (Lovejoy's "plenitude") nor accidental from possibility itself (Augustine's and Descartes' "God's will"),[46] but arises from actuality. What is already actual occasions what shall become actual. Thus all is actually free—but logically determined. This latter formulation, namely, that actuality furnishes the historical *occasions* for happenings but that possibility furnishes the logical *cause,* has rarely been understood. What follows always follows of necessity—yet not everything follows.

True realism calls for a perfect logical order of possibility and an imperfect (though none the less real) historical order of actuality. The actual world from its own point of view should be made as full as possible yet also as rational as possible. But the attainment of these ideals always falls far short of accomplishment, and hence short of the perfect rationality and complete fullness of the logical order of possibility. Lovejoy confuses the fullness of actuality, which is an ideal, with sheer diversity, which is an actual fact.[47] "The world is full of a number of things," as Stevenson's nursery rhyme reports, and it does not make us all "as happy as kings" for the simple reason that among the things in the world are numbered a great many bad ones. We are forced to face the undeniable evidence of shoes that creak, ships that sink, sealing-wax that burns fingers, cabbages that decay, and kings that are corrupt. Diversity, requiring evil as well as good, is a characteristic of actuality; whereas plenitude or fullness requiring only the good is a characteristic of the logical order of possibility, and has the

---

45. *Process and Reality,* p. 391.
46. *GCB,* p. 158.
47. *Ibid.,* p. 226.

relation to actuality of constituting a program for it. Were all things good, sheer diversity could not even present us with the evil problem of overcrowding!

These difficulties are avoided if we declare that the chain of being, with its plenitude, continuity, and gradation applies only to the logical order of possibility and not to actuality at all. Actuality has its characteristic properties, too. These are: privation, discontinuity, and inequality. It will be seen that in a sense they correspond to the properties of the chain of being. Since a plenitude of the good applies only to possibility, actuality suffers from privation of the good, which is evil; and the same is true of the beautiful and the ugly. History is characterized by the temporal sequence, which is largely irrational and discontinuous. Everything actual is exposed to the vicissitudes of finitude: accident, chance, eventual defeat. Although actuality, as we have said, is part of possibility, there is some reason for separating it as a definite part to be distinguished from that of which it is a whole by its peculiar characteristics.

What Lovejoy calls "the temporalizing of the chain of being" represents an effort to show the manner in which actuality is related to possibility. The theory of time in relation to the chain was represented by some as meaning that all possibles eventually become actual. But this was an attempt to retain an actual plenitude, and went too far. All that can be maintained for the future, even for the remote future, is that all possibilities *may* become actualized. There is no way to show that they *must*. As actuality progresses, however, we learn more of the nature of the logical order. Our abstract knowledge of the conditions of being increases. Lovejoy understands this increase very well in its proper function as is shown by a passage that is so apt it must be quoted.

Every discovery of a new form could be regarded, not as the disclosure of an additional unrelated fact in nature, but as a step towards the completion of a systematic structure of which the general plan was known in advance, an additional bit of empirical evidence of the truth of the generally accepted and cherished scheme of things.[48]

---
48. *Ibid.*, p. 232.

This is a description which accords with true realism—oddly enough quoted as a summary of Kant's position.

The temporalizing of the chain of being, or in other words, the eventual actualization of all possibilities,[49] is, however, more often wrongly interpreted by Lovejoy as the beginning of the breakdown of the principle of plenitude.[50] It is more truly the effort to avoid the absurdities of idealism and to return to the successive actualizations of the temporal order as a guide to the nature of the correct relation between possibility and actuality.

REALITY AND RATIONALISM

Some realists have asserted that the question of rationalism versus irrationalism primes all other metaphysical questions. They give as their reason for this the presupposition by all philosophical arguments of the principle of non-contradiction. They have been mistaken in this assertion, since not all rationalism is realistic. One form of nominalism which is known as subjective idealism admits of the efficacy of reason, and many subjective idealists have been ardent rationalists. Such rationalism, however, has succeeded in maintaining itself only by identifying logic with psychology and hence reason with reasoning, a position which was perhaps most in evidence in the nineteenth century.

Lovejoy points out that the great chain of being leads eventually to an anti-rationalism.[51] One of the strains of Platonism has overcome the other, he says. Translated into our terms, this means that historically idealism triumphed over realism. The fallacy of idealism, which consists in a crypto-materialism of a (supposed) really superior realm of essence, logically reduces to nominalism. But of course. The confusion does not lie in the history of these doctrines, although the victory of idealism would imply some lack of understanding of realism. It lies rather in Lovejoy's failure to understand that the two "Platonic strains" of which he speaks undercut the remainder of his problem, and in his further failure

---

49. *Ibid.*, p. 244.
50. *Ibid.*, p. 245.
51. *Ibid.*, p. 202.

to understand that the victory of one "strain" over the other is no more than the victory of idealism and the neglect of realism, followed by nominalism as a revolt against the excesses of idealism.

ATTACK ON LIMITED RATIONALITY.—In the light of these remarks, let us examine what Lovejoy has to say concerning points which bear on the question of rationalism. First in order is the consideration of the revolutionary theses of cosmography which were current in the sixteenth and seventeenth centuries. His concern is to take away the credit for the spread of these theses from Copernicus. For the question was not whether Copernicus' system is correct but, as Bacon expressed it, "whether there be a system at all." Lovejoy rightly observes that "The change from a geocentric to a heliocentric system was far less momentous than the change from a heliocentric to an acentric one."[52] Whenever a simple system proves inadequate in the light of more recent empirical findings, the question arises as to whether any system exists which is adequate to cover the facts. In other words, the failure of any inadequate system always calls into doubt the validity of all systems. This may be seen today, when the revolution in modern physics has cast doubt on the old Newtonian mechanism, while positivistically-minded physicists deny the validity of systematic implications of the new physics.

The failure of some particular empirical entity has never cast doubt on the validity of empirical entities in general. Phlogiston, which was once an empirical entity, proved to be invalid, but others arose to take its place. Systems seem so much less empirical than entities because they are so much higher in the organizational series. But the necessity for having some kind of system is as imperative to science, and consequently to rationalism, as the necessity for having empirical entities. And the substitution of new and adequate systems for old and inadequate should not be a signal to challenge the validity of systems. Rationalism is in danger from time to time but only in the understanding of philosophers and scientists and never in the constitution of the conditions of nature herself.

---

52. *Ibid.*, p. 109.

The Copernican (or cosmographical) revolution removed man from the center of the world and widened its boundaries.[53] The widening of boundaries entailed the substitution of irregular outlines for regular ones. Once again, realism (or rather idealism) gets a credit which should go to nominalism. The breaking up of old systems in order to make way for newer and wider ones is usually done in the name of nominalism. The showing that the boundaries of the world were wider and more irregular was a consequence of nominalism, and hence read irrationally. It is a persistent principle of logic, however, that history is not always right. Realism is not confuted by according a certain validity to nominalism. As Avicenna and others have shown, nominalism as the observation that universals are found in actual things is consonant with a realistic philosophy. The widening of boundaries irregularly does not argue for the invalidity of rationalism but rather for a more inclusive rationalism.

When Lovejoy is confronted with true realism expressing its attitude toward the logico-ontological structure of the world, his comments lead to the suspicion that he does not understand the position at all. The topic under discussion in one place is Robinet's claim that fossils have a certain measure of organization.[54] Lovejoy seems to think that any plausible reason must inhere in human minds (subjective idealism) and that the granting of rationality to any part of the inanimate world is "a peculiar sort of panlogism, a doctrine of the ubiquity of the rudiments of rationality in all natural things."[55] This is the very fundamental doctrine of rationalism maintained by true realism. There is nothing peculiar about it. It was maintained by Plato in at least one of his "strains"; it has been maintained still today, e.g., by such an eminent philosopher as Whitehead. The position as stated by Robinet and attacked by Lovejoy is that of true realism.

In the remaining passages which border on the question of ra-

---

53. *Ibid.*, pp. 112-14.
54. *Ibid.*, p. 277.
55. *Ibid.*

tionalism,[56] we find the same persistent error; namely, the failure to understand that the revolutionary indication of the limitations of prevailing truths is not irrational but comes in the interests of a wider rationality. It is true that most realistic philosophies sooner or later have made the mistake of closing the books of knowledge, of assuming that the widest system has been discovered, the greatest number of facts unearthed, and that little more remains to be done. This self-sufficient attitude which is so characteristic of long-established realisms always marks the death of realism for the time being; for some variety of nominalism then takes occasion to point out that the old realism has overlooked some embarrassing facts, has not, in other words, "kept up with the times," and must be removed from authority. But such cycles do not point to the inadequacy of rationalism and hence of realism; they point rather to the necessity of improving our rationalistic systems if we wish to retain our realism as valid and true.

SHORTCOMINGS OF THE CHAIN.—The implications of the chain of being in eighteenth-century biology[57] brought about some strange conclusions. As usual with Lovejoy, these conclusions are expected to illustrate the shortcomings of the chain of being. The blame is never laid upon the faulty historical understanding of the chain but rather upon the chain itself. It remains true, however, that when scientists begin to interpret metaphysics, or their own findings in terms of the metaphysical conclusions which seem to them to follow, some strange conclusions indeed are the result.

In eighteenth-century biological theory, the rigid division of organic forms into unalterable genera and species was taken to be an implication of the principle of gradation. The fixed hierarchy of forms called for by the principle of gradation issued in a set of organic genera and species taken as the actual application of that principle. In the same way, there was the contrary tendency to slur over the division of forms. This latter tendency seemed to be justified by another principle of the chain of being, the principle of continuity. In an effort to show that nature makes no jumps, the

---

56. *Ibid.*, pp. 288-89, 292-93.
57. *Ibid.*, Chap. VIII.

principle of continuity was appealed to as justification for the slurring of distinctions where no clear passage could be discovered in the hierarchy of forms as between one form and the next in the series. Thus, the inference goes, the chain collapses once again in a maze of contradictions.

This conclusion is, as we have already noted, unnecessary. The chain of being applies only to the logical order of possibility. Any effort to apply it with equal faithfulness to the mediated conditions of actuality is sure to bring about many insuperable difficulties. But these difficulties do not point to the invalidity of the chain of being; they point only to the shortcomings of the ill-advised efforts at its application.

The principle of plenitude, as Lovejoy implies, will always have the last word. In the historical flux, shortcomings are more in evidence than powers. But this is not an argument against rationality and the chain of being, rather it is in favor of them. The prominence of shortcomings is a demand for their abatement. It does not invalidate the standing and accomplishments of what has already been achieved. Those who smell the skunk avoid the smell and not the skunk.

Schiller sees the point. Lovejoy says of Schiller that "Since he holds that every unification must be incomplete, every aesthetic form or moral code prove in the end too narrow to contain the potentialities of humanity, it follows that the tendency to increasing diversification through perennial change will be, and should be, the dominant force in man's existence."[58] Correct. Behind this argument lies a comprehension of the perfect rationality of the conditions of being in the logical order of possibility. The principle of plenitude has the last word, because the urge toward actual fullness of perfection is immanent, and because the aim of actuality is the imitation of the logical order of possibility. Thus rationality and with it true realism is affirmed and not denied by this precept of Schiller's.

This, however, is not Lovejoy's own conclusion. His quotation

---

58. *Ibid.*, p. 303.

from Schiller is meant to show that in the end rationality is denied by Schiller in favor of life for its own sake. Lovejoy's quotations and summaries are so apt, and so neatly divided between those whose weak defense of an invalidly stated idealism make them seem ridiculous and those whose strong defense of a validly stated realism make it seem impregnable, that it is difficult to tell just where Lovejoy himself stands. The latter quoted passage and its surrounding context, as well as other such passages, lead to the suspicion that Lovejoy's explicit philosophy may be one which is opposed to all rationality. There is, however, the greater suspicion that Lovejoy is merely opposed to idealism.

SCHILLER AND SCHELLING TO THE RESCUE.—It was indeed Schiller, in Lovejoy's own account, who returned to at least one important aspect of the true realism. He posed the problem of the two orders of being and of the relation between them. He understood, as well as anyone in the tradition which Lovejoy has traced, the passivity of the logical order of possibility, the system of undifferentiated universals (or in Schiller's term, the *Formtrieb*) which "can never exact at one time anything but what it exacts and requires forever."[59] He understood the equal reality of actuality, and the force behind its drive for perfection.

There was, of course, the latent contradiction which Lovejoy notes, and which Schiller himself attempted rather unsuccessfully to resolve, of the question of reality with regard to the two orders of being: possibility and actuality. The wavering and indecision which Lovejoy observes in Schiller's refusal to make a choice of the superior reality of one order over the other came from Schiller's intuitive feeling for the truth. Schiller, unfortunately, was not a thoroughgoing metaphysician; and so he failed to work out the details of his ontology and the structure of an argument which could bolster both logically and empirically the refusal to elevate one order over the other in reality. His wavering was justifiable even if it went unjustified.

The last philosopher whom we shall have to consider in the

---

59. *Ibid.*, p. 302.

discussion of the chain is Schelling. Schelling accepted both "the One of neo-Platonism" and "a struggling, temporally limited, gradually self-realizing World-Spirit or Life-Force."[60] These are not contradictory, since "the latter is the aspect under which the former manifests itself to us." Schelling made no distinction with regard to reality between God and the world; between, that is, the logical and the historical orders. But he made the latter the source of all knowledge concerning the former. Primacy in matters of knowledge, however, does not indicate primacy in matters of being. Schelling understood the difference; he knew when to interweave the two orders and when to show their divergence. His writing in this respect often resembles Whitehead, both in regard to its emphasis on the dual nature of God and on its emergentism in actuality. Schelling said that "I posit God as the first and the last, as the Alpha and the Omega; but as Alpha he is not what he is as Omega...."[61] Whitehead's "primordial" and "consequent" natures of God are here, as also is the evolutionism of an historical order of actuality, striving toward greater inclusiveness and greater perfection as it half plans, half gropes, toward the ideal conditions of the logical order.

Schelling's shift of emphasis was in effect a turn away from idealism and toward the position of true realism. He thus chose one version of Platonism and refused another, and was no pioneer in this tradition which had often sought unsuccessfully to gain for realism the historical force of authority which had more or less constantly been in the possession of idealism. He did a service, however, in that the peculiar cast of his philosophy threw the issue into greater relief and demanded a decision from the ensuing generations.

Schelling ... at least showed the ineluctability of a choice between the two strains in Platonism, by making explicit their essential incompatibility. He put before the metaphysics of the succeeding century a forced option—though many of his successors have failed to recognize it or have ingeniously sought to evade it.[62]

---

60. *Ibid.*, p. 317.
61. *Ibid.*, p. 323.
62. *Ibid.*, p. 326.

Thus at last Platonism is correctly interpreted and the realistic fallacy of idealism in Plato "turned upside down."

But alas, Lovejoy intends by this latter phrase to indicate that all realism is thereby rejected. He may not mean what we mean. And finally, he may have even succeeded in misunderstanding Schelling's philosophy. For he mistakenly supposes that the "Chain of Being has been converted into a Becoming."[63] Schelling simply meant that Becoming works out the implications contained in the conditions of the chain of being, and not at all that one reduces to the other! Lovejoy would have it that in Schelling's transference of God from the logical to the historical order, the reduction to absurdity of the chain of being is completed. There is no justification whatsoever for this interpretation. By deifying Becoming Schelling meant to make it of equal reality with Being; but he did not mean to withdraw the attribution of deity from Being. Such a detraction would indeed be an impossibility without thereby also affecting to some extent Becoming. For deity, as realists from Scotus Erigena to Schelling have understood, "is found in the very entrails of the world."[64] Schelling is but one more name in the list of those who from time to time have sought to save true realism by modification of the excesses of the realistic fallacy. He is *not* the last reduction to absurdity of the realistic tradition.

GENERAL CONCLUSIONS

It is difficult not to infer from what Lovejoy says in several places that "the great chain of being" has been responsible for the extensity of interests and the intensity of accomplishment of the whole of Western civilization.[65] He says of the principle of sufficient reason, for instance, that "By this sort of faith in the rationality of the world we live in, a great part—probably, in spite of the recurrent and powerful opposing tendencies, the greater part—of Western philosophy and science was, for a score

---

63. *Ibid.*
64. Maurice de Wulf, *History of Mediaeval Philosophy* (London, 1935), p. 127.
65. *GCB*, pp. 304-5.

of centuries, animated and guided."[66] The thesis is that Platonic rationality gave us Western civilization. Thus the work concludes with the affirmation of a statement with which it began, a statement of Whitehead's that "the safest general characterization of the European philosophical tradition is that it consists in a series of footnotes to Plato."[67] This is the kind of enthusiastic claim which only the most ardent realist would make for realism.

But Lovejoy is prepared to go even further in its defense. The final conclusion is that the error of believing in the chain is due to a persistent philosophical craving for it. This is, of course, not argument against realism but pretty cogent argument in favor of it—the kind of extremist argument in favor of which cautious believers in realism would be slower to put forth. Here indeed the true realist must insist that Lovejoy has somewhat overstated the case, and given credit to realism for much of what has been historically occasioned by nominalism. And there are other instances. For example, the influence of Aristotle, who was a realist but according to Lovejoy no great believer in the chain, has had to be somewhat overlooked to make the case come out.

THE FAILURE TO EXPLAIN TIME.—Lovejoy's book, strange as it may seem from the foregoing, was written to refute realism and not to defend it. The virtues and accomplishments of the chain of being are as nothing when weighed against the failures of the chain.

Chief among these failures, according to Lovejoy, is that the principle of sufficient reason, a consequence of the chain, is unable to explain time. As Lovejoy says, the principle of absolute rationality in the cosmos "conflicts, in the first place, with one immense fact, besides many particular facts, in the natural order—the fact that existence as we experience it is temporal. A world of time and change—this, at least, our history has shown—is a world which can neither be deduced from nor reconciled with the postulate that existence is the expression and consequence of a system of 'eternal' and 'necessary' truths inherent in the very logic of

---

66. *Ibid.*, pp. 327-28.
67. Quoted in *GCB*, p. 24, from Whitehead, *Process and Reality*, p. 63.

being."[68] Apart from the tempting question whether if the whole of our Western civilization has been deduced from such an impossible contradiction it should not be immediately abandoned, one is forced to repeat again, that if idealism has proved historically and logically invalid, why should that be taken as the refutation of true realism? Is a philosophy demonstrated invalid by a review of the misrepresentations of those who have misunderstood it?

As to the charge that the principle of sufficient reason is unable to account for time, this we may for the moment admit to be true within limits. But does it justify the rejection of the chain of being merely to show that one of its implicates fails to explain what no other philosophy has succeeded in explaining? The fact that a primordial God, feeling the needs of his consequent nature, proceeds to forge the adventures of actuality, is one which has never been satisfactorily explained. The various surmises which have been put forward under the aegis of realism and the chain of being are as good as any that have been offered. This remains true even though Occam's "Razor" and the charge of dogmatism be levelled against them.

The temporalizing of the chain, the substitution of the theory of a slow and laborious ascending for the theory of a swift spilling over of perfect abundance, is to substitute what has been observed in experience for the dogmatism of authoritative hypostatization, that is all. But it is not to discount or deny the philosophy of realism. There may be an Unmoved Mover who started the wheels going, or there may not be: we have no way of knowing absolutely. In this sense, one guess is as good as another. Only, one hypothesis may explain more than another; and this would justify its retention.

Again, there may be an abundant plenitude of being which spills its actuality over, or there may not be: again we have no way of knowing. The explanatory indication here points the other way. But what we do have evidence for and what we do know is that the purpose of the universe is gradually being un-

---

68. *Ibid.*, p. 329.

folded in actuality; that actuality with all its imperfections, contradictions and disvalues, its limitations and its partiality, can only be seen as intelligible if we take it for granted that it is slowly and painfully moving toward an ideal and perfectly logical order of possibility.

PURPOSE: PUSH OR PULL.—It is a reasonably fair observation that if we could discover a purpose in the universe, this would presuppose that somebody or something had put it there. But this question of what lies behind ultimate purpose is removed from the reaches of human knowledge. We can probably never know who put it there, or why, but we can know it in so far as it *is* there. And we are interested in its exposition in so far as it is there. It is not the task of philosophy to penetrate any further than reason can go with the aid of empirical allowance and intuitional insight. Thus the conception of an Unmoved Mover is called into question, and there is substituted for it the conception of an infinitely remote *future* goal, Schiller's God as Omega.

What concerns us most is not how and where and why the actual universe started, but where it is now and where it is going. In the last analysis, we care more for where we are going than for where we have been. The reason for this is that the latter question is one which actual experience can aid us in discovering. Further, the past is unalterable but the future is at least partly open. Improvement, if there is to be any, lies in the future and not in the past. We can hazard as many guesses as we like as to where we have been; but we can actually investigate the question of where we are going, and somehow the latter seems vastly more important.

The substitution of the theory of a gradual evolution of actuality toward the logical order of possibility for the notion of a divine overflowing of possibility is merely the transfer of emphasis which brings about the substitution of true realism for the exaggerations of idealism. The Neo-Platonic misunderstanding of plenitude, which explains actuality as the spilling over of divine abundance, is done away with, and in its place the biologists inadvertently restored the balance of true realism: the gradual unfolding of logical possibilities in the world of actuality. Thus a pull in the universe became substituted for a push. The push of the Creator was abandoned as unknowable, and the pull of the universal goal was accepted in its place as the most general observation of empirical evidence.

UNSOLVED PROBLEMS.—Lovejoy charges that realism fails to explain the relation between the two orders of being. God as perfect cannot be reconciled with God as imperfect. In his words, "an Absolute which is self-sufficient and forever perfect and complete cannot be identified with a God related to and manifested in a world of temporal becoming and alteration and creative advance."[69] This may fairly be regarded as the age-old problem of realism, that actuality requires a logical order, whereas the logical order cannot be shown to require actuality. From the point of view of actuality, the problem is easy to solve. The logical order has to be supposed as real in order to account for the imperfections, shortcomings and incompleteness of actuality. Actuality is unintelligible and meaningless without the assumption that there is a real, universally perfect, order of being, having a one-to-one correspondence with the conditions of all potential happenings.

From the point of view of actuality, therefore, the problem is simple. But from the point of view of the logical order of possibility, the answer is somewhat different. Why does the real perfection of God (or the absolute, or the logical order of possibility) require the imperfect order of actuality? To this question, the answer, if it had come, would have been in terms which would finally have explained why being is in two distinguishable orders. But the explanation is not forthcoming, and the reason for this is also simple. In order to understand the purpose of the whole universe, it would be necessary to analyze it as a part of some larger whole. Purpose is always in terms of the relation of part to whole. But the universe is defined as that whole outside of which there is nothing. To talk about the purpose of the largest whole is meaningless. With this question, then, we reach the point past which the human capacity for reasoning,

---

69. *GCB*, p. 327.

being itself part of the universe, is unable to follow. The part can know nothing of the purpose of the whole of which it is a part.

Man as a creature living in the vivid world of actuality yet equipped by means of his intellect to aspire toward the abstract logical order, is caught between the two levels of being and, according to an eighteenth century view, strange to both. This is a tragic dilemma for man.

He is therefore—not in consequence of any accidental fall from innocence nor of any perverse machinations of evil spirits, but because of the requirements of the universal scheme of things—torn by conflicting desires and propensities; as a member of two orders of being at once, he wavers between them both, and is not quite at home in either.[70]

This is an awkward predicament—or a privileged position, whichever one chooses to regard it. From the point of view of the belief in the possibility of progress, it is a privilege. To be only partly involved with our animal destiny and to have been lifted, if only to a small extent, into a position in which we may share (if only minutely) that view which is *sub specie aeternitatis,* is to be the despair only of those who prefer a tidy and limited community to an untidy but also unlimited one.

For Lovejoy, the fact that Whitehead makes God the irrational ground of all rationality is the final absurdity. This fact yields for students of philosophy "its most pathetic interest, as a manifestation of a certain persistent craving of the philosophic mind."[71] In the light of a previous passage of Lovejoy's this condemnation of Whitehead is particularly inept. For Lovejoy has already observed several pages back that "rationality, when conceived as complete, as excluding all arbitrariness, becomes itself a kind of irrationality."[72] But does not Lovejoy understand that such a "certain persistent craving" is not locked up within the brain as one of its physiological defects? The "certain persistent craving" which the thirsty have for water, which the hungry have for food, and which the cold and exposed have for shelter, is no mere idle fancy but

---

70. *Ibid.,* pp. 198-99.
71. *Ibid.,* p. 333.
72. *Ibid.,* p. 331.

represents a real and objective set of conditions which it were ridiculous to deem entirely mental. The "certain persistent craving," which as Lovejoy admits has obsessed philosophers as far back as we can trace them, must stand for some real human need; some need, moreover, which is capable of being satisfied by something corresponding to it in the objective world. It is not a primitive and useless appendage which, like our tails, were better lost.

The whole question about the great chain of being is that it was simple enough to be misunderstood. Does the consequent misunderstanding condemn its validity as a whole, and with it the validity of the true Platonic realism? There is no reason to accept such a conclusion. Lovejoy has indeed knocked over a straw man: the extreme position of idealism has been in disrepute since the rise of empirical science first successfully challenged the Church's prohibition upon the discovery of further universals in an effort to save the limited realism of the Church free from questioning. But Lovejoy has only succeeded, and this inadvertently, in showing the great strength which the valid philosophy of true realism, in its modified form, has maintained, and therefore in hinting, though this too without intention, at its probably validity.

As long as those difficult questions of metaphysics which realism has failed to answer continue to go unanswered in the course of philosophic thought, the fact that the chain of being has failed to render any satisfactory account of them is not and can not be construed as an argument against the validity of the chain and thus also against realism. The burden of the argument is transferred to Lovejoy's shoulders, and the responsibility for the answers to the very significant questions he has raised fall upon him. He is expected by his own pleadings to extract their solution from some ontology other than that of realism. To accomplish such a task would more than any other argument expose the insufficiencies of the chain of being. This positive labor, however, he has not yet attempted.

LOVEJOY'S VIEWPOINT.—If Lovejoy's study proves anything, it proves just this, that there is only the one philosophy of rationalistic realism. The realistic philosophy is constituted by the equal reality of possibility and actuality, a balance which is extremely difficult to maintain. When the position is pushed too far in the direction of either order in particular, some kind of philosophic error results. When it falls off on one side into idealism, empiricists attack it. When it falls off on the other side into the nominalistic fallacy, rationalists attack it. Lovejoy seems to be at heart a rationalist who is attacking the irrationality of idealism.

Early in the work on the chain of being, Lovejoy acknowledges the authority and practical efficacy of the Ideas. This is especially true in the passage describing the effect of changing ideas upon the English gardens.[73] He is himself in this passage a perfectly good realist, a "friend of the Ideas," to use a phrase of Plato's. The promise made in this connection to show the same efficacy of ideas throughout the work is only partially fulfilled later. The effect of ideas upon lesser literary men is set forth, it is true, but not the effect on economics, politics, customs, institutions, etc.

Lovejoy does not explicitly maintain his thesis throughout but lets his selected items speak for themselves for the point of view from which they have been selected. Is he successful in this endeavor? Not quite in the manner intended, certainly; for the account frequently is eloquent for an opposite moral.

Lovejoy's argument, viewed in perspective, is seen definitely to face two ways. One suspects that he came to realism to jeer and barely escaped remaining to pray. The moral of the work as a whole would seem to be capable of being cast in the form of an incomplete argument. The chain of being has been very fruitful. The chain of being has proved invalid. And here Lovejoy stops, without drawing the very obvious but rather silly conclusion. Should we abandon the products because they have been drawn from a set of invalid metaphysical notions? We are never told.

It is impossible to avoid the suspicion that Lovejoy is almost a realist. He appears as a sort of philosophical victim of a period of transition, a Pompeiian figure, whose work has been frozen as he was in the act of trying to face in both directions: away from a philosophical revolution which he does not entirely admire, and toward a philosophical tradition which he admires but refuses to let himself accept. So he ends by attacking the latter.

---

73. *Ibid.*, p. 15-16.

V

Pragmatism and Inverse Probability

THERE CAN BE LITTLE DOUBT that the prestige of the day is generally accredited to science, and, more particularly, to scientific method. The success of the physical sciences, in both theoretical and practical fields, leads other studies to emulate science and to claim the scientific sanction. All types of thinkers, from philosophers to social scientists, including even practical men of affairs, are eager to justify their particular interests by proclaiming their scientific nature. In the field of philosophy, warring schools have in common at least the pretension of being that school which accords best with the procedure of science. Pragmatism, in the peculiar form in which it was advocated by William James, is no exception to this ambition.[1] Marked divergences have been noted between the variety of pragmatism set forth by Peirce, its founder, and that other variety made popular by James. James did not sharply define this divergence even if he was aware of it. He noted that Peirce's presentation was obscure, took it for granted that while he could not wholly understand Peirce, he was yet advocating Peirce's doctrine, and let the matter go at that. Putting aside for the moment the fact that Peirce was, in addition to being a philosopher, a practicing scientist while James was not (unless it is fair to describe literary psychology as also scientific), it will be the business of this chapter to inquire only whether James's pragmatic doctrine is in agreement with the method of science. We shall confine our at-

---

1. *Pragmatism*, (New York, 1940), Lecture II, med.

tention for the most part to James's theory of truth, as set forth in Lecture VI of his *Pragmatism,* and we shall compare the view there set forth with the modern theory of probability, as advanced by one of the leading authorities on its use in scientific method, R. A. Fisher, in his *Statistical Methods for Research Workers.* Since this is not a detective story, there can be no harm in admitting in advance the conclusion to be reached. The pragmatic theory of truth conforms not to valid statistical probability method but rather to the error which Fisher condemns under the name of inverse probability. If modern methods of calculative statistical average are right, and if the comparison to be made in this chapter is a correct one, then pragmatism, so far as scientific method can corroborate it or confute it, is wrong. That is the general thesis to be argued here.

Let us begin, then, by considering pragmatism's theory of truth. Accepting the general view that truth means agreement with reality, rival schools have split over the question of what is reality. James said that agreement with reality means nothing more nor less than verification and validation, and further, that verification and validation imply certain practical consequences of the idea which is verified and validated. It is possible to reduce these statements to succinctness in the following formulation. *The truth of an idea is its agreement with certain practical consequences.* Of course, the practical consequences are those which would be expected to follow from the idea, those that are relevant rather than those that are not. If the hypothesis that all cats have green eyes were being tested, obviously only the eyes of cats could be admitted to evidence; and all other animals as well as all other green things would have to be ruled out. Relevant practical consequences are those consequences which bear as evidence upon the hypothesis, either to support it or to disprove it. This particular point would probably be accepted by all pragmatists and non-pragmatists alike.

But before we can proceed any further, it will be necessary to make certain more debatable observations in explanation of the statement which we shall agree to accept as pragmatism's theory of truth. In the first place, by practical consequences James evidently meant *immediate* practical consequences. It is clear from his general point of view that he could not have meant ultimate practical consequences; he was always anxious to get away from first principles and to cultivate facts. The practical consequences of which he spoke existed in the present factual world, not in an indefinitely remote future world or in the infinite. Thus the agreement of an idea with its practical consequences for James would have to mean an agreement verified and validated in the actual world of the present, an agreement now.

In the second place, James did not think of an idea as we have come to think of a scientific hypothesis; that is, as something independent of our mental processes and as an objective proposition to be disproved or supported by investigation. He considered an idea to be a general thought whose agreement with practical consequences is sought, having merely a mental status: an idea in the mind, presumably, of some investigator. Thus for James, the pragmatic method was almost a branch of epistemology. The subject's thoughts about the object were to be tested by the subject, and the object's existence was fortuitous and incidental to the purposes which it could serve in contributing to the subject's fund of knowledge. What is the truth, as a question, was resolved into, what can we know. Universal theories concerning objective facts were not supposed to have any real being. The thinker entertained an idea; and, if he was a pragmatic thinker, he would proceed at once to enter upon the process of discovering whether the idea he entertained could be verified and validated by the relevant practical consequences in that part of the actual world which was available to his resources as an investigator. The whole affair of testing truth, then, is a unit-affair; conceived, and carried out as conceived, by an investigator acting upon his own suggestions.

In the third place, it would follow from the two notions which we have set forth above that the truths which were found to agree with the relevant practical consequences could not have had any being or existence prior to their verification and validation. For if hypotheses are nothing more than ideas in minds, and their verifications and validation a matter of immediate application, then the ideas are, so to speak, summatory of the facts and have no standing of their own. For ideas exist only in minds, and minds, like the bodies which maintain them, are mortal. We may presume that unless ideas possess the faculty of being able to hop from bodies which are old and doomed to those which are young and promising, they, too, must perish, never to be heard from again. But if ideas exist only in minds, it follows that they could never have existed before minds and cannot exist without them. As if to support this contention, James employed the terms of the old medieval argument concerning the status of universals; did they exist before the thing to which they referred, *ante rem,* or was their existence confined to the things in which their reference was found, *in rebus?* James decided in favor of existence *in rebus,* thus declaring that the existence of ideas, apart from their being held as concepts in the mind, was confined to the particular things in which they were to be found.

Here, then, we may have brought to light the crux of the pragmatic conception of truth. Such reality as truths enjoy is known by minds, which derive them from relevant facts; but reality is *dependent* upon the facts from which the truths are derived. In other words, the primary reality of the situation is accorded to the facts, and the reality of truths, being derived from this primary reality of the facts, can be described as nothing better than secondary. The reality of truth is a derived and secondary reality, emphatically mental by nature. We may sum up the argument thus far, then, by declaring that, in James's view, the truth of an idea is its agreement with certain practical consequences, and, moreover, that the reality of such truth is dependent upon and hence inferior to the reality of the practical consequences themselves. We wish now to contrast the position of pragmatism with that of scientific method, especially in reference to the question of truth. It will now be our task, therefore, to leave the question of pragmatism for a while, in order to shift our attention to the consideration of the status of hypotheses in that part of scientific method which is concerned with the statistical method of probability.

The position of the mathematical theory of probability statistics is mainly to be found in the introductory chapter to the book by Fisher already mentioned. Scattered throughout that chapter there are methodological statements and statements of fundamental position. We shall choose from these only the ones which will lend themselves to contrast with James's pragmatic theory of truth. For it is not the operation involved in the calculation of statistical averages which chiefly concerns us; it is instead the assumptions underlying such operations. Fisher's book has been selected for this purpose because of the clarity of his statement of these assumptions. He is rare among statisticians in being aware of many of the assumptions upon which his method rests.

Fisher states that in statistics we do not study individual results but rather do we try to make our experiments representative of the "population of possibilities." The word to be stressed here is possibilities. Fisher definitely affirms that we are dealing in scientific method not with actualities but with permanent possibilities. We work with actualities only in order to get at the possibilities. Possibilities, of course, can only be exhibited as infinite populations, and we are told that "actual observations can only be samples of such possibilities." The values of actual cases must therefore be interpreted as random samples of "hypothetical infinite populations," for what is being approached by the statistical method is the discovery of constants, called parameters, which specify mathematically the character of infinite populations. Thus what we are after is the constant character of infinite possibilities, by means of samples of actual cases made by means of actual observation and planned experiment.

It is worthy of note in connection with the thesis in hand that when Fisher sums up the statistical method so far as the general nature of its procedure is concerned, he finds it to be no different from the method prevailing in the various physical sciences. It is a process, he tells us, which begins with hypothesis, not one chosen at random but one conceived and then "defined with all necessary exactitude." The practical consequences which it possibly could have are explored by deductive argument. These consequences are next compared with the available observations, and if the observations do not differ from the deductions, the "hypothesis is justified," at least until more relevant data becomes available. The question of reality, of course, does not enter, since it introduces no distinctions; the constants of nature, the hypotheses, and the facts being equally real.

Another significant observation to be made is that in Fisher's formation there is no reference to an observer, a subject or an operator, and we can discover in it no assumptions implying the necessity for such a reference. Scientific method is a method which requires the existence of certain relations holding between hypotheses or general or universal propositions on the one hand, and sets of particular relevant facts on the other. It is operated by human beings working individually or in groups. But we may suppose that it is the internal relations of the scientific method which count, and that the method itself is one which could be carried out, let us say, accidentally and less well by monkeys, deliberately and more perfectly by beings superior to ourselves. Both of which cases, in so far as it was the scientific method which was being carried out, would afford valid instances of scientific method. The fact that human beings are at the present time the only creatures performing acts involving the scientific method does not in any wise suggest that as a logico-empirical method its validity depends upon them. Fisher is in fact concerned with method *qua* method, which is to say, with method quite apart from its relations to minds and actual things.

So much for the exposition and explanation of one phase of the theory of probability in statistics. Let us proceed to compare that theory with the pragmatic conception of truth. Science has been in possession of its valid method for hardly more than three hundred years, while the term, pragmatism, James hastened to assure us, in his second lecture in the volume to which we have already referred, is derived from the same Greek word meaning action. Is pragmatism, then, merely an *old* name for some *new* ways of thinking? Is James's experimental method consistent with that method of probability statistics which is so widely employed throughout the physical sciences?

We have noted that James's method deals with mental ideas and with practical consequences. Absolutes are not sought, but on the contrary their very existence is denied. The statistical method deals with infinite populations and with parameters or constants. Thus the statistical method cannot be said to rely upon mental ideas but only upon ideas derived from fixed relations which in no wise depend upon minds. Practical consequences are specifically denied by Fisher when he states that we are *not* concerned with "individual results." Thus where James relies upon mental ideas and practical consequences, statistical method is concerned with neither of these but only with hypotheses and with their verification. The fields of reference of the Jamesian terms and of the terms of statistical method may overlap, but they also certainly do differ widely, and the distinction between them is not a dim one which can be discerned only with great subtleties of meaning. The differences actually rely upon an extremely divergent underlying viewpoint. We can detect this in a general way, and we can also observe its effects through a closer scrutiny of what is intended by the use of the terms themselves. For the distinctions and differences between James's method and the scientific method of probability statistics do not end here.

We may consider, for instance, the question of the time categories, particularly as these appear in the temporal order of the steps of the method. James evidently meant immediate practical consequences, as we have seen, and it is obvious that immediate practical consequences cannot be ascertained about infinite populations even from the observation of random samples. Immediate practical consequences must be presumed to lie, temporally speaking, in the imminent future; it is hard to say just how long a run of time is required, but certainly not more than a few weeks or months, or, at best, years. There would be nothing practical to the experimenter accruing from an experiment to which he was forced to devote the best part of his life and perhaps the life of his successor. Practical consequences depend, then, upon results to be attained or ends to be achieved in the immediate present or in the immediate future; no more. Infinite populations, however, seem to be independent of time, or, if you like, dependent upon all time: it comes to the same thing. An infinite population of instances of some type of occurrence would have to include all those instances which have occurred, even though they may be forever beyond the reach of experimental investigation; all those instances which are occurring even as the theory of scientific method is being discussed, and which therefore in a sense are themselves partly beyond examination; and, finally, all those instances which will occur at some time in the indefinite future, however long they may have to be awaited. Thus the emphasis of the method of pragmatism is on the present and the immediate future, while that of statistical method is on the indefinitely remote, or infinite future, and includes also the past and present.

Then, too, and in many ways more importantly, the scientific method of probability statistics begins with the conception and definition of an hypothesis, thus implying the existence independent of actual things of the constant to be ascertained. James said that he preferred to find his truths in actual things. For statistical method, the formulation of the hypothesis precedes the investigation of its support by random sampling and the determination of whether or not it corresponds with parameters; only ultimate consequences accord with infinite populations. For the pragmatic method of James, the hypothesis is to be derived from the observation of practical consequences. James does not comprehend what statistical method assumes, namely, that hypotheses cannot be derived from facts, since random samples are all that we can hope to observe, and random samples are selected as relevant data for some hypothesis. Thus to derive hypotheses from facts is to derive them explicitly from facts selected in accordance with the dictates of some hypothesis assumed and employed implicitly. Thus the ideal aim of the pragmatic method is at best impossible; at worst, confusing. The pragmatic method denies the real being of the laws it pretends to set out to discover, while the statistical method, never expecting to ascertain anything more than a very high ratio of probability, makes its calculations with the explicit understanding that constants have their being among infinite populations, and that it is the knowledge of such characteristics of infinite populations which are being sought out.

Thus there is a wide disparity between the pragmatic method of James and the statistical method of modern science, a disparity so wide that in many instances it finds them ranged on opposite sides of the same question. James had an interesting habit of taking the modern evolutionary and progressivistic view of a topic, but of preferring to express it in the outmoded language of a metaphysics he thought it better to discard. On the vexed question of universals, a medieval controversy dating back to the Socratic consideration of the independent being of the ideas, we find quite naturally that James assumed the then modern view, or, may we say, the then post-modern view. The then modern view was more positive than James's, for it chose to lead away from the controversy over universals altogether, and to proceed to more advantageous fields; while James remained behind—or ahead—to express in a medieval terminology his contempt for the theory of the real being of universals. So far as universals were concerned, he preferred to think of them *in rebus* rather than *ante rem*, thus ignoring the fact that Avicenna had settled the problem to the general satisfaction by asserting that *ante rem* referred to ontology, while *in rebus* was a matter of epistemology. Modern statistical method in science returns to the adoption of an old position, though endowing it with an exactness and a practicality it formerly lacked. For this latter method assumes the being of parameters or constants among infinite populations: eternal truths to be known but independent of knowledge—universals. Statistical method sees a necessary relation between eternal truths and the methodological approach to them, and states that relation in terms of a reliable method of investigation. James sees an absolute antipathy between eternal truths and the approach to them, and wishes to deny the reality of the former as a necessary step toward saving the latter. The relation between eternal truths and the observation of random samples is exact and mathematical in the statistical method of science which utilizes both definition and calculation.

In contrast with the precision of this approach, we have something rather more nebulous and unanalyzed. The relation between mental ideas and their practical consequences is vague and rough in the pragmatic method of James, depending as it does upon the Cartesian properties of clarity and distinctness. James wishes to propose a method of clarifying ideas by supposing for each of our ideas the practical consequences that would flow from it. Despite the professed aim, this is extremely subjective in outlook. The statistical method wishes to count, to calculate, and to rely upon as well as to approach the discovery of unchanging laws of method on the one hand and of content or subject-matter on the other. The method of James is that of common sense; it deals with wholes. The method of statistical probability is analytical; it deals with parts. Scientific method is essentially analytical, if it is nothing else; yet Jamesian pragmatism never probes any deeper than the level of common sense which, whatever it is, does not lie at any deep analytical levels. The statistical method seeks a vague end by means of an exact method; the pragmatic method of James seeks an exact end by means of a vague method which pretends to nothing more than the clarification of conceptions. Science searches for universals with the aid of statistical averages; James searches for statistical averages with the aid of the absolute denial of universals. In the face of these differences, it can hardly be contended that the method of James is scientific while the method of statistics is less so.

We have reached the first half of the conclusion at which we predicted at the outset we should arrive: the pragmatic theory of truth as set forth by William James is not consistent with the statistical method of modern scientific probability theory. We are prepared, then, for the second half of our thesis; we are ready to ask whether there is any other kind of statistical method which does prove to be consistent with the pragmatic theory of truth according to James. The answer is that there is, and that it is described by Fisher in the same introductory chapter of his book as inverse probability. Let us describe first of all inverse probability and next the points which inverse probability and Jamesian pragmatism have in common.

Inverse probability consists in the attempt to deduce the properties of populations from the observation of random samples. It thus requires first the samples, then the observations, and finally the deductions; whereas the order of probability requires first the hypothesis, then the selection of the random samples, and finally, the ascertaining of whether the claims of the hypothesis are borne out by the samples. Probability starts with hypotheses; inverse probability starts with facts. Probability endeavors to ascertain whether its hypotheses are supported by the relevant facts; inverse probability endeavors to ascertain whether its facts will yield a relevant hypothesis. Instead of checking hypotheses for disproof or allowance by examining relevant cases (there is no such thing in scientific method as proof by relevant cases), inverse probability looks for the hypothesis itself among the relevant cases. Thus while it resembles scientific method, its procedure actually runs counter to it. Its results, therefore, for all scientific purposes, are worthless. Fisher has no hesitation in condemning inverse probability as an error which must be wholly rejected. The practice of inverse probability is widespread among the social sciences. The results which were to be expected, consisting either in a body of funded knowledge or in practical techniques, are pathetically missing. Social scientists assume that the method of physical science is that of inverse probability, while it is actually that of probability.

It will be immediately obvious to the discerning reader that inverse probability bears a family resemblance to the pragmatic method of James. If we recall here that in the method of James the truth of ideas follows from immediate practical consequences, it will be at once evident that this is a statement in other and more popular words of the pretensions of inverse probability: the fallacy of looking among facts for a theory, instead of looking with the aid of a theory among the relevant facts for those which will support it. Among *what* practical consequences shall we search for our theory? We cannot search among all; if we choose a few, on what basis is the choice to be made? James does not provide us with the means of answering these questions. He only provides us with a method which raises them as questions; and perhaps on his assumptions they cannot be answered. The method is sterile and self-refuting, since we can never hope to encounter among chosen facts any theory except that particular theory from which, implicitly perhaps, the facts were selected in the first place. Inverse probability and its philosophical counterpart, the pragmatic method of James, may look practical and hard-headed from a distance, but a closer inspection reveals that actually they maintain their existence in charmed circles, by denying the existence of absolutes to be sought, and by pursuing incessantly the chimera of facts which are able obligingly to produce their own theories.

In showing that the pragmatic method of James comes closer to the theory of inverse probability than it does to statistical method which is employed so widely among the physical sciences, we have reached the end of the second half of our thesis. Inverse probability stands as a condemned error in the procedure of physical science, while the statistical method of probability itself is held to be valid and is widely employed. Since the pragmatic method of James accords with inverse probability, and is inconsistent with the statistical method of probability, the scientific pretensions of this pragmatic method must perforce be abandoned. Whether the argument is strong enough also to force the abandonment in social science of Jamesian pragmatism itself is a moot question. Logically, it does have such strength, and it should leave the Jamesian pragmatic method only as a convenient and rough rule of thumb for purposes of clarification only and not for any profound analysis.

The announced thesis of this chapter therefore, is a negative one, and it may be presumed to have been accomplished; but we cannot afford to let the matter end there. Attacks upon positive positions are conducted largely for one of two reasons: merely to eliminate an error, or to clear the ground for the statement of another positive position. Ruling out the former alternative as insufficient for the genuine aims of philosophy, we are left with the necessity for stating a positive position. In order to avoid the risk of overextending the proportions of this chapter, we may limit ourselves to suggesting the existence of such a position, and even point out that it was referred to at the outset. For if there are marked divergencies between the varieties of pragmatism set forth by Peirce, its founder, and by James, its popularizer, then perhaps the Peirceian version of pragmatism was mistaken by James and does accord with the statistical method of probability better than the Jamesian version.

James did not attempt to conceal that his version of pragmatism was based upon that of Peirce,[2] that he did not fully understand Peirce,[3] and therefore (we may conclude) that his version of pragmatism was based upon a misunderstanding. The version of pragmatism set forth by Peirce implies that the conceivable effects of our conception are the same as the object of our conception.[4] This version neither limits the hypothesis ("our conception") to the effects (in which we can read "practical consequences") nor denies that there is an object to be known. It is a method which admits the existence of truth. From a number of passages in Peirce's collected papers, it is clear that by the conceivable effects of our conception he did not mean that truth was to be found in its consequences, but just the reverse: truth leads to true consequences.[5] In the Peirceian understanding of pragmaticism, a term which he adopted in order to distinguish it from false interpretations of pragmatism, the truth is independent of its consequences and therefore exists *ante rem*. Pragmaticism insists only upon conceivable practical bearings, not upon immediate practical consequences. Hence, it is consistent with the possibility of there being constants (universals) *ante rem* and with infinite populations.

It was Peirce, and not James, who set up the true pragmatic method, from which James created a diversion; and so we should not be surprised to discover that it is the statistical method and

---

2. *Ibid.*
3. *Ibid.*, Lecture I.
4. *Chance, Love and Logic*, "How to Make Our Ideas Clear."
5. *Collected Papers of Charles S. Peirce*, Vol. V, *passim*. See especially pp. 468, 503.

not inverse probability which agrees with Peirceian pragmatism. It is time for those who are concerned with true philosophy and true science to return to the pragmatic maxim of Peirce, and to the implications of a metaphysically realistic nature which that maxim supplies; and, correspondingly, to abandon the error which is inseparable from Jamesian pragmatism and inverse probability. The analysis of the method of science reveals that it relies upon constants of nature. Even the method of statistical probability, the existence of which has been such a comfort to those who deny that there are any constants to be known, relies upon such constants. And when James in theory declared that he wished to turn away in practice from first things and principles, he also turned toward inverse probability, which is invalid, and away from the valid method of science and from that interpretation of pragmatism which Peirce had so heartily advocated.

Part III
The Revival in History

VI

Have We Exhausted Greek Culture?

THE WORLD, IT IS GENERALLY THOUGHT, has moved forward rapidly in the last few centuries. Despite the successive disillusionments of war and economic depression there is a steady conviction in the continuance of some sort of progress. We understand our own history in the following terms. Once civilization had emerged from the darkness of the Middle Ages into the ripening atmosphere of unrestricted thought and action, inspired by the Renaissance and liberated by the Reformation, progress became an accelerated process. In the last two decades this acceleration, at least in scientific and political thought, has reached a maddening pace. It is all we can do to keep up with our own times. Consequently when we look back upon ancient times and other civilizations, they seem overwhelmingly out of date and inadequate. The Greeks in particular, although still regarded as the most civilized of ancient peoples, hardly seem to have deserved the acclaim which was accorded them as late as the last century. In the high light of modern science, technology, and politics, they appear to have been an extraordinarily precocious people, by some strange coincidence given to original explorations in those very fields which we ourselves have so greatly advanced. It is clear to us now, for instance, that the Greeks had in little the idea of science, represented by such figures as Thales in physics, Aristotle in zoology, Pythagoras and Euclid in mathematics. But Thales' physics is no longer acceptable according to present standards, Aristotle's biology is inadequate, and Euclid's geometry has been seriously challenged by non-Euclidean geometry. It is clear to us also that the Greeks were supreme artists, and art is a field in which they have never been excelled; but since we do not place much emphasis on this aspect of civilization we are only too apt to regard them as having been somewhat misguided in their interests. Generally we suppose that the Greeks were merely clever people, much given to unprofitable philosophical speculations and unfortunately held back by a youthful and even childish idealism.

It will be helpful to stop in our summary judgments and ask two questions concerning this modern deprecation of Hellenic culture: (1) from what viewpoint of our own does it arise, and (2) does it represent a fair estimate? An answer to the first question should throw some light upon the extent of the validity of modern opinions, and an answer to the second should lead toward both a revaluation of Greek culture and a reorientation of the modern viewpoint.

In order to comprehend the perspective from which we view Greek history today, it will be necessary to start far back in history—in the account of Greece itself, as a matter of fact. We must begin by considering the issue between Socrates and his rivals, the Sophists. Socrates maintained a belief in the real independent existence of abstract ideas or universals; he considered that universals are independent both of the thinking subject and of the object which is thought. This is the position which the Sophists were concerned with assailing; they held on the contrary a more relativistic view of knowledge, and did not accept the independence of universals as conveying anything. Universals for the Sophists are creations of the reasoning subject, and, since they thought man the measure of all things, universals must be otherwise meaningless. In this controversy it is no longer considered necessary to take sides. Nevertheless, it is a perennial one in philosophy. We find it occurring again in the later Middle Ages, this time as conducted between scholastic theologians and the new empirical philosophers. If there is a single idea on which it can be said the Christian Church was founded, it is this belief, inherited from Plato, in the real independence of universals. Consequently when the Church found its realism, as it was called, opposed by nominalism, the name given to the disbelief in the real independence of universals (or conversely put, the belief that universals are but voices or names), it made a vigorous but unsuccessful attempt to suppress the new heresy.

Nominalists, as an American philosopher has wisely remarked, are always politicians. The Sophists were practical men who sought by teaching the art of argumentation to advance the legal, financial, and political fortunes of those who attended to their teachings. But the mediaeval nominalists went a step further; they sought the practical establishment of a theoretical franchise: they wanted the way open to freedom for investigations of the natural world. Despite the opposition of the Church, the nominalists finally won, and the empirical research into the physical world went forward. But the victory of nominalism carried much more with it than the revival of Greek science. Concurrently with the discovery that the new freedom led to the finding of natural laws came the explorations of what nominalism implied in other fields. The unreal subjective and mental side of existence was explored, as well as the real, objective and physical; and so gradually nominalism became the world presupposition and has remained so since the seventeenth century. The explicit controversy between realism and nominalism has, of course, been for the most part forgotten; nominalism is usually not understood but all the more insidiously does it manage to spread as the unexpressed and unacknowledged premise of all our modern thinking and of much of our modern conduct. Thus the realism of Socrates, Plato, and the Church is thought to be false, and the world attempts to proceed on the basis of nominalism.

Nominalism does not admit of the real independence of universals. Thus everything of which we can have knowledge must be divided between man and the world in which he lives, between what Locke called primary qualities, which are the properties of the real objective world, and secondary qualities, which are the inventions and fictions of the subjective mind. According to this conception man must always remain a stranger in an irrational and indifferent world. But in the course of the years which have elapsed between the rise of natural science under the nominalistic incentive and modern times, man has grown weary and despairing, and has sought many avenues of escape from the nominalistic predicament. He has not liked to think of himself and his unreal mental qualities as shut out of the real physical world; and so he has decided, largely with Kant's assistance, that even if he could never know the real world, at least he could know his own world, and if he must remain confined to that world at least he could explore its confines and find perhaps in a thorough recognition of his limitations some relief from their strictures. This is the development which accounts for the sudden rise of the science of psychology, the attempt to make a science out of a study of the mind and its operation. Even reason today is understood nominalistically, and logic, the last independent criterion of existence, becomes subordinated to psychology, leaving nothing to bridge the broad cleavage between the subjective and objective worlds.

It is from the point of view of modern psychology, then, that modern judgments of history are made. Armed with this presupposition we have turned our attention to Greek culture, and what do we find there? Obviously, very little. Psychology is a field in which the Greeks do not seem to have had much interest and consequently one they spent no time developing. Moreover, their viewpoint of psychology seems to us to be wholly misconceived. It must still be admitted that the Greeks did at least lay the basis for modern physics and biology and for modern mathematics, but they seem to have failed in their task when it came to psychology. They were a people who simply did not anticipate the traditional association psychology; and since this knowledge was not given to them they naturally also lacked all our new insight into the human mind gained through behaviorism and psychoanalysis. Psychology, we suppose, has unlocked the storehouse of an infinite wisdom whose existence even was not known to the Greeks. Thus, it is thought fortunate that largely due to the rapid advances made in the science of psychology we have finally, after many centuries of struggle, left the Greeks and their rigid conceptions behind us and started on the path to new truths. Consequently it is now considered somewhat old-fashioned to be a Greek scholar, to dabble in a culture from which all of worth has been extracted and from which we have nothing more to learn. Greek culture is a dried-up well whose life-giving flow has been exhausted since the Renaissance. We can at best now but admire the superlative examples of Greek art and wonder a little at the brave race which could have flowered so beautifully and in so short a space of time. Pythagoras, Socrates, Plato, Aristotle, these are the names of precocious men who were almost but not quite modern; but the world has moved on and acquired fresh experience since they lived, and it is no longer progressive to turn to them for support. There are no more hints in the Greek writings to help us; we must turn and look forward, and in so doing leave the Greeks forever behind.

What small effort is required in order to demonstrate that this view of Greek civilization is false! Nominalism, the premise on which modern judgments are based, is a self-contradictory and untenable doctrine, since the formulation of nominalism is a universal principle which according to nominalism itself can have no real standing. What is more true is that we owe much of what we are, think and do, to the Greeks, whose influence is so widespread and profound that we are susceptible to it even when we fail to recognize the fact. This is illustrated in the two most amazing developments of modern times: physics and mathematics, which are in their foundations essentially Greek. It is Greek realism and *not* nominalism which makes modern science possible. Science is engaged in the study of the logical structure of an independent world, in the possibilities of existence, and this would be useless upon a genuine acceptance of nominalism. Modern science, in short, is allowable only on the view that an independent and real realm of ideas exists. For the laws of science are never confined to a summary of the actual occurrences they describe, but such laws approximate to the universal conditions which make possible the actual occurrences whenever and wherever they take place. It is not the relation between the diameter and circumference of any actual circle or collection of circles but the possibility of relation between the diameter and circumference of any circles ever to exist. As long as we hold on to both the philosophy of nominalism and the validity of science there must exist an unresolved contradiction, for modern science and mathematics which stand in such high esteem are dependent upon Greek and mediaeval realism which is now regarded as the ultimate error. Regardless of abstract considerations of metaphysics, however, the truth of realism is accepted by those who, having no familiarity with metaphysics, accept unquestioningly the validity of science.

But science is far from being the only field in which the Greek influence continues to be exercised. Let us take an example from politics. The central doctrine of Marx's political philosophy is the movement of the dialectic. This conception he inherits from Hegel who gave it a more idealistic meaning. So widespread is this idea today that Professor Morris Cohen tries to avoid Hegel and insists that his debt for the principle of polarity goes back to Nicolas Cardinal of Cusa; yet he still seems to the student of historical philosophy to be unfair. For the principle of polar opposites is none other than the principle of positive opposites which was already in ancient Greece enunciated by Heraclitus and refuted by Aristotle. Indeed, Heraclitus anticipated Marx in seeing that the belief in positive opposition calls for an approval of strife and a kind of development growing out of strife. The truth is that Greek philosophy at some time or other in its brief career touched on so many fundamental problems in metaphysics that it is almost impossible today to assume an attitude that was not anticipated by the Greeks.

Why then should we try to escape from Greek influences? We may not do so until we are certain that our debt to Greece has reached its highest figure. The prevalence of the nominalistic philosophy today gives evidence that we have much to learn yet from Greece. As long as nominalism remains the world presupposition, it must be insisted that the principal contribution of Greek civilization to culture has not even yet been adequately recognized. This contribution consists in the abstraction of the universal from the temporal occasions of its actualization and the recognition of its existence as prior to such occasions. In the relation between your house and my house, structures which may not look alike, we recognize a common houseness, a function which must have existed before any houses could have been built. It is indeed difficult to understand how there could be any human productivity without the employment of this principle. Even granted, however, that we do make use of the principle without recognizing the fact, this is not enough. Before any genuinely great advances in civilization can be made, the principle of realism, the belief in the prior existence of universals as possibilities, must be explicitly understood. The discovery of laws in every field is sure to be aided by the conviction that such laws exist to be discovered.

We have shown that nominalism accounts for the kind of psychology which yields our perverted view of the Greeks. The Greek philosophers, it is true, never did fully develop the study of psychology. But Greek psychology was developed far enough at least to indicate that the whole study of psychology was possible upon a realistic basis. If this assertion can be supported then there is a whole subject matter, namely, the subject matter of psychology, the favorite modern study, which can still learn from the Greeks. Let us turn back then and have a look at the kind of psychology the ancients were trying to build on the basis of realism.

First of all it must be understood that there was in Greek philosophy a sharp distinction drawn between psychology and logic, between the structure of mind and the content of mind, between the mind itself and that of which the mind is aware. For Plato and Aristotle the mind is a center not of creation but of awareness and apprehension. The Greek consciousness or *nous* functions in a logical world, a world built upon the framework of an intelligible and self-consistent system capable of being comprehended by the mind. Nature is a term standing not for an objective and solely real world of physical particulars but for the intelligible and all-inclusive order of the universe. Nature in this sense of the term is the theatre of human interests and practices, the scene of human efforts which succeed or fail to the extent to which they are or are not designed to accord with that intelligible structure. The mind, then, is not a rational affair laid in irrational surroundings which it yet struggles to understand, but part of the general intelligibility of nature, and consciousness together with all that can enter into consciousness consists of real elements in nature.

Clearly there is no need in such a world for the processes of human creativity, no need to worship the dark mysteries of intuition which create in a God-like manner a mental world of imaginings corresponding to nothing objective. This is an utterly modern, romantic, and nominalistic conception. Intelligence consists not in invention but in discovery. Degree of intelligence is measured by breadth of understanding and extent of awareness. In Greek psychology the dark clouds of romantic mystery are dispensed with and logic takes the place of creativity; minds are not expected to make something emerge out of nothing, but to acquire knowledge of and make known the intricateness and inclusiveness of the logical order of the universe. Value as well as logic enters into this Greek conception since the world, which is structurally logical, consists of value, and value reaches awareness through feeling. The feeling for values is in turn widened through the idea of understanding. We can love only what we understand; but on the other hand to understand is to love, and we must extend our sympathy by necessity to whatever we have sufficiently understood. Privation of understanding leads to privation of sympathy; in order to increase feeling it is essential to begin with an attempt to increase understanding.

The modern cosmogony has been nominalistically interpreted, and the view is authorized that man stands opposed to the irrational forces of nature, and dwells by virtue of some cosmic accident upon the inhospitable surface of a dead planet in a meaningless universe of innumerable other planets, fighting the elements for sheer existence and destined to be wiped out in the end by a sudden change in terrestrial temperature, a meeting of planets, or some other chance cause. This view is due to a most superficial study of the evidence; for the same argument can be turned around and made to demonstrate the opposite of what it seems to prove. The fact that man has come to exist at all in such a world, that there has been a favorable concomitance of entities and processes in the irrational natural world sufficient to make man possible, points not to the improbabilities of chance but to the presence of some order in the universe. The answer simply is that the universe is friendly—or man would not exist at all. Thus he is a natural part of the whole of nature and not something outside nature, contradictory and inimical to it.

Surely the understanding of psychology as it is to be found in Greek philosophy accords better with this latter and more optimistic view. Man is not a fungoid growth on a cooling and shrinking planet but an integral part of the rational plan of the universe whose ultimate purpose is withheld from us. This is not, however, to posit a pious and theological view of existence; it is not to substitute passive worship for positive human works. For although the ultimate purpose of the universe remain beyond the limits of our vision, the knowledge of its existence is sufficient to indicate a human direction toward a goal. We may learn from the Greek philosophers that what we are to do is not to despair of human productivity while aspiring toward it, nor yet to sink in the passive worship of an ultimate reality our feeling of the hopelessness of the human predicament, but rather to seek the knowledge of the logical and intelligible structure of the universe and to work with a slow but asymptotic success toward its final integration.

Modern physical and mathematical sciences have progressed to an almost incredible degree since the classic age of Greece, and still remain largely consistent with the principles laid down for them. But the case is different with modern psychology. It is a well-known fact that psychology has accomplished very little and is sadly lost in a maze of conflicting schools of thought. Not only is the behaviorist at odds with the psychoanalyst and both in opposition to the traditional association psychology, but all three are wholly inconsistent with the principles and points of view laid down by Greek psychology. Since we have followed the Greek lead in other sciences, why need it seem so backward to do so in psychology? By turning back to the Greeks psychology may be brought into line with other modern sciences and perhaps earn a share in their success. The state of psychology being what it is, there is nothing to be lost and everything to be gained by such a method of procedure.

The return to the orientation of Greek psychology should have other and perhaps more important implications than those which have to do directly with the advancement of the science of psychology itself. It seems that only by the adoption of the principles of Greek psychology would the modern world be in a position to appreciate the single most important contribution of Greek culture. This contribution, as we have already seen, consists in the recognition of the independence of universals, an independence which applies equally to the occasions or lack of occasions of their exemplification in actuality. The premises of science and mathematics lie outside those fields and in philosophy; thus it is not necessarily known to the scientists and mathematicians that the independence of universals moves forward already in their studies. But it is unlikely that this principle will ever be successful over a broader field until it is explicitly and abstractly understood, for in other fields than those of physical science the difficulties of the subject matter militate against an instinctive feeling for the right sort of procedure. The confusion in politics, in ethics, in economics, and in the social sciences generally, are instances of the bafflement experienced because of the failure to follow the hint of the Greek idea of independent universals.

Thus it may be said, in conclusion, that we shall not have exhausted Greek culture until we have extracted this last word, which is not merely something left over from innumerable gleanings but the essence of Greek wisdom itself. The theory of realism, it is true, is not unknown in modern philosophy. However, it is there regarded as one philosophical viewpoint among many which are of purely academic interest but which are lacking in practical import outside the confines of that abstruse study. This is to place philosophy among intellectual exercises, on a par with chess or contract bridge. Whosoever judges Greek realism, the real independence of universals, in this manner does not truly understand the principle. The Greek philosophers were thinkers who abstracted to a very high level, but always with a view to discovering laws which would have a very wide applicability to actual problems and to the practice of living generally. Independent real laws are conditions of what Aristotle termed possibility. This category itself should give the clue. We shall not progress very far until we comprehend the distinction between actuality and possibility, that possibility is independent of actuality but only has meaning in relation to it. Possibilities, although real and independent, do not exist in a vacuum but are possibilities of actualization, of exemplification, that is, in the world of action and reaction. The full grasping of this idea means learning the most from that Greek culture which made European civilization what it is. Therefore it is not by means of a complete break with the past that we can progress beyond our present stage. Only by returning to seek what we have overlooked in the past shall we find that the Greeks, who uncovered vast vistas of knowledge, uncovered also the vista of the possibility of knowledge itself as an independent, wholly real, and natural affair. And when we have learned this method and followed it into its various implications in the separate fields of human endeavor, we shall be face to face with genuine progress.

VII

Toynbee's Theory of History

To UNDERTAKE, in the brief compass of a chapter, the evaluation of a work as comprehensive as Professor Arnold J. Toynbee's *A Study of History*,[1] is to assume a labor for which only the most ignorant have sufficient daring. The very voluminousness of the work, the many problems of enduring perplexity which it raises in every field of theory and practice, and the immense amount of ground covered, would be enough to cause any cautious individual to withdraw. But the merit of Professor Toynbee's volumes is such that it behooves anyone who is appreciative to endeavor to call them to the attention of a larger public. Professor Toynbee has attempted to "expound and illustrate a system of ideas" (I, vii),[2] and it is just possible that there exists no single individual competent to judge both the self-consistency of the system and the relevancy of the illustrations. The difficulties of this situation clarify themselves by their very enormity: since secondary sources have furnished much of the material, it becomes advisable to call upon a host of specialists to verify the facts. In the present chapter, the relevancy of these illustrations will be, for the most part, at least, assumed, and the estimation of truth and falsity will be directed chiefly toward the "system of ideas" around which the work as a whole is constructed. As this

---
1. London, 1934-39, 6 vols.
2. All references in the body of the chapter, otherwise unspecified, will refer to volume and page of Toynbee's *A Study of History*.

chapter was being written, only six volumes of *A Study of History* had been published, volumes IV to VI having just appeared at the outbreak of the second world war. This event, together with the fact that the six volumes contain all the elements of Toynbee's system, justifies to some extent the effort to make a tentative estimate of the value of an unfinished project.

We shall begin our consideration of Toynbee's history with a brief sketch of the main features of the system, one which perforce will omit much that is vital but which will at least suggest the approach. This sketch will be followed next by a statement and examination of the postulates, method and conclusions of the system, and then by an attempt to sum up the worth of the work in detail and as a whole.

I

According to Toynbee, the intelligible fields of historical study are not states or nations but the larger units called societies or civilizations. There are six such societies in existence today: the Western, the Orthodox Christian (main body), the Islamic, the Hindu, and the Far Eastern (main body and branch in Korea and Japan). And there have been in the world some fifteen more: the Iranic, the Hellenic, the Syriac, the Indic, the Sinic, the Minoan, the Sumeric, the Hittite, the Babylonic, the Andean, the Mexic, the Yucatec, the Mayan, the Egyptiac, and the Orthodox Christian in Russia. Thus there are recognizable some twenty-one members of the species.

The genesis of civilizations is a problem closely connected with their relatedness. Of the twenty-one we have named, some are related to others, while some are unrelated. Those unrelated owe their origins to primitive societies, through "transition from a static condition to a dynamic activity" (I, 195) by a sort of mutation. Those related owe their origins to something of the same change but one which takes place in a member of their own species which is "apparented" to them, and to which they are "affiliated." It will make clear not only the genesis of civilizations but the whole span of their existence to quote the passage explaining how this transition comes about.

... when a civilization begins to lose its creative power, the people below its surface and beyond its borders, whom it is all the time irradiating with its influence and attracting into its orbit, begin to resist assimilation, with the result that the society which, in its age of growth, was a social unity with an ever expanding and always indefinite fringe, becomes divided against itself by the sharp lines of division between a dominant minority and an internal and external proletariat.[3] The minority, having lost the power to influence and attract, seeks instead to impose itself by force. The proletariat, inwardly alienated, remains in, but not of, the disintegrating society until the disintegration has gone so far that the dominant minority can no longer repress the efforts of the proletariat to secede. In the act of secession, at length accomplished, a new society is conceived. (I, 187-88.)

The genesis of civilizations of the species is stimulated in both related and unrelated societies by challenges of many natural kinds in the environment, to which a certain response has to be made. Challenges are of various sorts: they may be physical, as for example the stimulus of a hard country or new ground; or they may be social, as for example the pressure of neighboring peoples or of a penalization of some kind. The challenge must be of the right strength. Too small a challenge does not require any response; too large may not receive any. The golden mean is a challenge which can be met with effort.

The growth of civilizations consists in the transfer of their fields of action from some low level of material endeavor to the higher level of the spiritual, from an objective social field to a subjective individual field. The process is one described as "etherialization." "Civilizations grow through an *élan* that carries them from challenge through response to further challenge and from differentiation through integration to differentiation again" (III, 128). Such differentiation is individual. In increased mastery over the external environment (the "Macrocosm") and in increased self-determination over the internal environment of the individual (the "Microcosm"), growth proceeds. The

---

3. The term "proletariat," employed by Toynbee throughout his work, is not used in the Marxist sense. "It is used in the sense of the Latin word *proletarius* from which it is derived... a group in a community which has no 'stake' in that community beyond the fact of its physical existence." I, 41, n. 3.

rhythm in the individual is that of withdrawal-and-return, withdrawal from action to contemplation followed by return to action with increased powers. The growth of civilizations is finally a matter of individual response, of mimesis, in the transference of the field of action from the material (and hence social) to the spiritual (and hence personal) plane.

The breakdown of civilizations has already been described in the case of "apparented" societies. It usually occurs from within. Civilizations break down when their attempts at mutation fail. Society as a whole finds itself unable to follow the individual mutation achieved by the saint, who is a higher type of being, existing at the next stage of humanity and achieved by a leap from the level of civilization with which we are familiar. Thus collapse begins when, through an outbreak of internal discord, the creative minority forfeits its faculty of self-determination, and hence loses its creative power. The dominant minority tries in vain to make up for this loss with various archaistic substitutes: with ephemeral selves, institutions, or techniques. The internal and external proletariat respond with the withdrawal of true mimesis, bringing about the consequent loss of unity in the society. In this extremity, the *ci-devant* "creative," now the "dominant," minority appeals to sheer militaristic repression to hold its position but receives only a mechanical mimesis.

The disintegration of civilizations continues the process begun by their breakdown. As the external proletariat fail to be charmed by the dominant minority as they were formerly by the creative minority, there takes place the "estrangement of the proselyte": feeling themselves threatened by the militarism of the dominant minority, the external proletariat, in the form of barbarian warbands, instead of following as they were accustomed, takes the initiative and, breaking through the frontier, overruns the territory of the civilization that has gone into decline.

The process of disintegration has three distinct phases: a "time of troubles," a universal state, and an interregnum. The universal state is the protective institution which the declining society throws up when it finds itself threatened with imminent dissolution in the culminating paroxysm of its time of troubles. The rally of its moral forces wins a momentary reward in the shape of a reprieve, an "Indian Summer" which visits a storm-tossed world under the universal state's aegis.

The three factions into which societies disintegrate: dominant minority, internal proletariat, and external proletariat, have their own characteristic expressions. The dominant minority displays its power in the construction of universal states and schools of philosophy; the internal proletariat gives rise to "higher religions" or universal churches; and the external proletariat expresses itself in heroic, epic poetry. The higher religion is the gentle response made by the internal proletariat to the violent challenge by force by the dominant minority, a contrast which eventually wins the master over to the side of his subordinates. The epic poetry is the commemoration by the barbarian war-band of the heroic age in which he assaulted in vain the ramparts of the decaying civilization.

Such in brief is the outline of Toynbee's system. It furnishes but the most rudimentary presentation of a scheme whose complexities must overflow the confines of any short account, from which is missing the enormous mass of illustration and example, which in Toynbee's books is presented with a wild profusion, as though its source were endless. There is no way to depict this mass or its fascination. Toynbee seems at home everywhere, in tiny hamlets of anyone's native land, in the remotest corners of the earth in every age—a pan-provincial whose touch turns every episode to interest. It is impossible here to do justice to that aspect of the work. We can only treat of the main scheme, and even that not completely; and yet the essentials are here, sufficient to reveal the trend of the argument.

II

Of the postulates of Toynbee's approach to history, some are frankly avowed and openly acknowledged in the course of the development, while others are not stated and are only present by implication and as presuppositions. We shall discuss next the acknowledged postulates, together with the hidden presuppositions which such postulates perforce carry in their train.

Toynbee sets up primary categories which immediately involve him in an ontological dualism, an epistemological subjective idealism, and a theological transcendentalism. The first is precarious and tentative, the second partial and tenuous, and the third total and absolute; all three are nominalistic.

The dualism in ontology consists in a fundamental division of being, and of everything in existence, into spirit and matter. The latter terms, despite their importance and recurrence, are never defined but are employed as though they could not possibly involve any misunderstanding. This is, unfortunately, far from the case, inasmuch as the long use of both terms in different meanings by different schools of philosophy and religions has made definition a prerequisite of their employment today. Moreover, the terms are employed in a special sense. Matter, as we may gather from the overtones of the work, is equivalent to everything actual, while spirit proves to be some evanescent and exclusive quality of the individual human soul by virtue of which that soul is enabled to survive the material body in which for a time it is encased. The spirit, we discover, is assumed to be a casual and uncomfortable visitor to this earthly realm, and waiting only the day when it can leave the flesh and return to a heaven from whence it came and where alone it is at home. The earth, in short, is all material, and Heaven is all spiritual.

Since on earth it is only within human beings that spirit is to be found, we should expect the theory of knowledge to be just what in fact it is: despite an underlying conviction of the reality of social events, the focus of value, if not the determination of being, centres in the mind (and spirit) of the individual human being. Truth is a partial correspondence to actuality, since social events do take place, but since the value of being does not intimately associate with happenings, truth must consist in a correspondence with the spiritual realm, and on earth this correspondence is to be found only in the human individual. Thus the theory of knowledge upon which Toynbee relies is an inconsistent compromise between objective correspondence and subjective idealism.

The understanding of Toynbee's old fashioned metaphysics is made easier by a criticism of its now obvious inconsistencies. It rests upon that notion of a static substance having attributes which has been exploded by relativity physics. It may not be possible for scientific discoveries to tell us what kind of metaphysics to hold; it is possible for such discoveries to tell us what metaphysics *not* to hold. We may be sure that there is no such static substance as is intended by the term matter. Similarly with spirit, the term has no longer any standing, but for another reason. In this case, the term intends something so vague as to be meaningless. Its epiphenomenal nature must be apparent to everyone. For Toynbee, however, these terms are still alive, and he uses them with firm adherence to their old meanings, for a reason which will be made apparent to us as we proceed. He remarks that the statement, "The use of material means toward a spiritual end is always a dangerous game," is a truism (IV, 545), though one that is often very true. But we may well inquire what other alternative there is. Until we are disembodied spirits, we are forced to work through matter, be we churchmen or militarists, and the only difference between us on this score seems to be one of degree. Toynbee, however, is not arguing relative differences but absolute principles, and so he faces a dilemma of accepting the situation as he finds it in actuality or of holding onto his principles; reconciliation of the two would seem to be impossible.

The third primary category in which Toynbee is candidly involved is transcendentalism in theology. Value as such is, as we have seen, equivalent to human value, and such human value is essentially at home only in another world where matter is not to be found. Earthly existence is an ordeal, and if we are found worthy we are ready for the after-life. For we exist in this world only for the sake of forsaking this world in favour of another world whose superior reality is finally made clear when it is bathed in theological perspective. The view here is the basic

Christian eschatology, shared alike by Catholic and Protestant. It is irrefutable since it involves, as does the acceptance of an ontology, an act of faith. Its refutation here must rest only upon the negative results which its application to history brings about. Suffice to say that no sadder theology could have been chosen by a historian, whose ostensible chief concern is with the sequence of actual events and their pattern.

Two secondary categories accompany the ones we have listed. These are super-naturalism in morals and determinism in history.

The morality which the Christian theology entails is too well known to require extensive explanation. The good life, according to it, is not in this world but the next. The good life in this world means no more than preparation for the next. All temporal satisfactions are evil in themselves and therefore must be shunned. Matter is evil; spirit is good; therefore we are enjoined to seek otherworldliness and to live this life only as a preparation during which we are forced to put up with the indignities of matter. Those who have tried to adhere to orthodoxy of this sort will attest to the impracticality of trying to live a proximate life as though there were no proximate and intermediate goals.

One of the main aims of Toynbee's volumes is to abstract from history the unchanging pattern discernible in the course of civilizations. The system which results from his inspection of the twenty-one societies of the species is one which admits of no exceptions. The time-span occupied by the genesis, growth, breakdown, and disintegration of civilizations may be longer in some cases, shorter in others, but the form remains essentially the same, and the succession is absolutely inevitable, as are the fundamental causes for the changes, causes conceived to be essentially the same. The result is a strict determinism of the temporal order, at least so far as the succession of social events is concerned. Societies are born, they come to fruition, and then die, with an unfailing regularity. We may well wonder whether such determinism is justified by the facts. We may ask whether it does not rest upon a confusion of history with logic, of time with cause. The number of societies which we have at hand for examination is, as Toynbee himself admits, exceedingly small, barely twenty-one, in fact.[4] We can say that most of those which have come into existence have sooner or later perished; we cannot even yet say that all of them do, since five are still alive. But even if we could claim that all past societies have perished, it would not prove that all future ones must. The sheer repetitiveness of the past lays no necessity upon the future. Events continue to happen with some regularity because there is a cause at work, and not merely because they have done so for so long.

Toynbee's association with philosophy is on internal evidence a brief and unpleasant one. He has not anything like the familiarity with philosophical works that he has with history and historiography. Nor does he assign philosophy a very high place among the elements of his system. Philosophy, we learn, is a product not of the people but of their masters who are in the minority, and not of the creative minority, at that, but only of the minority in the decline when it becomes dominant. But even so he does not consort with the philosophies that we should expect him to, judging by what we know of his philosophical postulates. The philosophers most often quoted are Smuts and Bergson: emergent evolutionists who subscribe to the superior reality of actuality and change. What interest can Toynbee find in the works of men who believe that novelty is the most important element in the universe? For one as opposed to evolutionism as Toynbee, who attempts to retrieve from world-history its changeless pattern of characters and events, to seek out Bergson, the most uncompromising of evolutionists, is certainly inconsistent. Bergson's whole philosophy is one of change; Toynbee's, one concerned with what can be saved from change—with the changeless. At first sight contradictory, the relation is one in which we may see a clear connection when we understand that Toynbee shares with Bergson a distaste (unconscious in the latter)

---

4. In response to a request made by J. W. Friend and the author of the present work, for clarification on certain points raised in *A Study of History*, Professor Toynbee admits, "Of course I myself am on weak ground here, as I am venturing to generalize on the strength of only about twenty instances of civilizations."—Letter of January 16, 1940.

for the proximate truths, the partial values—the general worth, of actuality. Perhaps the position is excusable when it is realized that these men, like ourselves, are born into an age when the survival of anything good, beautiful, holy, and true seems dubious indeed: Toynbee tells us that all historians are born at the end of an age; yet the logical invalidity of the contention is independent of the extenuating circumstances of social history. Suffice to say that Toynbee is not in agreement with their ontological principles based upon the primary reality of change, even though he may find some use for them in his own theology.

In conclusion, it must be admitted that the postulates and presuppositions upon which Toynbee's argument chiefly rests are not of great merit and validity. Why, then, is his work of such importance? Obviously, valid deductions may be drawn from false postulates, since truth can follow from falsity. But such a sequence is usually a result of accident and not of planned logic. Usually, whenever a work has merit despite its avowed postulates, we may assume that its true presuppositions are not the postulates supposed. Toynbee's argument as a whole does not hold up, but what is valid about it must rest upon hidden true presuppositions. Just what these latter presuppositions are will be revealed later.[5] Suffice to say for the moment that the validity is there in the system, despite the invalidity of the avowed postulates.

III

Before we proceed to a consideration of the specific points raised by the details of Toynbee's theory of history it will be necessary to discuss the method he employs in setting it forth.

The range of historical knowledge covered by Toynbee's work is encyclopaedic. Few men ever before have attempted to include within the sweep of their theories the same amount of factual material obtained from so many societies. The effort involves a weakness, which we may as well admit at the outset of our examination: Toynbee has had to rely for much if not all

---

5. In Sections X and XI.

of his factual material upon secondary sources. The specialist who has made his life work the intensive study of one particular epoch or of one particular people will tear his hair over the references to his specialty; and probably in most cases not without some justice. There is no reason to believe that all the secondary sources employed by Toynbee are absolutely accurate; most men have made mistakes, to say nothing of the ordinary differences of opinion among experts with regard to controversial and moot questions of historical veridity. There can be no doubt about the existence of errors arising within that immense superstructure which Toynbee has erected on what are in many cases hazy conjectures as to fact.

The accusation was inevitable because it is not entirely without foundation. The defense must rest entirely upon the necessity for such a method, given the same ambition. The large picture of world-history that Toynbee has drawn for us could only be attempted by means of such a method, since it would be impossible for one man to verify his facts in so many empirical fields and also to construct a theory. To this defense, that only on such a plan can so wide an ambition be even partially fulfilled, the specialist in history will probably reply, but why do it? Why throw the net wider than the separate strands will bear? What is to be gained by constructing a theory of such magnitude that it cannot be verified, so large and yet so self-consistent that it must collapse if the facts are found not to bear it out as they were supposed to do?

The reply to this final criticism is that Toynbee's system is not entirely overthrown even if certain of the facts upon which he relies were to be proved wrong; more than that, it would not be overthrown even if certain of the theories advanced were to be proved equally insupportable. The wide suggestiveness of broad speculation is an essential part of historical research, and its effect must be felt by all historians who come into contact with it despite its failure to be an all-inclusive theory. There are in all sciences two movements: the movement toward greater differentiation, by specialists, and the movement toward greater unification, likewise by specialists. We have many of the former, yet few of the latter. It is men like Toynbee who must be encouraged, if the field of history is to be properly circumscribed.

It is possible, however, that it is not the factual material which is the most at fault. Toynbee has described a pattern of the life of society which is applicable, presumably, to all twenty-one of the species. But where did he obtain it? From hints taken from an examination of these societies? There is an indication here and there that this was not the case; that the method was rather to abstract the entire pattern from a single family of societies. This family was the Hellenic-Roman-Christian, or as Toynbee calls it, simply the Hellenic. Genesis and growth seem to derive from the Greeks, universal states from the Roman Empire, universal churches from the Christian church, philosophers as members of the dominant minority from Plato and Aristotle, the inevitable failure of proletarian political leaders from Cleomenes and the Gracchi, and external proletariat or barbarian war-bands from the Germanic tribes. The list of analogies is almost endless. The whole thesis is lifted from the curve of this family of societies, and it is possible that other societies, in whom these same elements are sought and not infrequently found, are carved up to make them fit wherever they prove refractory. Throughout the volumes we run across one phrase, "the exception that proves the rule," used as an argument that would be enough to make a good logician wring his hands, since the exception does nothing but disprove the rule. There is nothing exactly wrong with this method in general except that it has a tendency to be coercive, and to endeavor to read into history what we have come to suppose ought to be there. This may do as a conjectural method of filling in blanks in our knowledge; but where the knowledge exists and does not work as we had hoped, there should be no effort to force it into a mould into which it does not easily fit.

One of the difficulties which perhaps contributes most to this condition is the low abstractive level at which the system exists. Toynbee has abstracted from history certain leading characters and patterns of action. But the abstraction as a whole is not one of very high degree. Toynbee, we feel, has strained through a mass of elaborate illustration and extended imagery in search of the structure of the organization of culture and its purposes. The result is not the highly abstractive logical and quantitative structure which it ought to be, but something still qualitative and indeed almost literary in its approach. From an analytical point of view, the failure to reach high levels of abstraction vitiates much of the value that a work of this sort could and ought to have. The scientific method is one of abstracting from a qualitative subject-matter the quantitative functions which are relatively quality-free. This can only be done by seeking, at a high abstractive level—a level arrived at only by abstracting from abstractions—the invariant functions of actual situations. The constants of Toynbee's scheme are highly qualitative; they lack the abstractiveness of quantitatively described functions.

Yet it is a lack which is not without its compensations. The approach, as can be readily admitted, is a most charming one. The style is full of tricks, but they are tricks which are effective. We grow through habit to like the Homeric-like adjectival repetition, the barbarian war-bands who always come from "behind the beyond" and who break through the "marches" of the *ci-devant* civilization. We feel at home in "successor-states" but fear their "time of troubles" as though it were our own. The far-flung sentences carry us along almost without effort of our own, and we grow so accustomed to the unassuming plainness of the names of leading characters ("external barbarian," "creative minority," and so on) that we are quite unprepared for the novelty of phraseology of subordinate conceptions which, as a consequence, fill us with delight. We find high literary value in "the Margrave turned Moss-trooper," the "Estrangement of the Proselyte," "The Philosopher Masked by a King." Toynbee has a neat way of referring to all periods as though they were equally past, a technique which is especially applicable to the present. "In the year 1937 it was possible to note, etc.," or again, an event is mentioned which happened in the "first quarter of the twentieth century of the Christian Era." Smuts is referred to as the famous "South-African philosopher-statesman." The work evidently has been written by one who expects his touch to endure, his work to live and to be read by people in another society somewhere else in another epoch. Such complete indifference to the literary conventions, in the hands of a master, leads to the effect of sweep and inclusiveness. Toynbee will use all the personal pronouns in one passage, almost in one paragraph; and he changes from "the present writer" to "he," "I," and "we" in a breathtaking way (V, 509). Suspicion of strict accuracy is aroused, however, by obvious literary tricks, which could not have been coincidental in every case with strict exposition. Toynbee gives in easily to literary advantages; he has a fondness for alliteration, which he manages to make very effective. Alliteration abounds in subtitles: "Pammaxia and Proletarianization," "Fossils in Fastnesses," "The Problem of *Peripéteia*," "Schism in the soul," etc. The whole Study is a strange mixture of logical analysis conducted in dispassionate terms and historical melodrama with a most perfervid cast of characters.

We have examined the postulates and presuppositions of Toynbee's system, and the method he has employed to present it. Several broad observations of the system as a whole are still necessary as a preliminary to the detailed examination of his categories.

The absence of exact logical definition is an obstacle to any effort at thorough understanding. What is culture? We are never told by Toynbee; although he insists that "the cultural element in a civilization is its soul and life-blood and marrow and essence and epitome" (V, 200). Despite this extravagant insistence upon its importance, culture, like the "spiritual" and so many other key terms in the work, is never defined. It appears, however, that culture is something which has its origins in the origins of society, and grows with it, breaks down and disintegrates in much the same way. Thus it would appear to be synonymous with societies and their life. We are given quite another picture of culture when we see that the whole purpose of societies is to give birth, in their death-pangs, to "higher religions." For then culture appears to be something which is capable of development only in the soul of the individual. On this showing, culture would appear to be individualistic in the last analysis, and not social at all. This contradiction in the understanding of culture, which sometimes appears to be the essence of society and sometimes appears to be the essence only of the individual, is never resolved.

For one who is chiefly preoccupied with religion and the way of "gentleness" as final human aims and goods, Toynbee devotes a large amount of space to the account of wars of conquest and defense, and generally to the military aspects of civilization. Where are the arts (and sciences) of peace? Where are the moral laws and all that contribute to the positive side of culture? They are hardly to be found in Toynbee's analysis. The reason is that Toynbee's system is rigged in favour of religion, moreover in favour of a certain kind of religion: Protestant Christianity. In order to lead up to it, he has had to take his lessons from a certain kind of society: the Hellenic-Roman. Since the Hellenic-Roman society existed only in order to give rise to its "universal religion," Christianity, it could have no other purpose. Hence religions, and even churches, are always good, while universal states are always bad (except in so far as they give rise to churches). Cultures fail when they lose battles and when they become universal states. But religions rise only within universal states; and religions, with their saints, are the apex of human achievement. Here is a further latent aspect of the contradiction: the failure of human culture is the salvation of mankind.

It is possible that the model for the examination of the life pattern of cultures may have been constructed on a false analogy. The Roman Empire was something more than merely a Hellenic universal state, and also something less. The Hellenic universal state was the Hellenistic society, centered in Alexandria. From Greek to modern times there have been four distinct societies, not two. These four may be apparented-and-affiliated, but they are four nevertheless. These are: the Hellenic, the Roman, the Christian (medieval), and the Western (modern).[6] The Christian society was affiliated to three older societies: the Hellenic, the Syriac and the Roman. The modern Western society is affiliated to the Roman, Hellenic, and Christian, but differs from the Christian sharply, in exchanging the Christian for the scientific cosmology to say nothing of the marked change in the practical way of life. This is not altogether Toynbee's plan, although it is partly suggested when he says that a universal church can make a contact between two societies in time.

The truth is that the iron rigidity of Toynbee's system, like the medieval torture device of the iron woman, closes in upon him more and more as his exposition develops, until he is completely hampered in his movements. Finally, although he began with a wealth of illustration, he can only contemplate the bare bones of the system itself. He is faced with the alternative of being consistent with his explicit system or with his implicit beliefs; and in the latter case he must break through the system himself, in order to square with his assumptions the statements he feels compelled to make.

IV

Let us examine in some detail the four successive movements of civilization as these are set forth and described by Toynbee. In this and the following three sections of this chapter we shall discuss in turn: genesis, growth, breakdown, and disintegration. We shall begin with an examination of genesis.

The origins of civilization, Toynbee tells us, consist either in the mutations of primitive societies into unrelated civilizations or in "the emergence of 'related' civilizations through secessions of proletariats from preexistent civilizations" (I, 189). "We have now ascertained the nature of the geneses of civilizations," Toynbee says later. "They are particular beats of a general rhythmical pulsation which runs all through the universe" (I, 205). And he

---

6. "I do not myself feel that there was any break, sufficient to be reckoned as a break between two different civilizations, at the transition between the medieval and the modern chapter of our western history," Toynbee insists in his letter of January 16th, 1940.

adds that "evidently this is as far as we can go in understanding how the genesis of civilizations occur."

Toynbee's analysis of the genesis of civilizations has thrown some light on the problem. But having said this much we are almost at once constrained to criticism. What he has done is to describe the genesis of civilizations after the fact and from a common sense and concrete point of view. "Mutation" is a term borrowed from biology, where it is used to describe a process concerning which not so very much is known. In the case of civilizations deriving from primitive societies, it merely circumscribes the blank spot which exists in our knowledge of the cultural distance between primitive societies and civilizations. That there was no intermediate stage is of course possible, but seems to be a contention which is undemonstrable. Primitive societies may have evolved into the species called civilizations by some very gradual process which is not susceptible of definition at any stage.

The second alternative, that civilizations emerge from the disgruntled internal proletariat who decide to secede, is one which can be easily exemplified; for instance, the Christian from the Roman. But to erect the abstraction from this example into a necessity and to read back into other affiliated civilizations a similar genesis calls for some strong assumptions in favour of fact. This explanation has the advantage, at least, of showing how the emergence comes about, but its generality is something which does not appear demonstrable given the lamentable paucity of historical knowledge. It may not be possible just at present to offer any satisfactory account of the genesis of civilization, since our familiarity with history does not extend into the remote reaches with the necessary detail.

The chief explanation offered of the genesis of civilizations is the movement described as "challenge-and-response," the "particular beats of a general rhythmical pulsation." Challenge-and-response is by no means an isolated system; it cannot be both vague and exact. We have to make an arbitrary decision as to what is challenge and what response.[7] Response to something may be challenge to something else. There is also a large accidental character to it. The explanation of anything must be in terms of necessary, causative factors; necessity rather than accident must be shown, since accident is that from which true cause attempts to abstract. But Toynbee tries to raise accident into a causative factor, an attempt foredoomed to sterility of further explanation. The discovery of genesis as a product of challenge-and-response may bear out one great lesson, however. This is that the genesis of societies may be inexplicable on the basis of the isolation of societies alone. We may be unable to explain the genesis of societies on the basis merely of what takes place within the societies themselves. It may be necessary to go outside the societies to examine their environment and particular elements in that environment: physical as well as social. Human social history may prove impossible without the inclusion of its background and setting of natural or world-history. In effect this lesson, namely that human society is only for certain narrow purposes a valid isolate, is one which Toynbee discovers and then almost as suddenly drops. No hint of it appears in the later movements of civilization: growth, breakdown, and disintegration. In fact, the analysis turns the other way, toward an attempt to explain every development from the inside.

V

The growth of civilizations is a movement not unlike the movement of genesis: it depends chiefly upon rhythm, and in it the attempt to bring in the environment in which societies are bathed is abandoned altogether. A completely internal explanation is attempted, and growth is explained entirely on an individual basis. Indeed it is on the spiritual plane that growth proceeds. The con-

---

7. "I do not think it possible to predict what the response to a given challenge will be. At the two extremities of the scale, if the challenge is extremely weak or extremely formidable, you can make a guess as to the probable character of the response, but even at the extremes there is no certainty, because the response is made by a spiritual personality, and 'spiritual forces' are not, I believe, subject to scientific measurement."—Letter of January 16th, 1940.

ception of "etherialization," however, is inconsistent with the movement of genesis. Why would a civilization whose genesis was social be enabled to grow only by a movement which is personal? That the elements of social growth may have their correspondent effect upon and interrelation with the individual is to be expected; but that they should be exhausted by that aspect of society is not logical. Does etherialization have no social and objective counterpart? Is there nothing in the objective relations between individuals, and between social groups, which corresponds to what is happening within the individual? There is a strong temptation to suspect that there must be. It is curious indeed that etherialization goes into the individual and not upward on a social basis at all. Toynbee declares himself a subjectivist in insisting that higher levels of cultural value must be exclusively confined to the individual's soul, and that these higher levels can have no existence in the objective social and natural world.[8]

As the creative minority work toward etherialization, the charm of their creativeness captivates the masses who are thus obliged to follow—voluntarily. The obligation to explain all actual events by material entities or spiritual forces leaves out a third alternative explanation. Toynbee's division is nominalistic. The consideration that the masses may be following not persons at all but rather what those persons represent: certain truths and values, is left out. Could it not be that while the minority are engaged in translating certain valid truths into actual events the proletariat are more than glad to give their allegiance, but that when more "practical" ideas are selected by the minority, ideas which still parade as "truths" but which only serve narrow purposes, the allegiance of the proletariat, which sees through the change, is lost? This explanation would posit some external criterion of truth and falsity to which the creative minority would

---

8. Cf., "I do think that higher values are achievements of individual souls, and that they cannot be created by anything else. At the same time, the spiritual achievements of souls will always be reflected in social life, if I am right in regarding society as the field of intersection of the activities of different individuals."—Letter of January 16th, 1940.

itself have to be faithful in order to keep the masses with it; and would no longer allow the whole hypothesis of leadership to hang upon a romantic and subjective and mysterious power of "creativity" to inhere in the minds of a few persons. Thus growth might be represented as the discovery by the few and the voluntary acceptance by the many of more and more important truths and values, a minority held, therefore, strictly accountable for its faithfulness and honesty in pursuing the greater truth and the higher value irrespective of any other consideration.

The movement described as "withdrawal-and-return" has an element of truth, yet is arbitrary and serves chiefly to confuse the issue further. Withdrawal-and-return is described as a wholly individual movement. It is "a disengagement and temporary withdrawal of the creative personality from his social milieu, and his subsequent return to the same milieu transfigured: in a new capacity and with new powers" (III, 248). First of all, the movement so described is to a large extent conventional. Is withdrawal from worldly affairs to a state of contemplation which constitutes a preparation for return with "new powers" to interference in those affairs a necessary pattern for the creative leader? It would hardly appear so. Napoleon and Abraham Lincoln are examples of men whose leadership, so far as it lay within their decision to control their own destiny, was unremitting, and there are many others who could be named. It may not always be necessary to withdraw; and, further, withdrawal may be fatal if there is no return. How many potentially creative leaders may there have been who retired to contemplation, but because of some unforeseen factor, external or internal, failed to take up again an active life? On the other hand, for the saint, perhaps, the participation in the affairs of this world may constitute a withdrawal, while return may be understood in terms of preoccupation with spiritual matters.

The contention seems to be that the period of growth in civilizations, like that of genesis, is unfruitful, that in short nothing good comes from civilizations while they are in their formative stage or their prime. The argument, as we noted at the beginning of this chapter, is that nothing good comes from growth, only universal churches from periods of decline! Culture, through the failure of other contenders to put in their claims in the course of the argument, goes by default to religion, and culture becomes synonymous with religion. Growth, then, is only an intermediate stage, necessary to produce the civilization which is capable of going into disintegration. The fruitfulness of the period of growth in every civilization refutes this portion of Toynbee's theory.

VI

The breakdown of civilization is given a psychic and individual cause. The failure of creativity on the part of the creative minority is never explained, it is only posited. What occasions the loss of creativity? How is it lost? No account of this process is given. But it is this loss which causes the internal and external proletariat to withdraw their mimesis, the creative, now dominant, minority to attempt to stay in power by force, and a mechanical response to be made by the proletariat. Thus considering that the external proletariat, although outside the borders of a civilization, is part of its radiated effects, it is asserted that civilizations collapse from within and never from without—always from internal causes.

Such a contention is untenable on the basis of other evidence which Toynbee has to offer in other connections. The barbarians who are driven to seek their economic salvation in the land owned by the civilization across the *limes,* by the "bouts of aridity" which occur in the no man's land "behind the beyond" initiate its breakdown without ever having been within the radius of its charm. This may be said to be a breakdown begun from without. And, again, breakdown may come from without by the incursion of an alien civilization. Toynbee gives a good example of this in the invasion of the empire of the Incas by the Western Spanish explorers, the breakdown of the Andean civilization by members of the Western.

To put the failure of a civilization to continue at its originally healthy rate and in its normal condition to the failure of the creative powers of the leaders, without explaining what causes those powers to fail, is simply to remove breakdown to a place of safety inside the psychological workings of a minority where it will not have to be explained any further. Some further explanation is offered of the process, however, if not of its original cause. We are told that breakdown consists in "resting on one's oars," or in the resort to militarism, the passive and the active response to the internal seaming of social unity. Although still not causative, these are interesting descriptions of the operation of breakdown at its start. But somehow and somewhere, subjective responses must be the result of external and objective challenges; how these challenges themselves originate is never shown. It is like attempting to make an abstract study of smoke without planning even a preliminary investigation of fire. Its future value, as the basis for constructing canons for the prediction and control of societies must therefore be minimal.

The failure of the masses to follow the saints into sainthood may be the failure of one stage of biological mutation as Toynbee asserts. But what evidence have we that the saint represents a biological mutation? The suggestion is not sufficiently supported by argument, although it is an interesting one. We cannot help but wonder, if Toynbee is correct, what a society of saints would be. In actual life we rarely gain something without losing something else. As animals we have lost our physical strength by gaining an intellectual cunning, for instance. The saint, a rare enough creature in these times, seems dependent upon those of us who have not accomplished the mutation. It may be that the existence of a higher type of individual, a Bach, a Velasquez, or even a St. Francis, is developed in the interior of a country only by virtue of the maintenance of a strong army at the border.

Toynbee paints, however, a wonderful picture of the first difficulties consequent upon the breakdown of societies: the "intractability of institutions" no longer fit for the society for which they were made; the efforts to return to a former condition when social relations were better; and finally the tragic disaster of appeal to force in the militarism of those who attempt to maintain their position of power. Although we may suspect that antagonisms always exist between social classes, that former conditions may to some extent be restored without justifying the accusation of archaism, and that militarism is a characteristic also of periods of growth—that, in short, the social maladies and attempted remedies which Toynbee denotes so acutely are not peculiar to periods of breakdown—yet the picture which he draws is instructive and suggestive in the extreme.

VII

If we are compelled to give a disproportionate amount of space to the disintegrations of civilizations, it is because the emphasis placed upon this phase by Toynbee justifies it. When we examine the products of the disintegration process we cannot help but feel that for him it is this stage of civilization which alone is worthy and which justifies all the others. All three factions of the rapidly disorganizing social body take this occasion to make their creative acts: dominant minorities develop universal states and philosophies; internal proletariats give rise to universal churches; and external proletariats invent heroic epics. And all this in a stage of disintegration when creativity has supposedly been lost! How can the dominant minorities give rise to universal states and philosophies in a period when they have just exchanged creativity for dominance? There is bound to be an emphasis on disintegration since it is in this extreme period of civilization's decline that all the good things for which civilization deserves its name take their start.

In the movement of disintegration, the fallacy or historicism, to which Toynbee is constantly subject, comes to the fore. He is forever assuming that things which have happened together in history must belong together logically, an assumption which is confuted by the nature of things themselves. For instance, tobacco, which was obtained from the cultivation of the American aborigines, is held by Toynbee to be *in se* a primitive thing. Similarly, he assumes that since no universal language was ever constructed artificially, none can be (V, 493). But the failure of Esperanto or some equivalent to win over masses to its use may denote a cultural lag, and nothing more. The past lays no injunction upon the future except in the way of demonstrating what cannot be done; and even such demonstration requires logical proof. There is no evidence to show that because an artificial language has never passed into general use it cannot do so in the future. The same historical argument is at work in the analysis of disintegration into three and one half beats. There is assumed to be in a failing society enough creative energy to return to the same challenge, which it fails to meet and which thus is presented to it again, three and one half times only, after which the society is destroyed altogether by the challenge. The point here is that even if this could be assumed to be true (and it is far from demonstrated) it would certainly lay no injunction upon the future. Even if we could assume the truth of Toynbee's contention, namely that every civilization of the past has failed exactly three and one half times to meet its challenge before disappearing as a civilization, this would not mean that currently existing civilizations or others in the future must follow this pattern. An historical pattern has been shown, but not a logical cause; and it is causes that compel the following of patterns, not the patterns themselves.

Let us take up one at a time the three creative results of the process of disintegration: universal churches, universal states and philosophies, and epics.

The products of the internal proletariat are "higher religions" and "universal churches." In discussing "universal churches" and "higher religions," Toynbee fails to show what these have in common and where they differ. On Toynbee's grounds, salvation seems to be a personal affair, and yet the institution of the "universal" church would seem to argue against any such contention. The failure of religious institutions to measure up to the requirements of the religion in whose name they exist is notorious; yet Toynbee constantly speaks as though universal churches were integrally religious affairs, without flaw. The flaws are evident, however, on the basis of Toynbee's own argument. Religions, he says, owe their start to some "alien inspiration." The internal proletariat is stimulated by some source outside the borders, from the external proletariat perhaps, to initiate a universal church (V, 338 *et seq*). But the fact that the higher religions depend for their success under the sponsorship of the internal proletariat upon alien rather than indigenous inspiration points to some weakness in the institution of universal churches. It is something of an admission of the fact that religion dodges the practical problem of building a good life in this world to see it as an escape, as the creative effort of an internal proletariat in a disintegrating civilization, stimulated by an alien source.

The assumption that religion is a product of civilization in its disintegration stage involves certain other assumptions to which Toynbee accedes willingly. Life in this world, as attested by the decline of civilizations, is a failure, and therefore religions arise to lead us into the next. This account is marked by the preference for theological transcendence over immanence. Of course, Toynbee's argument could be turned around on him and it could be maintained that since religion is a product of society's decline, it is a decadent affair, and to be valued in the same way as the arts and sciences which are products of the growth of civilization. It should be remembered that the doctrine of immanence is also a perfectly good theological tenet. Toynbee prefers the path laid down for the Colossians by Paul: from Man through God to Man (VI, 10), but it must be remembered that the road from Man through Men to God is also a religious path. The doctrine of immanence is also theocentric, and it is a doctrine altogether neglected by Toynbee.

Toynbee's argument is that no organization based upon force can continue forever.[9] If Toynbee means by force violent physical

---

9. This is the Christian version of the "liberal ideology, that suppression is always ineffective and that in the end it defeats itself. This, however, is not always true. Of course, all human arrangements succumb to the attrition of time. But taken over a limited period, which is generally as far as human prevision can go, suppression has often achieved its goal. Paganism was suppressed in Christian lands and so were various forms of heresy. Spain got rid of Protestants as well as of Jews and Moors, and France achieved unity by suppressing the Huguenots. The ruthless eradication of the Paris Communards by the Versailles troops of Thiers, of the Socialists in Finland by the counter-revolutionaries, and of all liberal and dissident parties by the Bolshevik, Fascist, and Nazi governments, are a few of the examples that can be cited of the successful achievement of unity by deliberate

force, of course he is correct in his assertion. Violence is too intense a state to maintain for long at a time. But it should be remembered that a certain amount of force is involved in the actual existence and pursuance of purpose of all organizations. All of them are doomed eventually, since nothing actual persists forever. But the problem of force is a relative question, a *quid pro quo*. Is the end large enough to justify the means employed in obtaining it? No actual organization is permanent. Political organizations, such as civilizations, being to some extent of this nature, are doomed. But what about the militarism of the religious orders? What about St. Dominic and the Albigensian wars, for instance? Sometimes, more often than we care to remember, religions choose the way of violence rather than the way of gentleness. But even the way of gentleness has its aspect of force. The exemplitude of the saint is expected to be, and is, a compulsion of some sort and therefore a force. Moreover, "universal" churches, like all other organizations, seem to perish in time. Toynbee has placed upon himself the necessity of showing that actual organizations, churches or any other, not created by extreme force or coercion, do not come to an end, also. In view of the sad fact that all actual organizations come to an end sooner or later, it is hard to discover what has been proved.

The truth is that Toynbee's entire argument, in all six of the volumes which have been published thus far, is bent in the direction of formal religion. Civilizations are born and grow up only in order to break down and decline, and they break down and decline only in order to give rise to universal churches! To this end, although militarism is constantly deplored as the "way of violence," it is perfectly all right for the "Warden of the Marches" to fight the barbarians at the frontiers (IV, 501), although civil war is one of the worst evils. Civilization, it turns out, is only

---

and systematic suppression."—Morris R. Cohen, "Minimizing Social Conflicts" in *The Annals* of The American Academy of Political and Social Science, of May, 1939.

Whether such suppression redounds to the benefit of those who exercised it, or not, is another question. Possibly everyone involved suffers, those who exercise the suppression as well as those who are its victims. But Cohen is here going no further than to refute those liberals who assert that suppression never is effective.

made possible by militarism, which is an essentially evil institution. Yet when societies fight to preserve or to expand they are bad, and when they fail to do so they are decadent! On the basis of this contradiction it would appear that there is really nothing that a civilization can do that will please Toynbee except to collapse and then, after having given birth to a universal church, to get out of the way! In the light of this underlying thesis, it is amazing how much of Toynbee's volumes is devoted to an analysis of the military aspects of cultural developments, in terms of which the life of civilization takes place. The error is to assume that "gentleness" and "violence" are absolutes, and they can both be obtained in the pure state. Toynbee is an absolutist who cannot understand how good can sometimes issue from evil, how gentleness and violence are limits, evident in greater or lesser degree in every actual event. An event is never actual without some gentleness, nor possible without some violence. All universal churches owe their existence to the employment of compulsion, just as all temporal powers have made their successes only by the final employment of gentle persuasion and the abrogation of force.

The antithesis between absolute gentleness and absolute violence is carried further in the four ways of escaping from the defects of the present: Archaism, Futurism, Detachment and Transfiguration. These are divided into a "violent pair" and a "gentle pair" respectively (V, 383). The violent pair are both dismissed as false ways of escape. They are "archaism" and "futurism." Archaism is an attempt to return to some Golden Age of the past; futurism an attempt to establish a better order in the future. These, Toynbee insists, are on the same plane: both seek an escape to some other period of time in This World; both are involved with the way of violence. Are they on the same plane, however? Social situations which have occurred in the past are less in number than those which may happen in the future; therefore having to choose from the past is a greater limitation than being allowed to choose from the future. The temporal order runs from the past through the present toward the future. Any attempt to return to the past must be an attempt to return to some past *actual* situation; whereas a plan for the future is a plan for a *possible* situation. The future contains all possibilities; the past, only some. Thus archaism is anti-rational, while utopianism is not.

Any attempt to alter social conditions as they exist in the present perforce involves violence, or so Toynbee maintains. This is hard to see. The issue depends upon the rate of change which has been adopted. Swift change by force is of course violent; but many changes have occurred in history which were of a slow tempo, depended upon persuasion rather than physical force, and involving no more than that minimum of violence which, as we have seen, is a necessary part of everything actual, churches and saints not excluded. Both archaist and futurist are defeatists, we are told. It is easier to understand defeatism in the archaistic way of escape from the present. But is futurism also defeatist? (V, 385). Why? Why is the futurist "bound to tumble over into reaction" (V, 384)? The point of view is asserted but by no means demonstrated. Toynbee agrees with St. Augustine in condemning those who regard the present as an opportunity, and who work for a better social world in the future without regard for their own personal welfare either in this world or in the next, and joins him in denouncing them out of hand as being not unlike the Roman heroes who "hoped to live, even after death, a life of sorts in the mouth of an applauding Posterity." Toynbee approves St. Augustine's scorn (VI, 369), but are we not out of sympathy here, and in sympathy with the hero who works in any field, the field of science or politics, for example, not so much to earn a life in the mouth of an applauding posterity as to earn a life in the pattern-of-life of posterity? And can we regard such a man, one who prefers gentleness to violence so far as the choice does not interfere with the improvement of human living, one who labors all his life with no interest in the outcome of his own reputation in any form, and who seeks only to discover a little more of the truth than is known in order to turn it over *gratis* to society, as a futurist, without at the same time applauding him out of our own mouth as one who has chosen a rational path, the path not of escape from the present but toward the proper use of the present?

In contrast with the "violent pair" of archaism and futurism, there is the "gentle pair" of detachment and transfiguration. Of these, detachment is passive and transfiguration is active (V, 383). Detachment is the way of the oriental religions: detachment from the affairs of this world without energetically seeking to participate in those of the next. "It is a way that leads out of This World; its goal is an asylum; and the fact that asylum excludes This World is the feature that makes it attractive" (V, 394). The impulse that carries along the man who seeks the way of detachment is "a pull of aversion and not a pull of desire."

Transfiguration, Toynbee's choice among the four, is another name for spiritualization, the way of escape from the present which consists altogether in individual preparation for the next world. Its goal is the Kingdom of God (VI, 171), and it consists altogether in a renunciation of this world in favour of an active preparation for a life after death. The ground has already been prepared for the choice of transfiguration by the premise—taken for granted and never argued—that this world is a place to avoid in some fashion or other, and the acceptance of this premise is insured by cleverly contriving to have the choice occur at the birth of religion, i.e., during a time of disintegration of civilization, when there seems to be no actual life worth having in this world. The ground has further been prepared by the prior preference shown for transcendence over immanence.[10] Is it possible that we have been put into this world with the sole purpose of seeing our handiwork, which is civilization, crumble away, in order to teach us the lesson that this world itself is not worthy of our attention, which should be directed toward the world to

---

10. Paradoxically, Toynbee makes a "pragmatic" defense of otherworldliness. "Personally I believe that the pursuit of otherworldliness is like Solomon's choice. If you make otherworldliness your goal the most fruitful forms of success in this world will probably follow, just because you are not aiming at them. Perhaps the surest way to miss the attainment of worldly goals is to aim at them directly and for their own sakes."—Letter of January 16th, 1940.

which we go after our death and from which presumably we must have come before our birth? Is the chief lesson of life to consist in the moral that life is unworthy? We were dead so long before we were born, and from every indication, we shall be dead so long after our death, it seems hardly logical to assume that the brief period during which we are allowed to play in the sun is senseless and stupid and of no account—except to teach us the moral lesson that it is of no account. This is a lesson which man is no longer prepared to accept as he marches, in the words of J. G. Frazer, from magic through religion to science. There are, no doubt, elements in religion which science will overlook, and which will necessitate the reassertion of some kind of religion, a religion of immanence, most likely. But that does not mean that we shall be compelled to return to the old-fashioned kind of ascetic transcendentalism which was in vogue during the centuries since Jesus. For the tradition of immanence, though stifled in the main, has always existed, and can be brought into prominence in connection with the increase of present natural knowledge.

The two products of the dominant minority, during the period of disintegration, are universal states and philosophies. We may discuss them in that order.

The term universal in the phrases "universal state" and "universal church" must be intended by Toynbee in a metaphorical sense, although to be sure he never says so.[11] There are great churches which are "world-wide" in the sense of having members in every corner of the globe, but there are no universal churches,

---

11. The point about the use of the term universal in connection with states has been clarified by Toynbee in his letter of January 16th, 1940: "One of the criteria in my mind for regarding a state as a universal state is that it should have united, in itself, all states within the whole civilized world as known to the members of that society. Political unification of previously separated states, as in Germany since 1871, or in the United States since the foundation of the Union, is not enough in itself to give a state the character of 'universality,' in the sense in which I have used the term. On the other hand, both the Roman Empire and the Chinese Empire, in the second century of the Christian Era, were universal states in my sense, because each of them did include in itself the whole of the civilized world as far as the knowledge of its own members extended. In other words, the universality of universal states is at least partly subjective."

if by universal is meant all-powerful, or world-wide in any exclusive sense. There has always been more than one church in the world at any given time in known history. Similarly with the universal state, this must mean empire, since no state has ever been omnipotent throughout the world, not even the Roman Empire or the British Empire. Perhaps by universal, it is meant to describe aspirations rather than accomplishments. We have seen that there is nothing good about the universal state, so far as Toynbee is concerned. Small states are deemed abortive, and scorned; large states are accused of being themselves symptoms of disintegration, peaceful respites from the "time of troubles," yet nothing more than that. The only value of a universal state that is worth mentioning is that it forms a protecting shell, or carapace, beneath which the universal church gets its start in life. The arts and sciences which may flourish under the same social order which makes the birth of religion possible are held to be of little account.

Universal states are supposed to exist by force and to be maintained in the same way. Being the products of the minority which has long ceased to be creative and which exists in power only by virtue of its dominance, they have no charm. And yet Toynbee tells us that the late Roman Empire received states in its fold which came and begged for admittance, having been charmed by the orderliness and peace which existed at the time within the confines of the Empire. Thus we can see that even Toynbee has difficulties in deciding upon the constitution and characteristics of the universal state. The fact is that it is hard to decide just what is a universal state and what is not. As we have already noted, the universal state of the Hellenic society is the Roman Empire, according to Toynbee, although we might read that particular historical sequence another way and propose that the Hellenistic civilization be deemed the universal state of the Hellenic society.

The second product of the dominant minority is philosophy. When touching on philosophy, the shortcomings of the attempt to construct a whole theory of history on the analogy of the Greek society make themselves keenly felt. Because Plato and

Aristotle were members of the ruling class, philosophy comes from the dominant minority, and because they preferred logic to experience, philosophy seeks another world "only for its negative value of being an *alibi* from this one" (V, 395). The philosopher is condemned because he is only pretending to prefer the next world, when he really prefers this one. Is this a fair judgment upon all philosophers? Is philosophy as a whole not rather a house in which there are many mansions? Toynbee himself relies to a large extent upon the philosophy of change, as exemplified by Bergson and Smuts, but seems himself curiously unfamiliar with philosophy.

Toynbee agrees with the mass of mankind which has failed to follow philosophy into rationalism. He holds that the emotions of religion are higher than the reasons of philosophy, as if these were opposed (V, 558). If philosophy is as bad an affair as Toynbee maintains that it is, why have his religions always sought it as their justification? Christianity hastened to embrace Greek philosophy and only with its aid vanquished the rival religions which were competing for public acceptance. In justice to Toynbee it must be admitted that he seems to prefer the least philosophical branches of each religion that he discusses: he prefers Protestant to Catholic Christianity, and Mahayana to Hinayana Buddhism.

Toynbee tells us that his reason for preferring religion to philosophy is that philosophy begins with doubt whereas religion consists in acceptance; philosophy springs from the revolt against religion. But the positing of doubt as the basis of philosophy is Cartesian, and there are many other schools which disagree on this point with Descartes. Only *one* school of philosophy out of many begins with doubt. And again, just as philosophy may spring from the revolt against religion in one period, it may spring from the acceptance of religion in another. The philosophy of Thomas Aquinas, one of the great systems of the world, was nourished in religion and built upon a deep acceptance of it. That religion "is a movement that comes from below" whereas philosophy "is a movement that comes from above" (V, 562 n.) is an accident of origins in one case, and untrue in another. When this description of origins happens to be true it proves nothing, since the attempt to prove something by it is an instance of the historical fallacy. When it happens not to be true it is disproved; and it happens not to be true in a number of cases. Many philosophers arose from the proletariat, notably the following: Socrates, Antisthenes, Epicurus, Diogenes, Epictetus, and Spinoza. On the other hand, many religious leaders have come from the dominant minority: Ikhnaton, Moses, Gautama, Lao-Tse, Mani Mahavira, St. Francis, Nanak, and Ghandi. The generalization does not hold.[12]

Toynbee simply fails to understand the function of philosophy. Logic was never intended to replace feeling, nor ontology eschatology. Not one of the valid fields of human endeavor has any right to usurp the function of the others. We can no more look to religion to the exclusion of, say, politics, than we can look to philosophy as, say, a rival of religion. The different fields exist on different planes and should be understood as mutually implicative and not as competitors. Everything valid has its place under the sun, and Toynbee is as much in error in assuming that religion can supplant philosophy as the contemporary scientists are in assuming that science can supplant it.

The product of the external proletariat, is, we are told, heroic poetry. One of the most interesting minor themes in Toynbee's great work is that devoted to the consideration of the creation of heroic epics. The epic "ignores the greatest events of the age" and "exaggerates the importance of the affair which it has taken for its theme," creating "'a possession forever' out of the fruitless deeds and ephemeral experience of one particular set of barbarian

---

12. On the questions of the necessity for higher religions to rationalize their faith, the philosophers who arose from the proletariat, and the religious leaders who were members of the dominant minority, as well as the general point of the derogation of philosophy as a sterile affair, Toynbee writes as follows: "I may have been unfair to the philosophers. This happens when one is taking living personalities and historical movements as types of a particular attitude of mind. One is always in danger of making too radical an abstraction. Your two points about philosophy being one of the necessary elements of a higher religion and about the social origin of certain philosophers and religious leaders are both of them very fair and useful criticism."—Letter of January 16th, 1940.

war-bands" (V, 238). Thus the Homeric Epic ignored the sack of Cnossos *circa* 1400 B.C., and the Teutonic Epic ignored the sack of Rome in A.D. 410 in favour of the celebration of lesser heroes and events. "It is not the military or political effectiveness, but the literary 'availability' of a barbarian war-lord that makes his literary fortune" (V, 607). As the events in the epic diverge from the factual truth, with all its limitations, it begins to approach the broader and more general truths of mythology as contained in the legends recounted by the unknown bards who write the folk epics.

There is little doubt that here Toynbee has got hold of an important aspect of cultural development. The cloth, however, is always cut to fit the occasion. There is too much arbitrariness about which group is to be the civilization and which the barbarians pounding at the gates. For instance, the Alexander Romance becomes an epic of the external proletariat only by making the Macedonians, under Alexander the Great, the external proletariat of the Syriac society! Can the Macedonians, tutored by the Greeks, be classified as the barbarian thrust which finally "broke through the marches of the Achaemenian Empire"? Can one civilization be said to be the external proletariat of another? In the passages in which Toynbee touches upon the contacts between civilizations, this does not seem to be the case. Toynbee himself is aware of some difficulties when he asks, "How came the figure of the Macedonian war-lord to be kidnapped and carried off bodily into Fairyland in the broad daylight of Hellenic rationalism?" (VI, 441) a question which is not satisfactorily answered. There is more genuine justice in the account of the French with their Epic of the *Chanson de Roland* and the Byzantine Greeks with their Epic of Basil Digénis Akrítas as the Western and Eastern wings respectively of the external proletariat of the Syriac society (V, 260). The Europeans of that day, like the Asiatic who bordered on the Arab civilization, were primitive by contrast, a fact which the textbooks of history of our own day, in concentrating upon the importance of the rise of the European civilization, are apt to overlook.

Toynbee fails to account for the 'civilized epics,' the conscious literary creations of single individuals in the heart of a civilization: the epics of a Dante, a Milton, and a Goethe, which recount not the heroic deeds of a barbarian war-band without the boundaries but rather the cosmology, in its most exaggerated and mythologically affective terms, of a civilization from inside its centre and in its heyday. These epics are, it must be admitted, in many ways inferior to the epics of the war-bands, composed by many hands and reflecting the varied experiences of a people, but in other ways the epics of the literary artists are superior, carrying as they do the basic beliefs not of an external proletariat but of a whole civilization. They, too, must be included in any satisfactory account of the poetic writings of history.

VIII

Having commented in some detail upon the four movements of civilization, we may now turn to a judgment upon the larger aspects of Toynbee's history. First we shall take up the shortcomings of the sytsem, and of its application to the Western society of our day, and then we shall attempt to indicate something of the virtues of the work, its superiority to other histories and its merits as a whole.

What may be described as the larger shortcomings of Toynbee's system are its failure to comprehend the place of art and of science in civilization, and the attempt to found the system upon transcendental theology.

Toynbee concedes a distinction between what is and what ought to be, between the fixed and the flux, but will allow the distinction to be valid only for religions. Something of high value is admittedly saved from the flux, insusceptible to accidents, and possible always. But this something, Toynbee insists, must be a religion. One consequence is that art and science, along with lesser human endeavors, is swept along with the other accidents of actuality that are hardly worth saving. Needless to add, it is impossible on any such premise to expect to see justice done to the work of art. We are prepared for the wrong-headed judgment that the contemporary vogue for so-called "primitive art" is an example of "barbarization" (V, 482). The acceptance of primitive art by members in good standing of the Western civilization marks for Toynbee the decline of that civilization and the archaistic yearning of its members to return to a primitive state. This is seeing things in simple terms indeed. For "primitive art" means works of art executed by primitive *peoples;* it does not mean primitive *art.* As one art critic and appreciator has already warned, there is nothing in common between archaism and primitivism in art.[13] The primitivism which is resuscitated in contemporary art is not evidence of an archaistic revival but only of an attempt to purge civilized art of its extraneous elements, to "purify" it. All of the attempts to borrow from the past could not be on a level unless the past as a whole was on a level. But there are equally elements in the art of the past which are of value irrespective of the period in which they were discovered. The historian of art is keenly aware that there is no such thing as progress in art. The cave drawings in Spain are as sophisticated in their way, and as validly works of art, as are the latest examples of the modern master—say the best work of a Velasquez or a Cézanne. Art, like science and religion, and any achievement of logic or value, is independent of its origins and does not have to rise or sink with them. Primitive art is not "primitive" simply because it has been developed by a primitive people. Art is not to be confused with its creators.

Analogous to the confusion between the circumstances surrounding the creation of a work of art and the work of art itself, is the confusion, which is rife in Toynbee's volumes, between science and its application. It is well-known by now that there are two distinct movements in science: the work in so-called "pure" science, which is the search for truth concerning the laws of nature irrespective of their usefulness; and the application of those laws in the many useful ways that their discovery makes possible. The former may be called science proper; the latter,

---

13. Elie Faure, *The Spirit of the Forms,* trans. Walter Pach (New York, 1937), p. 77.

technology. The distinction may be exemplified by the difference between Faraday's work on the dynamo and any public utilities corporation of today.

Now, the error that Toynbee makes concerning science is the confusion of science with technology, the consideration that science consists in the application of technological mechanics to problems of material well-being, and in nothing more. He understands neither the essential method of science (I, 441), its two tendencies, namely toward greater diversification as well as toward greater simplification (III, 181), nor its purposive aim (III, 101); and he holds science to be mechanistic and materialistic, a mere affair of application (III, 101). Such a view of science leaves out of account the detachment and singleness of purpose of a Newton, a Planck, an Einstein, men whose work is not primarily intended to further practical interests but to discover the truth about some tiny part of physical nature and so add to that small but growing body of human knowledge upon which some reliance can safely be placed, and, more, upon which future scientists can safely build as they go about their business of enlarging the scientific purview so as to show previous theories to be but special cases of a more inclusive theory. Such work must have its practical application in time, if it is valid at all, and this technological application is of immense importance. Yet there remains the other aspect of science which Toynbee overlooks altogether: the aspect of science as the search for truth, and the social consequences of the faith of a large public in this integrity of the scientific pursuit. Surely this is science, too, and something more than mere material utility.

However, for Toynbee science is an affair only of immediate practicality, of the manipulation of material nature, and accordingly he accepts Spengler's view that science is a product of its own time, and that nothing of it can be saved beyond the period of its discovery (III, 380). Both men agree that science has already passed the zenith of its possibilities, and is on the downgrade, together with the culture that produced it. We are, Toynbee insists, already discounting the faith which we had put in science to lead us to truth.

Already we are beginning to doubt whether our classic nineteenth-century scientific method of weighing and measuring, in which we have put our intellectual trust, is really a talisman which can be counted upon to transmute subjective thought into objective truth (V, 177).

And he almost rejoices in the possibility that the twenty-fourth century A.D. will see some

> Rumanian Iamblichus, or the twenty-fifth century some Mexican Proclus, to conjure a rank Neohuxleyian theurgy out of a senile experimental technique (V, 177).

Of course, science is not trying to transmute subjective thought into objective truth, but rather to extract objective laws from equally objective events. One is reminded, by Toynbee's description of nineteenth-century scientific method as that of "weighing and measuring" merely, of the modern neo-Thomist attack upon science, which deems it to be confined to surfaces. The method of weighing and of measuring is ages older than science in the modern sense, and constitutes only a tiny part of scientific method as a whole. Can an experimental technique age? Will the logic of scientific method perish, along with great works of art, while religion is saved from the fate which is meted out to all other actual things? There is, at any rate, no reason to believe that it must.

In all this underestimation of science there is a failure to understand the modern Western civilization, in which the institution of science is the chief vehicle for the pursuit of truth. In any civilization it would appear that the search for truth and reality dominates and is the chief occupation of the leading institution. Religion is only a name for the dominant institution whose task it is to seek out the real and the true. The "higher" religions of civilizations have differed qualitatively from the primitive religions. Why can we not suppose that science differs from the "higher" religions in the same way? With good reason or bad, our religion has become that of science, and our high priests scientists. We look to them for knowledge concerning the nature of the real. We have replaced supplication at altars with investigation in laboratories as our procedure. Admittedly, by this exchange, as Toynbee would insist, something has been lost; but as he would probably not admit, something equally valuable has been gained. There is every reason to try to save the institution of science as well as restore that of religion. Applied science may be a symptom of the decline of civilization whenever it occurs without the pure science which gave it birth. But pure science itself is a sign of growth, of vigorous creative powers, of the high noon of human culture.

The second large shortcoming of Toynbee's system is its transcendental theology. Transcendentalism is indefensible as a working philosophy; and no philosophy which is indefensible as a working philosophy, although philosophy is not entirely a matter of working, is defensible. The saint, who is held up by Toynbee as the human archetype, shuns this actual world and all its concerns as a vale of evil and error; and so the best possible aim of mankind in its journey through life is to—avoid life. But the avoidance of this life is something none of us need worry about; we shall achieve it soon enough. Whether we are in love with this life for what is good about it, or shun it like the plague for what we recognize to be its shortcomings, the end will be the same for us; and the death which terminates all our attitudes and brings to a close our perspectives will approach soon enough. Death is automatic until men become immortal; so that the human problem is one of life and not of death. How to make actual living as good, as beautiful, and as holy as possible: that is our problem; and the civilizations that have gone before have striven toward this same solution, more or less. The theological attitude which seeks to justify preoccupation with mortal problems is termed immanentism. It gives way to no compromises with the absoluteness of the goals, but seeks to approach them, if not to reach them mediately in an actual indefinite future. Toynbee's adherence to transcendentalism allows him no consideration whatsoever of the immanentist alternative.

The result is that Toynbee's wealth of detail with regard to human history points in its admirable bulk away from human life altogether and the things of this world, and toward a world to come. The history of civilizations proves that everything ends with decline and disintegration: civilizations together with all they contain. All organizations, in fact, must sooner or later perish. In the face of this catastrophic truth, Toynbee feels constrained to endeavor to save the churches, since they and they alone stand for what does not perish. Here we meet a difficulty which we have met before in our examination of the problems of churches. Has not Toynbee confused churches with what they stand for, institutions with religious values? For churches, being actual organizations, must perish too, a stubborn fact which Toynbee is loath to confront. But if churches are to be saved because, although they themselves perish, they stand for things which do not: the holiness which remains always possible; then other institutions and endeavours must be saved on a like basis and with equal argument: the arts and sciences which seek beauties and truths beyond what exists at any given time, and even states which seek good beyond what any man living under any actual government has known.

If the only moral of such an extensive survey of actual existence as Toynbee has conducted is to point away from actual existence altogether, then the investigation has been a failure unless the moral is read in reverse. The transcendental doctrine to which Toynbee clings will not allow such a reading, but an immanentist approach will. We may say that past civilizations have gone into their decline so soon only because they have not been good enough. In the future we must not deny life but rather seek to build in this world something which the saints advise us to await in the next: a more perfect life, filled with goodness, beauty, and holiness to a greater extent than what we have known in the past. It will not be perfect; we know that—not until men themselves are perfect. We cannot expect that it will be more than a little better than past efforts have produced. But that itself will be an advance, and will be evidence of the fact that those who have advanced have not lived in vain but have served an actual indefinite future of actual life in this world.

Toynbee condemns this method of approach to the problems

offered by the continually occurring decline of civilizations, and terms it "futurism," holding it to be condemned to violence, a condemnation hardly proved. Yet it issues as the only feasible solution. That Toynbee himself was aware of the viewpoint as well as the validity of the doctrine of immanence is made evident in at least one passage. "Perhaps," he says, "the truth is that no created thing can ever be evil intrinsically and irremediably, because no created thing is incapable of serving as a vehicle for the virtues that flow from the Creator. 'The military virtues' are virtues none the less for being jewels set in blood and iron" (IV, 647). Not such immanence as this, which sees positive if limited value in everything actual, but a transcendence which shuns actuality altogether and wholeheartedly, is the leading conception which dominates the whole of the *Study of History*. Why, the question must arise, did Toynbee make the choice he did of denying actual existence in favor of a transcendental goal? The explanation can be made evident in the solution of still another paradox. There are two parts of Toynbee's position which at first glance appear to be contradictory, but which are, in point of fact, reconcilable; their reconciliation reveals the fundamental point of view which Toynbee holds. He prefers the Western religion of Christianity to all other religions, and yet prefers Eastern civilization to the Western.

The period of the greatest acceptance of Christianity was in the Middle Ages in Europe, and in Christian civilization, as in the oriental civilizations, culture is (or at least was) integrally and fundamentally religious. All other pursuits were not separated out and pursued independently; the sciences, the arts, ethics, logic, and philosophy were not separated out and cultivated on their own account but existed undifferentiated, just as they do in Eastern civilization.

Now, it is the single great contribution of Western civilization (understanding by Western civilization the continuous tradition from the Greeks to modern Europe) that these different pursuits can be separated out and placed in quasi-isolation for purposes of detailed examination and acute analysis. Logic, like the separate sciences, goes further when it is considered alone—as though it had nothing whatsoever to do with anything else—than it does when it is included in theological treatises as a holy exercise and considered an adjunct of religion. And the same is true of every other study. If the sciences had remained undistinguished in theological theories and practices, the application of physical waves to human organisms for therapeutic purposes would have remained unknown; and yet who can deny that the Roentgenologist performs to some small degree at least the work of God in helping to save human lives?

Toynbee, however, is opposed to such specialization because it is not candidly God-fearing. Eastern mysticism and Western science struggle for the possession of the Western way of life. Is science, that glory of the Western civilization, to be allowed to develop its own social notions, or must we return to classic religion prematurely? In the East things are different; there, religious mysticism has had no competition, and consequently has held mankind in a vise-like immobility which resembles death— which is death. Toynbee has no use for science, for actual life, for anything mundane, and envies the "absolute detachment" of Buddhism (VI, 143). He mistrusts the sciences since their advance is conducted with "dry" reason and not with emotions appropriate to their ends. He prefers the integral cultures which do not get very far because they advance as great unwieldy wholes, dragging their immense burden of emotional content along with them over every step of the way, only to sink down exhausted in the end, admitting that such paths as they have been attempting to pursue exist for traffic only in another world where angels have wings and the streets are paved with gold.

The value of science, Huxley once declared, is that any fool can advance it a little; but the kind of civilization which Toynbee prefers can only be advanced by saints, and so he chooses the transcendental rather than the immanentist doctrine, omitting as he does so the immanentist aspect of Christian doctrine. For it is possible to be a good Christian and a scientist, or a logician and a good Christian; but only by choosing, over the Jesus who said that we should give up earthly considerations and cleave only unto him in the life to come, that other Jesus who proclaimed that he came in order that we might have life and have it more abundantly. Although intermittent in history, immanentist theology is also good Christianity.

IX

"Christianity," declares Toynbee, found Western man a "barbarian and has promoted him to the lordship of creation" (V, 438), a statement which ignores that science and philosophy which *Homo Occidentalis* inherited from the Greek "barbarians" who antedated Jesus. Erroneous as such a statement is, it yet sounds the note which is the *leitmotif* for Toynbee's predictions concerning the future of the Western civilization, a note which, we may hasten to add, is consistent with Toynbee's predictions on the whole but inconsistent with many acute observations that he has made.

One of the benefits to be expected from any system of such dimensions as those of Toynbee's is the light which we may expect it to throw upon the future of our own civilization. Where are we in the life-cycle of a civilization according to Toynbee, and what may we expect to happen to us in the future? These important questions immediately raise the further one of whether Toynbee's system can be employed as a canon of prediction at all. There is, according to his calculations, a prescribed pattern for the life of a society, but its pace is not determined, so that disintegration may be put off; but on the other hand each civilization has only three and one half responses to make to a challenge, after which it must accept complete defeat. Toynbee is not absolutely sure of what can be predicted from his system. In one place he warns of the dangers attendant upon any attempt to ascertain from inside a civilization just where that civilization itself is in the life-pattern of civilization. Nevertheless, the attempt must be made, and Toynbee goes ahead bravely to make it. We may set forth first his short-term predictions, and then, before listing his long-term efforts, try to show what is characteristic in his views of the present.

Toynbee has demonstrated how democracy and industrialism, institutions which are inherently international in scope, have been perverted to the purposes of sovereign nation-states (IV, 156 ff.). Nationalism, having served its turn as an instrument of consolidation of lesser political units, was falling into decline before the newer demands of internationalism, when democracy and industrialism arrived upon the scene and put new "drives" into nationalism, thus reviving an outmoded form of goverment. On this basis he predicted the Russo-German Pact of September, 1939:

The convergence between the nationalism of the Soviet Union and the socialistic nationalism of her neighbours is unmistakable; and we can already make out the lineaments of the new common standard type of community towards which our post-war Capitalist and Communist states are thus all tending (V, 186).

He likewise predicted the present war as a second in the series of "totalitarian wars" (i.e., not merely wars by totalitarian states but wars of "areas" rather than "fronts," in which nations as a whole are engaged). Our chief danger, as Toynbee understands only too well, consists in "an infatuation with the sovereignty of national states" (IV, 319), which makes the present conflicts, their predecessors and successors, inevitable.

So much for short-term predictions. When we come to examine the predictions of the long-term, we find the old preconceptions now aiding, now standing in the way of the implications we should be prepared to expect from a knowledge of the system.

First in the order of present misunderstandings is Marxism. Toynbee refuses to give it any credit whatsoever. There is nothing new in Marxism, nothing, that is, which does not derive from and is not to be found in Hegelian, Jewish, and Christian elements (V, 582). Even the socialist element in Marxism existed in Christianity. Apart from the fact that Toynbee confuses the Marxist movement as a whole with Russian communism, he misses the main issue, and does not feel obliged to account for the peculiar form of Marxism at this particular time. Even if economic socialism did exist already in Christianity, why was it the variety known as Marxism which happened to revive that issue now? Toynbee is always given to confusing issues with their actual advocates, another example of the fallacy of historicism. Even if Marxism as a militant movement is defeated, is it not possible that certain virtues of Marx's social emphasis may survive in whatever form of government eventually adopted, just as certain admirable planks in the platform of Norman Thomas' American socialism were adopted and put to good effect by the "New Dealers" of the Democratic Party headed by Roosevelt?

Science (by which Toynbee means applied science and physical technology) is condemned out of hand because it has failed to distribute properly its material benefits to a sufficiently great part of the population (V, 163 f.). The accusation is just, but is this difficulty to be laid at the door of science, or blamed upon the maladjustments of the economic and political system under which we live? This failure in understanding, which is a result of the failure to understand the function of science in general, is equalled only by the failure to understand Western philosophy. The humanism of Comte (IV, 300), the ontological dualism of Descartes, and the dialectical philosophy of Hegel (IV, 328), these are the only philosophies coming from the Western society whose credentials Toynbee will accept. But are they the only ones whose papers are in order? What about Kant, the so-called philosopher of Protestantism; and what about the English realists, from Moore to Alexander and Whitehead? Apart from omissions, have the philosophers nominated by Toynbee ever received such sufficiently widespread acceptance as to acknowledge them the official philosophical representatives of the Western society of our day? Many philosophers would be strongly inclined to disagree.

The paramount problem of our times, Toynbee holds, is the decline of religious belief (V, 671). Here Toynbee's accusation does square with the facts. There is no doubt about the decline of religion in our day, and this despite the enormous numbers of the population who still give lip-service, the "Sunday Christians" and "Sabbath Jews." The same indifference with regard to religious practices pervades the members of all faiths equally. The seriousness of the situation is partly made up for by the reverence for facts and for the discoveries of laws: a reverence for the method of science, on whose efforts and often on whose conclusions we feel that we can rely. Toynbee would probably pronounce this substitution a sad one, and he would be right to the extent that science fails as an object of search for the realities on the emotional side which cannot forever be neglected. Yet we must recognize that although one belief has declined, another has arisen at least partly to take its place. And we must recognize further that the final solution may come in the discovery of a new religion just as well as in the revival of an old one.

The decision to revert to the past, and to seek our salvation in the universal church of an apparented culture is not made by Toynbee hastily. The fact is that his theory of history does not lead back to Christianity. Nothing in his theory leads backward at all. He has had to twist the theory itself in favor of an institution of the past which he wishes to see revived.[14] Toynbee is so much of a nominalist that he does not contemplate the retention, or revival, of ideas without the retention, or revival, of the institutions which served at a certain date and place as the vehicle for the conveyance of those ideas. Accordingly, therefore, he first looks around for our own universal church, but when he fails to find a new one, he expresses hope in the possibility of turning to one taken from the past and purports to detect "the sap of life visibly flowing once again through all the branches of our Western Christendom" (V, 193). In this revival it seems the Protestant churches take the lead, and there is hope even in the Oxford Group movement (V, 439), although the Catholic Middle Ages would appear to be the ideal period of Western society, and Toynbee longs for another Gregory VII to restore the spiritual conditions that were prevalent in the eleventh century.[15] Toynbee is

---

14. See end of Section 3, p. 179.
15. "I think that in its modern phase our Western society has been keeping itself alive on the principles which inspired it in the mediaeval period; in so far as we are in a bad way now it is because we have fallen away from those principles; if we retrieve our position, I believe we shall do so by returning to the Christian tradition."—Letter of January 16, 1940.

here unfaithful to his own system. In the first place, any return to an institution of the past is archaistic, and archaism has already been condemned in favor of transfiguration. A revival of the Christian church at this particular stage in our development would represent one of those backward movements in history which Toynbee has already said involve violence and accomplish nothing of value. In the second place, the fact that we have no universal religion of our own in the Western society, except Christianity, from which Toynbee admits we are rapidly departing, was to be expected, and could not possibly, according to Toynbee's own postulates, be otherwise. It will be recalled that Toynbee has already said that universal religions are responses made by the internal proletariat, on inspiration from the external proletariat, to the challenge of oppression by the dominant minority, in a universal state. Thus we should not be expected to develop a universal church until we have our own universal state. Have we achieved a universal state for the Western society? Toynbee says no, we have not. On his calculations, we are at present in the "time of troubles" preceding our universal state (IV, 3-4). Assailed by doubts as to the accuracy of this calculation (IV, 108 n. 2), he finally concludes that it is correct (IV, 318). Toynbee has predicted a series of "totalitarian" wars in which one of the contenders will inflict upon all the others a "knock-out blow," and bring about the *pax oecumenica* of a universal state in which democracy and industrialism will find their natural field of operations (IV, 179). The time of troubles is to end with this "knock-out blow" sometime during the twentieth century (IV, 179). After which, presumably, there will spring up a universal state, and within it, as within a carapace, a universal church and its "higher religion" will flourish, only to mark the decline of the Western civilization, and to bridge the gap between this civilization and some other.

Thus the future of our civilization is to be expected to follow the same sad fate of other civilizations, and we can look forward only to despair and to the destruction of everything that we have built up and hold worthy. The prospect is too much even for

Toynbee himself to accept. Accordingly he leaves a way of escape. Although the odds are against us, "odds of sixteen to ten and possibly twenty-five to one, that Death the Leveller will lay his icy hand on us likewise" (IV, 38), there is left with us the suggestion that perhaps the past does not after all lay any absolute injunction upon the future, that maybe we can be the first to escape from the wheel of existence which carries civilizations down to their destruction even as it carries them up to the height of their growth.

"The dead civilizations are not 'dead by fate'; and therefore a living civilization is not doomed inexorably in advance" (IV, 39). We may, after all, survive with our Western civilization, keeping intact with us that Christian orthodoxy which Toynbee holds to be alone worthy of survival. Or, lacking even this slender thread of argument, there is still the final "hope-against-hope" to keep us going in our daily round. As Lucretius says, "The door of death is not closed."

Why does Toynbee want to save the Western civilization? The fact that he does is consistent with his humanity but inconsistent with his logical system. If we are in our time of troubles, then the sooner we disintegrate further the sooner we shall develop our universal state, and under cover of this state, the universal church and higher religion toward which all our efforts should be directed. In a sense, to try to save the Western civilization means only to hold back the development, held to be inevitable, of our higher religion. The point hinges upon the absoluteness of the inevitable. As an advocate of historical determinism, Toynbee is inflexible, yet he cringes before the consequences of such a hypothesis; and when confronted by his system with the demand that the disintegration of Western civilization continue in order that the higher religion may issue from the ruins, he winces, for it is not *a* higher religion that he wishes, but *the* higher religion of Christianity. Human effort is predicated upon the hope that the future may be made to mark an improvement over the past; determinism calls upon the future to reduplicate the past. Toynbee solves the contradiction by positing a possible but remote mutation of mankind to a higher species—and then hoping against hope that the mutation waits just around the corner and may at least begin to take hold before the present civilization disintegrates altogether and the good works of the present are totally lost.

X

We have concluded our brief summary and comments on Toynbee's argument. Those who have come thus far in this study will wonder, perhaps, why it was undertaken. If Toynbee has made so many mistakes in his volumes, what can justify such close perusal and detailed criticism? The answer to this question will be contained in this and the next section. In this section we shall consider the superior virtues of Toynbee over other theorists of history, and in the next we shall abandon the method of comparison and consider simply the chief merits of Toynbee's achievement.

The historians with whom Toynbee almost immediately challenges comparison are Vico and Spengler, and to a lesser degree, Marx also.

The comparison between Vico and Toynbee is an interesting one. There are many similarities; both historians share a high regard for religion. Vico, although more attracted to the possibilities of science than Toynbee, and holding them in higher esteem, yet clung to the conviction that human life could not be worthy without the preservation of religion, a conviction which Toynbee shares. Vico stood between two worlds: a world in which the Middle Ages still echoed and the modern age was born, a child of the late seventeenth century. He managed to combine with his love for the church and for science a wholly modern understanding of myths as containing the essential truths of history. Of course, neither scholar has ever been wholly understood in his viewpoint on myths, and Toynbee must face the combined scorn of a host of historical specialists to whom mythology in any connection whatsoever with history spells anathema. Yet it is probable that his observations in this field will in the end survive such condemnation. For Toynbee's ability to leap from factual details to mythological essentials and back again, with perfect ease and complete logical justification, is a power that has been possessed, even in lesser degree, by only few, if any, historians.

Although inclined to regard emotional rather than rational achievements as of prime importance, and thus preferring to take religion rather than science as a touchstone for the consideration of cultures, Toynbee, in contrast to Vico, is himself more analytical in his historical investigations. Extenuating circumstances may be set forth for Vico, circumstances of a historical nature; for it is clear that Vico did not have available the wealth of historical scholarship of archeological findings, and of other theories of history, that are at hand for Toynbee. Yet in making a non-temporal comparison of the accomplishments of the two historiographers, there are very evidently large areas of interest in which Toynbee's analysis is vastly superior. As has been shown elsewhere,[16] Vico's work contains much of value to the modern world; yet it is probably Toynbee's which will claim, as indeed it deserves, the greatest attention today.

Next in the chronological order of theorists with whom Toynbee challenges comparison is the political and economic philosopher, Karl Marx. No systems could be further apart than that of Toynbee on the one hand and that of Marx and Engels on the other. Toynbee is concerned to save Christianity, Marx and Engels to develop an atheistic form of socialism. Yet there are similarities. Both Marx and Toynbee are close in their analysis of the tendency of institutions to change over into something directly opposed to what they had been at first, after a certain stage in their development has been reached. Marx and Engels call this the tendency of an institution to "turn into its opposite," Toynbee calls it *peripetéia,* the "reversal of roles" (IV, 246). Essentially the conception is the same, although it is put to different purposes. Another similarity is that of the class-war. Although, again, put to different

---

16. James Feibleman, "Toward the Recovery of Giambattista Vico", *Social Science,* XIV (1939), 31.

purposes, the conception is fundamentally the same. Both Marx and Toynbee regard the seaming of society into different classes, one of which has enforced power over the others, as a symptom of severe social maladjustment. Marx regards it as the fundamental malady of the state, eradicable only in the establishment of a classless communistic society; Toynbee regards it as an infallible symptom of social breakdown, eradicable only upon the genesis of a new civilization to take the place of the old. Last in our brief list of similarities is the semi-determinism of history evident in both systems. Both Toynbee and Marx toy with the notion of determinism, and although they appear to be committed to it wholeheartedly by the implication of their fundamental postulates, both seek to evade its terrific consequences by assuming that history can be altered just a little by well-intentioned persons.

The differences between Toynbee and Marx are, however, enormous. Marx is almost exclusively preoccupied with the economic aspect of history and deems it of first importance. Toynbee is not unmindful of this aspect, as witness his excellent discussion of the Solonian revolution in ancient Athens (IV, 200 ff.), although it is true that he does neglect the economic aspects in other periods of history. But his superiority over Marx as a theorist is that he recognizes the vast number of other factors which go to make up a full-sized civilization, and is mindful of the many lines of force which converge upon the movement of a culture, so that none can be called exclusively causal. In Marx, history is oversimplified and the careful reader becomes more and more persuaded that the understanding of human social events in the past is a comparatively easy matter; all events at the higher social levels are caused by events at the economic level. Toynbee disabuses us of any such illusion, and, if he fails to solve all the problems of history, he at least awakens us to the vast complexities of the problem itself, which is as much as any one historian can hope to do.

Perhaps the most obvious comparison which springs to mind is that between Toynbee and Oswald Spengler. Among contemporaries these two names stand out as the authors of the most comprehensive and suggestive surveys of human history. We may best understand the differences between them by glancing first at their similarities.

These are indeed many. Both men are anxious to construct a theory of history in such a way that every civilization which has ever existed, or which exists today, can be shown to be a single species of the genus civilization. In both studies a cyclical theory predominates, and the cycle of the life of civilizations is divided into four stages. Toynbee's quartet of genesis, growth, breakdown, and disintegration is analogous to Spengler's spring, summer, autumn, and winter. Genesis and growth are flourishing periods as are spring and summer; and in both systems the two latter periods mark a decline.

Both systems rest upon a fundamental distinction between human beings and physical nature. Spengler, in fact, sees history as "opposed" to nature,[17] a doctrine inherited from the Cartesian distinction between thought and extended things (which in turn is a distinction inherited from the medieval formulation of nominalism), while Toynbee makes his separation of man from nature rest upon the transcendental independence of the human soul from all that happens in this world, a doctrine eventually derivable from Christian theology, also. Thus both historians are guilty of a subjectivist turn of thought, so that their fundamental theories set forth history in terms of what has been thought by men, rather than primarily in terms of what men have been led to think and do by virtue of what has happened to them. Again, both belittle philosophy and the rôle of philosophers in social history, and modern philosophers in particular. We have seen that for Toynbee philosophers play an unimportant and rather disgraceful rôle as members of the dominant minority; for Spengler their importance consists in their non-philosophical activities, and he finds contemporary philosophers woefully confined to their own profession, and lacking in significant avocations.[18] Both students take the same pessimistic

---
17. Oswald Spengler, *Decline of the West*, Atkinson trans. (New York, 1926), I, 48.
18. *Ibid.*, pp. 42-45.

view of the modern Western civilization; they agree that the period of creation is over, and that only the period of expansion is left.[19]

As great as the similarities are in the two studies of human history, the differences are more indicative. It is in the differences between Toynbee and Spengler that the superiority of the former over the latter rises to the fore. For where Spengler is mystical, Toynbee is rational; where Spengler appeals to a vague "destiny" to account for change, Toynbee attempts to show the mechanics of change. Spengler, writing his history during the years of the World War of 1914-18, and witnessing the defeat of Germany, attempted to save Germany's leadership by demonstrating that if Germany was decaying, that must be the fate of West-European nations, and Germany's defeat marked in fact a leadership in retrogression; if Western nations were going to decline, then Germany was going to show her leadership by leading the decline! Thus Spengler's chief preoccupation was the salvation of German superiority; he was "proud to call" his history "a German philosophy."[20] Toynbee, on the other hand, at the outset disabuses the reader of any notion that England is the hub of the universe, and attempts to judge the development of history impartially. He, too, has something which he wishes to save; but since this something is "higher religion" in general and what appears to be Protestant Christianity in particular, we may at least mark the superior generality of his object of choice over that of Spengler, and accordingly give him credit. Thus, marking German decline, Spengler asserts that "there are no eternal truths"[21] to be discovered or known (since Germans could not know them), while Toynbee accepts the existence of eternal truths even if only as the prerogative of universal churches.

The last and most important point of contrast is that describing the rise and fall of civilizations in general. Spengler, employing the method of analogy, compared the life-pattern of the human

---
19. *Ibid.*, p. 40.
20. *Ibid.*, p. xiv.
21. *Ibid.*, p. 41.

society to that of the human organism, a comparison which Toynbee finds that he cannot accept (III, 219-23; IV, 12). Toynbee graphs the life of civilizations in the same four-part pattern but, working not with analogy but with analytical logic, attempts to discover and to show *how* civilizations rise and fall. Spengler offered an analogy between significant persons in different cultures merely by asserting that they represent the same movements of society and indicate, in different societies and under different names, the same stage of culture. He asserted, at a time when the fact was little understood, that all activities in a given culture are related. Toynbee, however, has attempted to show how these relations come about and why they are true. The virtues of analysis over analogy are evident to nearly all logicians. If Toynbee does not succeed in saying the final word on the analysis of the rise and fall of civilizations (and there is little doubt that he does not), what he does say is of immense importance, and the fact that he attempts an analysis at all marks his work as of greater importance than that of Spengler.

XI

The disproportionate amount of space devoted in this chapter to a criticism of Toynbee's history must not be taken as evidence that the point of view taken here is chiefly critical and negative. Criticism occupies more space than praise, since in the case of criticism, reasons must be given, evidence set forth, and arguments offered for the adverse position taken; while in the case of praise, an acceptance of the arguments and the point of view of the work under consideration is all that is required. By virtue of praise, the author is the critic's advocate; while with criticism, the critic is his own, and frequently his only, advocate. Criticism demands support in logic and fact; praise requires nothing but enjoyment. On the whole, Toynbee deserves more praise than criticism, since he has done a magnificent thing. Indeed, the grandeur of his work makes it impossible for the appreciator to render due justice. Toynbee raises and attempts to resolve all the leading problems in a large number of the fields of human endeavor: religion and politics, science and art, philosophy as well as history. As a result, an adequate discussion of the problems developed in the *Study of History* would require as many volumes as that work itself is planned to comprise. Our primary aim, therefore, despite the space devoted to criticism, is not to criticize but merely to suggest a preliminary criticism, and more, to call attention to the immense suggestiveness and importance of the work.

As we have seen, Toynbee may be said to be the first historian who has attempted to make a profound analysis of the form of human history. He brings together many strains in human culture, in an effort to discover the laws of the organization of culture. He tries to analyze cultural structure, and in doing so takes the first step toward the establishment of the empirical field of human social culture as the empirical field of a science. Laws represent what does not change in history: the invariant functions of change. History as sheer change could interest nobody, since there would be no way in which interest could take hold: none of the similarities or differences by means of which reason operates. What all historians are seeking are the functions of historical change, and Toynbee goes a long way toward suggesting what these may be.

The search for the laws of society, the analysis of the structure of social organization, and the implicit first step toward the establishment of the field of human culture as a social science, collectively presuppose certain assumptions of a metaphysical nature. These assumptions do not prove to be the candid nominalistic ones which we examined earlier in this chapter.[22] They rest rather on a realistic understanding—realistic in the medieval sense of that term. According to this shift, science would not be derogated as a study preoccupied exclusively with surfaces but would become recognized as the search for independent and objective laws, according to the logico-empirical method. Thus if all laws of social action could be theoretically ascertainable, social life could be controlled in such a way that the errors of the past would

---

22. In Section II, above.

not have to be repeated in the future, civilizations would not have to continue to decline inevitably, but would find a way to increase their organization of values. Churches would not have to bear upon their shoulders the immense responsibility for the transmission of civilizations as these contact each other in space and time. Truth would not remain the sole property of the universal church and would not have to be apprehended solely in emotional form, but rationality would be recognized as a surer if only approximative means of ascertaining truth. And the goal of human endeavor would not be exclusively that of a transcendent otherworldliness but would include in its labors the improvement of the conditions of actuality in the light of a perfection of theory and practice which is always possible and which is called for by an immanentism of "this worldliness." To some of the implications, at least, of this latter metaphysical standpoint, Toynbee is committed, and proves himself an eloquent and able advocate. For he combs human history as few other students were ever equipped to do, in search of social laws and their exemplifications, for the invariant functions of the social order illustrated in human history.

But whether Toynbee has discovered any of the invariant functions of human history in candid abstract form or not, there is much of value in his work that must remain to guide later historians as well as to benefit those who count as one of the necessities of an education some acquaintance with the past. Toynbee's history is a mythological drama, with all the world at all times and in all places as a stage, and with a cast of characters made up of all the great individuals who have ever distinguished themselves, acting as protagonists, and with all the masses who have ever surged toward a goal, acting as choruses. Toynbee is not afraid to quote Goethe and other mythologists, for he understands that there is a sense in which mythology represents the essential truths of history. Thus it may be claimed that Toynbee's *Study of History* maintains some truths which transcend the factual errors and oversights which no doubt are scattered throughout the volumes. And what a wonderful scene these truths depict! What a plot the image of civilization unfolds against the background of an organized topography! If the test of such a work is its inclusiveness of fact and suggestiveness of theory, its representative realism of what the past has been, and charged depictiveness of what the future may be, then the requirements of permanence are met to a very great extent indeed. We are broader in vision, richer in understanding, and keener in appreciation because Toynbee has written. For one who has read Toynbee's history thoroughly it must become impossible to see the world, and especially human history, without looking to some extent through Toynbee's eyes and from the perspective that he has discovered.

Part IV
The Revival in Science

VIII

Science from the Standpoint of Realism*

THE PROFESSION OF PHILOSOPHY has fallen on evil days. The opinion of scientific men with regard to philosophy is far from flattering, but it is no worse than the one held by the men of good-will who have only common sense to guide them. An elderly lady recently confronted me with the rumor that I was a philosopher. There was nothing to do except to plead guilty as charged. Whereupon she looked somewhat startled, and said, "But you are young to be so resigned." Since the Middle Ages, philosophy has been thought by one and all to be the private consolation of men who are impotent to face the real world. Naturally, the subjective method of seeking truth is looked upon with scorn by scientific men who have found for themselves a more objective method: the method of science.

This particular understanding of philosophy by both scientists and philosophers has led to just the antagonisms we might have expected of it.

The scientists have only one attitude: they regard the philosophers as camp-followers. The attitude is well exemplified by one remark made by Einstein. "It is significant," he observed somewhere, "that the conclusions of philosophy usually agree with the physical science of the day."

The philosophers, on the other hand, seem to have three well-

---

* Read to a seminar of the Department of Physiological Chemistry at Yale University, September 27, 1940.

defined attitudes. Most philosophers, and especially the positivists, go whoring after science with the cry that *it* has most of the answers, and *they* have very few. Others adopt a snobbish attitude based largely on ignorance. This point of view may be exemplified by a recent statement made by Santayana. "If I ask the inventors what they have learned of the depths of nature ... they may be chewing gum," he wrote.[1] The third group understands that philosophy, like science, has its own reasons for being, and that only if each stands on its own feet can they be of use to one another. It is this third viewpoint that I wish to explain here.

The explanation will be clearer if you will permit me to make several observations concerning the history of science. For science today is scarred from the accidents of its birth. The history of science may be characterized by its efforts to free itself from philosophy. The fifth-century Greeks had a good philosophical method but no scientific one. They had no instruments; nothing but crude observation. They knew so little science that they saw no reason to set it up as a separate discipline. Science and philosophy were lumped together under the heading of the knowledge of nature. The extraordinary efforts were mixtures of childish error and shrewd insight. We may laugh; but there is much to be learned from them yet. With the rise of the Macedonian power, however, the synthesis was broken up, and science and philosophy went different ways. Science followed Alexander to Egypt. Philosophy migrated to Rome, where it busied itself by becoming the theology of Christianity. But both science and philosophy suffered from the separation; science became sterile through its preoccupation with practical technology, while philosophy became sterile through its labors as apologist for the sins of the Christians.

For a long time nothing happened to ease this situation, except that the scientific tradition kept on the move. It went from Alexandria to Byzantium and was taken over into the Arab culture. The Arabs did little with it except to keep it alive, but this was a

---

[1]. *Some Turns of Thought in Modern Philosophy* (New York, 1933), p. 71.

very great service indeed. For through the Arabs it managed to reach Europe. The point to be emphasized here is that when science did come back to Europe, brought by travellers from Spain and North Africa, it came as a rebel. It could have been united again with the philosophical tradition in peace, but was assigned the postion of a challenger by theology which felt itself under attack. By the thirteenth century, philosophy was a vested interest; its method was felt to be the only true method, and the Church which was the repository of its truth was thought to contain *all* the truths, so that there were no new ones to be discovered. Despite the fact that Aquinas himself indulged in scientific experimentation, the Church soon learned that the success of science meant the decline of ecclesiastical authority. Those who felt the restrictions and who suspected that the truths known by the Church were not all that could be known, took up the cudgels for science—and the fight was on.

Quite naturally, science as a rebel adopted all the rebel slogans. The Church stood for philosophy and defended the cause of reason. Very well, then, science would attack philosophy and hold aloft the banner of anti-rationalism. The method of philosophy leaned on deduction; then science would adopt the inductive method. Philosophy was realistic; of course then science would have to be nominalistic. Let me pause here to call your attention to this last pair of terms. By realism is meant the doctrine of the absolute existence of universals apart from the minds which apprehend them. Nominalism is the denial of realism, and regards universals as mere names, having no corresponding realities in the objective world.[2]

Philosophy had always been rational—perhaps I should say it had grown rationalistic—but science added the empirical investigation and check to the rational method. There is nothing irrational about empiricism, however, unless it is done to death. Science won and the Church lost. That was all to the good; but credit for this success was attributed to the irrationalism of

---

2. The realistic nature of science has been emphasized by F. E. Abbot, *Scientific Theism* (Boston, 1885), Introduction, and persistently by C. S. Peirce, *Collected Papers*, e.g., 1.20.

science, and that was bad. The fact is that there has always been a discrepancy between the professed irrationalism of the scientists and the rationalism of the scientific method. The professed irrationalism of the scientists had perfectly good political reasons: they wanted science to survive the onslaught of the Church's attack. But nevertheless the success of science has been due to its combination of rationalism with empiricism.

Suppose that we have a look now at the scientific method with this orientation in mind. Science assumes that there is a governing "uniformity of nature," a realm of law which actual events obey as far as chance contradiction will allow them to. All bodies are constrained to fall *in vacuo* toward the center of the earth at the rate of 32 feet per second but few even reach its surface. From a study of the events of the actual universe, science endeavors to discover the conditions which govern that universe, on the assumption that the actual universe and everything in it is involved in a constant process of change, whereas the conditions which govern themselves or, in other words, the system of natural law—do not change at all. Thus the system of natural law, of which we seek knowledge through science, is independent of the processes of thought and of the history of events, both of which are changing things.

Just what is the constitution of that system of natural law? Peirce illustrates it when he tells us that "Nature syllogizes from one grand major premiss."[3] The system of natural law is a set of possibilities for the universe, a network of logical relations which have their being independently of anything actual. It was not made by man and is not exhausted by any cross-section of the spatiotemporal manifold. But men of science have devised a method for seeking the knowledge of it.

The scientific method, whereby knowledge of the system of natural law is sought, has three steps. The first step involves logical induction primarily. Induction consists in the adoption of an hypothesis. From the logical point of view, this means the choos-

---

3. *Collected Papers*, 6.66.

ing of a premise. Quite obviously, however, such inductions have a long deductive background, in that they do not occur to men in general but only to such men as have a familiarity with the deductive system of a given science through training in the particular scientific field in which the induction has relevance. Hypotheses concerning physics occur only to physicists because it is physicists alone who have sufficient acquaintance with the deductive system of existing knowledge in physics. Nevertheless, the choosing of an hypothesis involves imagination, or the ability to put known things together in new relations.

An hypothesis is a candidate for law, and the scientific method consists in a testing of the eligibility of the candidate. Once the hypothesis has been adopted, it is tried in several ways. The first test is that of experimentation, which is a test for allowance. If no relevant facts can be adduced to disprove the hypothesis, it is deemed to be allowed. The ingenuity of the experimentor is brought into play by his efforts to set a trap for the hypothesis, to devise some situation in which it will be proved contradictory or inadequate. He might, of course, so cleverly devise his experiment that mere conformity of the hypothesis to its isolated conditions would constitute strong supporting evidence, and this sort of experimentation is positive. But the conclusive findings of experimentation are of necessity negative, since we can never be sure that one more test might not disprove our hypothesis. We might call this first test by demonstrated allowance the method of correspondence.

The second way in which the hypothesis is tried is the test for consistency. The hypothesis, having been allowed by experimentation, is now submitted to comparison with the existing body of knowledge in its own field. There it must prove itself to be not inconsistent. A chemical hypothesis must fit together with the existing knowledge of chemistry, either as a subordinate part of that knowledge, or, if it is wider, by including what is already known as special cases of its own generality. Of course, some ingenuity on the part of the scientist is required here, too, since the hypothesis which at first glance appears to contradict a previously established scientific formulation might turn out to be conformable with it. Relativity theory seems to be incompatible with Newtonian mechanics, until we learn how the one subordinates the other. We may term this second test by demonstrated consistency the method of coherence.

We thus have two distinct and complementary movements in the method of science: the movement toward greater specificity in the devising of the proper experiments with isolated and controlled phenomena, and the movement toward greater generality in the discovery of the universal laws which are operative in such phenomena.

The testing of an hypothesis involves logical deduction primarily, just as the choosing of the hypothesis involves logical induction primarily. We can see at once, however, that all steps involve both induction and deduction. The choosing of an hypothesis presupposes deductive training behind the induction; the testing of it requires an inductive acumen to facilitate the deduction. Overemphasis upon either step to the degradation of the other involves a fallacy. The fallacy of extreme empiricism consists in holding that actual experimentation, or allowance, is the only and sufficient proof of an hypothesis. The fallacy of rational dogmatism consists in holding that the demonstration of consistency is the only and sufficient proof. But in a completed scientific operation, neither is sufficient without the other.

A mathematician once told me that if you put a rope over a pulley and balance it by suspending a dead weight from one end and a live monkey from the other, and then let the monkey begin to climb the rope on his side, it can be proved mathematically (1) that the weight would go down, (2) that it would remain where it was, and (3) that it would go up. He said that since the authorities disagreed, the problem was evidently insoluble. I proposed another approach to him: I suggested that we might get a rope, a monkey, a pulley and a weight, and try it; but this suggestion met with his scornful and emphatic refusal. "It would be too vulgar," he said. That is the fallacy of rational dogmatism.

The fallacy of radical empiricism is illustrated by a recent paper in the field of sociology read before a learned society. The author had gone to investigate a small and isolated Creole community in the Ozark mountains. He studied them for some time with great impartiality, because he felt that their relatively long isolation from neighboring communities would make them an excellent subject for social science. His conclusions appeared in his paper, which he read with a perfectly grave face. The men of this community, he noted, went to work in the morning and returned to their homes in the evening. The women sent the children to school and then did the house work, washing and cleaning, and preparing meals. In the evenings, they foregathered in each other's houses to play cards, to talk, or, on week ends, perhaps to dance. And so on. And that, he concluded, was his account of the strange customs of the Ozark Creoles.

The fact is that inquiry can be instigated from either end of the scientific method so long as it eventually embraces the whole method. Investigation into sheer empirical material is likely to lead to some more definitely directional avenue of exploration; but on the other hand, deductive systems themselves have frequently been instruments of discovery. In every case, however, there must be an empirical check as well as a consistency check: correspondence as well as coherence.

Although the avoidance of both these fallacies in the skillful combination of the several steps in the execution of the scientific method will go far toward the establishment of an hypothesis as a scientific law, we still have the question of the status of that law to consider. For we can never be absolutely sure that a scientific law has had or will have no exceptions. Chance contradiction can never be exhausted in the actual universe so long as there is an actual universe, which means that we can never take the absolute rule of natural law for granted. Absolute truth, or law, is known in only two ways: through the experience of sense and through the tautologies of mathematics. There is no error in sense experience, but only in its interpretation. We do feel what we feel, but we do not always interpret it correctly. As for the tautologies of mathematics, they are absolutely truistic, which is to say—absolutely true: $2 + 2 = 4$ because that is what we mean by 2 and that is what we mean by 4. But neither the validity nor the value of the equation is impugned by the admission of its tautological nature. Let us hope that we have left at least this part of Kant's teaching behind us.

How do scientific formulations of empirical hypotheses, or laws, fit into this scheme? We may admit at the outset that all such scientific formulations are probabilities. But this does not mean that they are opposed to causal laws; it only means that they are approaches to it. That is to say, probabilities are imperfect approximations of the absolute truth of natural law. All scientific investigation can be traced back to its ultimate source in sense experience. The feeling of hunger has prompted an interest in the prospects of satisfaction in the physical world, and hence has led eventually to the formulation of the governing conditions of satisfaction in the physical sciences. The feeling of love has prompted an interest in the prospects of satisfaction among other organisms, and hence has led eventually to the formulation of the governing conditions of satisfaction in the biological sciences. The absolutes of sense experience are the starting points of scientific inquiry. But the tautological truths of mathematics constitute the ideal toward which the probability laws of the sciences aspire. Needless to add, it is an ideal which is more closely approximated by some scientists than by others. But it is never reached by any, since in the sheer nature of the problem attainment of this sort is impossible. There is an enormous probability in favor of—let us say—Newton's second law; and even though in this case we go further than probability in understanding the causal factors at work, we can never be absolutely sure (and here "absolutely" is the key word) that a small body will not hesitate for a fraction of a second on its way to the ground, some day, in the remotely distant future. Thus the condition of tautology is, like all ideals, a limit of empirical knowledge. It is what we strive to get our empirical scientific laws closer and closer to. But the fact remains that what we seek is a causal law and not merely a high probability. Newton could have counted falling bodies forever and never arrived at the gravitation theory. A high probability is a signal to look out for cause.

With the rational and empirical method of science in mind, we may return to the assumptions of the system of natural law which lie behind it, the system which is the ideal and limiting goal of this method and indeed of all the professional activity of the scientists. For the system of natural law, concerning the conditions of which we seek knowledge, occurs in the actual world as the functions of organization. Functions may be described as the unchanging truths about changing things. They are fixed relations between fluxing actuals. In physics, for example, rate of change is something remote from change. All empirical scientific formulations are functions, that is to say, they are relations between terms within an organization, or relations between the organizations themselves. The question of whether the functions are within one organization or between organizations is merely a question of how large the isolate under investigation happens to be. For the whole of the system of natural law is a complex of parts and wholes, such that each part is a whole to its parts and each whole a part to its whole.

This system of parts and wholes, and indeed the entire hierarchical structure of the system of natural law, is illustrated in empirical science by the hierarchy of the sciences. Each science consists in a system of laws and the sciences taken together form a still wider system. Each science presupposes those other sciences which lie at levels below it and of which it is a further complication. For instance, crystals are complexes of chemical elements and chemical elements analyze into the entities of subatomic physics. All biological organisms must have the physical properties of mass, density, dimensions, etc. Roughly, this hierarchy runs as follows: the physical, the chemical, the biological, the psychological, the social. There may be intra-physical or supra-social organizations of which we know nothing. There are no absolute boundaries between these divisions, so that sciences such as physiological chemistry and social psychology exist in the hierarchy. These may be termed the empirical sciences, to distinguish them from logic and mathematics, the logical sciences which serve both as auxiliaries and ideals to the others.

The last sentence illustrates how the method and the goal of science fit together. The goal of science can only be approached by the method of science. But the method is shot through with the quality and conditions of the goal. Induction and deduction in this sense are both directions in a network of knowable relations. That is why a knowledge of the logic of scientific method is of such inestimable value to the scientist, and also why a knowledge of the empirical laws of a science, plus a laboratory, while necessary, are not by themselves enough in the way of equipment for the scientist. We may define science as a set of propositions having a one-to-one correspondence with the system of natural law which has its being independently both of cognition and of history. Scientific method is a unique combination of induction, experimentation and deduction which has been devised in order to ascertain the laws of science.

I should perhaps warn you before I go any further that the philosophy of science which I have been propounding is that of realism. It is that third view of science which I promised to explain; it is my own view, and I think it is also the implicit view of science if not always the explicit view of the scientists. But it is certainly not the most popular view held at the present. The most popular view is that of positivism. I should like to devote a few words of criticism to this prevailing but erroneous philosophy of science.

The modern version of positivism is variously termed logical positivism, logical or radical empiricism, or operationalism, by its followers. They are the contemporary proponents of that nominalism of which I spoke earlier. Their theory, quite simply put, is that only facts are real, while laws are mere summaries of facts. They refuse to accord generalizations any real standing except, of course, their own generalization, which is to the effect that no generalization has any real standing. The only unchanging thing they admit is their own statement that there is no unchanging thing. They deny the independent and possible being of that system of natural law, which the realists affirm as the goal of science. On this theory, practice is substantial but theory ephemeral. Metaphysics, they say, is nonsense.[4] This is thoroughly honest but hardly profound; since it is only what they think they are saying. What they are actually saying is that *your* metaphysics is nonsense, while their own nonsense is perfectly good metaphysics. For they sometimes admit that they are nominalists, which identifies their views with an ancient and well-recognized metaphysics. There is a good illustration of the viewpoint of positivism in *Alice in Wonderland*. We recall that after Alice and the animals emerge from the pool of tears they are trying to think of some way to get dry. When the Dodo suggests a caucus-race, Alice confesses that she does not know what a caucus-race is. "Why," says the Dodo, "the best way to explain it is to do it."

This story is perhaps applicable only to the naive positivism of Bridgman and to what he calls operationalism. A more subtle, and hence more dangerous, version of the doctrine is the variety of positivism set forth by Carnap and the other members of the Vienna Circle. For they wish to make an absolute cleavage between theory and practice. All sentences of empirical science, they say, are "object sentences"; while those of philosophical analysis are "syntatical sentences."[5] The reference of the former is to facts; that of the latter, to words. But facts can be subsumed by general statements (and one aim of science is to see that they are). Moreover, every general statement refers to a number of actual or possible facts, and a universal refers to an unlimited number of facts. Moreover, there are general statements which may be regarded as facts, so that the whole position only serves to increase confusion by its efforts at clarity. The flat-footed distinction between sentences in the "formal and material modes of speech"[6] seems clear because it is simple, but not all clear and

---

4. L. Wittgenstein, *Tractatus Logico-Philosophicus* (London, 1933), p. 4.003.
5. Rudolf Carnap, *Philosophy and Logical Syntax* (London, 1935), pp. 64-66.
6. *Sic*, in *op. cit., loc. cit.*

distinct ideas are either profound, or, for that matter, true.[7] To talk about the physical language as "the universal language of science" on the epistemological basis of "intersubjectivism"[8] is only to insist further upon the cleavage between knowledge and the external world which has already been advanced in the "modes of speech." Verification as a criterion of meaningfulness is an extremely subtle doctrine, easily perverted. Those sentences in the "formal mode" which contain contradictions cannot be described as meaningless; the difficulty with them is they mean too much. The test of the meaningfulness of a proposition is not whether it can or cannot be veri*fied,* but whether it is conceivably verifi*able.* As for the desire to stick to the facts with a minimum of theory, expressed in the canon of verification, it is highly praiseworthy; Occam's "Razor" is correct. But we must not forget that there is another side to the caution that hypotheses must not be multiplied beyond necessity. That is, that they must be multiplied *to* necessity. Theory is as real as fact. The evidence consists in the logical situation that you can get from fact to theory by means of induction, from theory to theory by means of either induction or deduction, but that you cannot get from fact to fact at all without the interpolation of theory.

The widespread influence of the positivists is a danger to the continuous progress of science. The positivists would inadvertently choke off scientific inquiry by closing doors instead of opening them. They wish to reduce all sciences to the science of physics; this crude "physicalism,"[9] as they call it, is the rankest nominalism. They wish to exclude from science certain avenues of research as being "theoretical" or "metaphysical." But the history of science is full of instances of accomplishments performed shortly after the positivists of the day had proved they could never be

---

7. It is interesting that Bertrand Russell in a work declaring his sympathies with the logical positivists appeals to Descartes. He maintains that "the whole subject of Epistemology is a product of Cartesian doubt." Bertrand Russell, *An Inquiry into Meaning and Truth,* p. 16. In contrast to this, see the arguments against Cartesianism set forth by another pioneer of symbolic logic, Charles S. Peirce, *Collected Papers,* 5.264 ff.

8. Rudolf Carnap, *The Unity of Science* (London, 1934), p. 67.

9. Credited to Newrath by Rudolf Carnap, *The Unity of Science,* p. 28.

done.[10] The charge of unverifiability, launched so often by the positivists, only serves to block inquiry. For we can never know absolutely that anything is unverifiable. A doctrine is valuable to the extent to which it preserves the freedom of inquiry of science, harmful to the extent to which it interferes with that freedom; it is as simple as that.

A similar error, albeit one not doctrinally held, is the preference of some theoretical scientists for practice, to the neglect of theory. We all agree that there is a certain unity of theory and practice in science. Any theory is a theory of practice, and any practice is the practice of some theory. But certain scientists, forgetting that the theory of the unity of theory and practice is a theory and not a practice, are fascinated with the importance of practice, and hence with the demand for their services that prevails in the going concerns of industry. It is a gain, of course, if industry can avail itself of the scientific results of the university and foundation laboratories. But in so far as the attraction for this affiliation leads scientists to neglect theory, science itself is being destroyed. There is no doubt that results important to pure theory are often found while pursuing some practical problem. But this is not enough; science is not an accident. It may avail itself of chance findings but cannot rely altogether upon chance.

There will be no theory to practice if we concentrate on practice to the exclusion of theory. Thus far, Europe has furnished the theories while we have been bent on applying them. In the 1939 report of the Rockefeller Foundation, Mr. Fosdick recorded that much of the funds of his organization had to be given to scientists engaged in pure science in Europe because he could not find enough of them in this country. As a consequence, the plight of the industrial corporations is sometimes paradoxical; having bent the university scientists toward practice, they find themselves forced to promote their own workers in pure science, as a practical investment for the future. Theory and practice are not chronologically simultaneous. The attempt to make theorists out

---

10. See the list of examples in J. W. Friend and J. Feibleman. *What Science Really Means* (London, 1937), p. 90, n. 19.

of practical men has proved a failure in more than one attempt in Soviet Russia, and, as one observer somewhat ruefully concluded after describing an unsuccessful experiment in turning factory workers into scientists, "Progress in scientific research apparently depends on the invention of scientific ideas, and not directly on the invention of ingenious apparatuses."[11] No, pure science must be pursued without any regard to practice—if it is to have any practicality. Hence the pure science of one day is usually the applied science of another. Pure science is the investment which society must make to insure its own practical advancement in the future.

The emphasis on operations and on practice, to the exclusion of independent law and of real theory, is evidence of positivism, the modern nominalistic error. We named it earlier, if you will remember, irrationalism, and later we described it under the fallacy of empiricism. Broadly speaking, what it denies is that there is an objective science of philosophy, and that there is an affirmative philosophy of science.

The denial of a science of philosophy is based upon its private method and its public failure of agreement. Philosophers are pictured as subjectivists who continue to look into their own minds for the truth about an objective world, and who can be brought to agree among themselves about absolutely nothing. These are to some extent misconceptions. The philosopher works in his mind and at a desk with paper and pencil. But so does the mathematical physicist. Philosophy, despite some appearances to the contrary, is based on experience with the objective actual world. The area of disagreement in philosophy is large; but this is not to say that there is no progress in the history of philosophy. The progress of philosophy is an actual dialectic; it pursues a zigzag course, like a river, sometimes for a little distance backward, but generally forward. And although its dialectic is not as direct as that of science, it makes gradual but inevitable advances.

The denial of the philosophy of science implies that science is free of philosophy and has nothing further to gain from it. This

---

11. J. G. Crowther, *Soviet Science* (London, 1936), p. 46.

is equally untrue but has a long history. You will recall that I mentioned earlier that the history of science was characterized by its efforts to free itself from philosophy. To the extent to which a science succeeded it made rapid strides; hence science came to look upon philosophy as a hindrance. Thus any return to philosophy now seems to science to be a step backward into an old confusion—a prejudice not lacking in justification. But we should not forget that it was philosophy that brought science up to the point where it could live a life of its own. Philosophy, so to speak, sets the fundamental problems; science is a technique for finding the answers.

Science and philosophy have to be separate disciplines in order to fructify each other. They must be able to come together for mutual benefits, like a man and a woman, but for this purpose they must exist quite independently. Fastened together like Siamese twins, they suffer and eventually die. The effort of science to free itself from philosophy was not an easy one. The poet Shelley could still call his tubes and retorts at Oxford "philosophical instruments," and physics is still referred to in Edinburgh as "natural philosophy." The scientists had to struggle so hard to get free of philosophy in order to pursue truth in their own exact way that they mistakenly thought that they must agree with the positivists in opposing all philosophy.

You can measure the success of science by the extent to which it has succeeded in separating itself from philosophy. Physics is the most free of philosophy, biology next, psychology less so, and sociology hardly at all. Hence the psychologists and sociologists are loudest in their professed scorn for philosophy. On the other hand, physics has been free of philosophy for so long that the physicists feel they can safely indulge their penchant for amateur philosophical efforts without harm to their professional standing in physics.

Please understand that I am not advocating the return of science to philosophy. In my view, philosophy is enriched to the extent to which its former subdivisions are enabled to leave it and to stand on their own feet as sciences. Parents never feel themselves impoverished when their children come of age and start in business for themselves; they only feel proud. It was never the purpose of philosophy to make empirical findings; that is the sphere of science. Those philosophers who fear the shrinking of philosophy because of the growth of science fail to understand the function of philosophy. The province of epistemology, or the theory of knowledge, seems to have passed to psychology. Ontology, the theory of being, now answers to the findings of physics. Cosmology appears to have become the property of astronomy. Logic is said to be only rudimentary mathematics. This is discouraging to many philosophers, when from the best interests of philosophy it should be counted all to the good. For in these philosophical studies there are still large regions which remain open to the philosopher. One of the chief purposes of philosophy is to develop a problem to the point where it can be taken over for investigation by an empirical science. Wherefore the rise of a new science is something of a triumph for philosophy.

Apart from the nurturing of immature sciences, philosophy has other duties which it can perform for science, duties which are both negative and positive.

On the negative side, it is the task of philosophy to examine from the logical point of view the assumptions, the method, and the conclusions of a science. This may be of purely scientific value. For instance, the physical sciences have an infallible method, and yet the American emphasis on practice to the neglect of theory, which we have already noted, is a threat to the continuance of these sciences. The physical sciences may have to become self-conscious about their method and aim, if they are to continue their advance. From the point of view of undeveloped sciences, this negative function of logic can be of inestimable value. For instance, the social sciences ape the *laws* of physics instead of the successful *method* of the physical sciences. Carey's law, that "The attraction of cities is directly as the mass and inversely as the distance,"[12] seems an amusing and extreme case but is perhaps typical. By abstracting the successful method of the

---

12. Quoted in E. A. Ross, *The Foundations of Sociology* (New York, 1915), p. 48.

physical sciences and offering it in applicable form, the logic of science can contribute enormously to the establishment of social science. Science, in other words, has a philosophy, and is aided by knowing what that philosophy is.

On the positive side, philosophy has its greatest task. This is the organization of a synthesis of knowledge, based on the facts of common experience, plus the contributions of all the sciences. If philosophy, as Whitehead suggests, "asks the simple question, what is it all about?"[13] it will have to go to the sciences as well as to other disciplines, such as art, and then make a vast synthesis out of its findings.

In order that we may distinguish between the subject-matter of science and the subject-matter of the philosophy of science, the following criteria may be found useful. Any proposition concerning only one scientific level is a proposition in science; any proposition concerning more than one scientific level (that is, concerning the relation between levels) is a proposition in the philosophy of science. Further, any proposition concerning a relation between science and another topic is also a proposition in the philosophy of science. Such an understanding of the philosophy of science provides philosophy with a very great sphere of activity indeed, and moreover one in which it could work side by side with science, each having its own private interests as well as its value for the other, while remaining completely independent disciplines.

I think I have said enough to show what the standpoint of realism is with respect to science. First, I have tried to indicate how the sciences came to hold philosophy in contempt, which is to say how the scientists came to hold the wrong philosophy. Then I have tried to indicate through a glance at the history and method of science that while the scientists profess the wrong philosophy they actually proceed in their scientific work on the basis of the correct philosophy. Thus the procedure of science implies a realism even while the scientists themselves often swear allegiance

---

13. "Remarks," *Philosophical Review*, XLVI (1937), p. 178.

to some form of nominalism. After an examination of the completely rational method of science and a study of its completely realistic assumptions and aims, I have endeavored to attack the continuation of the nominalistic philosophy under its present name of positivism. I have attacked also the wooing of the pure scientists by practice, because of the harm this might do to the progress of science as a whole. Finally, I have tried to show the proper relations between science and philosophy. I have pointed to the dim outline of a science of philosophy, and given evidence of the negative and of the positive functions of a philosophy of science. The test of any point of view is ultimately a pragmatic one, in the sense that it is useful if it leads to further inquiry, and dangerous if it stops inquiry. I sincerely believe that the viewpoint presented here offers the greatest possibilities to the future both of science and of philosophy, but I will be content if only I can be sure that I have successfully raised these problems and brought the issues which they represent once more to your attention.

IX

The Definition of Science

IT IS FASHIONABLE among scientists to profess a disdain for philosophy. Bertrand Russell, although himself a mathematician, has expressed the prejudice of scientists in a notorious epigram to the effect that mathematics is a subject in which one never knows what one is talking about nor whether what one is saying is true. We may take this expression as being intended by most scientists for philosophy. Of course this is very glib, and very amusing, and very typical. It is also a very understandable attitude when viewed in the light of the origins and history of science. But the fact is that philosophy cannot be dismissed so easily. Philosophy is a constant mistress who cannot be denied by being denounced. Even when the philosophers themselves turn traitor and join in the general chorus of denunciation, the problem of philosophy remains. The fact that the leading scientists in this age of the triumph of science have published books which are reputedly popular expositions of their work but which turn out to be excursions into philosophy, strikes us as most astonishing until we remember that the triumphs of science are what they are only through the solution of certain problems, the discovery of certain laws, which in turn give rise to other problems and the search for other laws. And these other problems and other laws are not available for settlement by science. As a consequence, scientists being human like the rest of us and gifted with the capacity for reasoning, which is the need to get at the bottom of things, turn to philosophy for an answer to the questions which vex them.

I said that I believe the situation becomes clearer upon a survey of the history of science. But this is not the task I have undertaken in this chapter. I propose rather to ask "What is science?" and to seek an answer among the suggestions which have been put forward recently by scientists and the philosophers of science. We shall see that some of these proposals are invalid and we shall have to dismiss them, but we shall also find some which are valid, and out of the latter endeavor to formulate our own solution.

We may begin with the definition by a mathematical physicist, Professor P. W. Bridgman of Harvard. He defines science in terms of the procedure of the scientist, a subjective interpretation. "In general," he says, "we mean by any concept nothing more than a set of operations; the concept is synonymous with the corresponding set of operations."[1] In other words, scientific concepts are merely symbols or convenient signs standing for certain physical operations. For example, when I say "three" I am indicating nothing more than the fact that I have counted, or can count, three objects. And when I say "gravitation" I am indicating nothing more than the fact that I have dropped, or can drop, some body, or, more broadly, that bodies can be dropped. This theory allows no objective validity to scientific laws. Indeed the subjective character of Professor Bridgman's conception is seen clearly by him. He tells us that "the nature of our thinking mechanism essentially colors any picture that we can form of nature,"[2] and that "from the operational point of view it is meaningless to attempt to separate 'nature' from 'knowledge of nature.'"[3]

This is the view which is known today as positivism. One of the founders of logical positivism, Professor Wittgenstein of Vienna and Cambridge University, has seen that positivism is involved in subjective idealism or solipsism, the theory that the

---
1. P. W. Bridgman, *The Logic of Modern Physics* (New York, 1928), p. 5.
2. *Ibid.*, p. xi.
3. *Ibid.*, p. 62.

mind of the individual actually creates his entire world, and he does not reject it.[4]

From the position of Professor Bridgman, the objective agreement which is achieved by scientists is impossible to explain. Science is left with no objective world for subject matter and must rest content with the behavior of scientists. But behaviorism, the study of behavior, which is a branch of psychology, has failed even to account for the whole of psychology; why should we accept it as adequate to account for the whole of science? You could watch a scientist working in his laboratory for hours, but if you did not know that he was a scientist and if he did not tell you what he was *trying* to do, you would never be able to understand what he was doing. It is clear that although an opinion such as Bridgman's be expressed, it is not deeply held, nor, what is more to the point, followed by any scientist. Professor Wittgenstein has proved more logical and inexorable in pursuing to their conclusions the implications of his premises. As has been noted many times in the history of philosophy, subjective idealism is finally irrefutable. If I choose to believe that my mind has created everything I feel and know of the external world, that, so to speak, the world is my oyster, there can be none to say me nay. So with a growl and wholly without envy we shall leave Wittgenstein literally to his own devices and pass on to the next definition of science.

The next definition we have to examine is that offered by Professor Morris R. Cohen. He says,

In turning to the sciences I emphasize their method rather than their results. For, in an age of scientific expansion, not only are the methods the more permanent features of the sciences, but the supposed results are often merely popularized conventions, utterly misleading to all those who do not know the processes by which they are obtained.[5]

Earlier, in the eighteenth century, Linnaeus, the botanist, had asserted the same position. "All the real knowledge which we

---

4. Ludwig Wittgenstein, *Tractatus Logico-Philosophicus*.
5. Morris R. Cohen, *Reason and Nature* (4th ed. New York, 1932), p. x.

possess," he wrote, "depends on method."[6] The definition of science as scientific method has at least the merit of being more objective than those of Bridgman and Wittgenstein, and of granting more objective validity to the world. Scientific method is something more than a set of operations; it is a definite method, susceptible of abstract formulation and available to all who choose to learn its nature and to follow it. It is more certain and dependable than the random, wayward and inscrutable behavior of the scientists, when that behavior is expected to be self-explanatory. We know that scientific method stands independent of any scientist or group of scientists, that it can never be lost or destroyed and that it yields results which are gratifying.

Yet even here we cannot stop, content that we have found the proper definition. For it is just the little independent validity which is granted to science by means of this definition which demonstrates its insufficiency. For by the conventional definition, a method is a procedure, a *means* toward an end and *not* an end in itself. So then we must ask Professor Cohen and ourselves: what is the end which the method of science is to accomplish? Science, to put the matter bluntly, is the method *of accomplishing what?* But Professor Cohen has already admitted that scientific method is expected to get results. He is, however, properly suspicious of them, and hastens to assert that "Dead or detached results lend themselves to the mythology of popular science, and ignorance of method leads to the view of science as a new set of dogmas to be accepted on the authority of a new set of priests called scientists."[7]

But this is where we must be wary. Cohen has played the old trick on us of showing the preference for one alternative over another, with the hidden assumption that the possibilities are exhausted by the two alternatives. By comparing the method of science with its "dead or detached results," he has made us see the advisability of accepting the definition of method. If this were

---

6. Quoted in W. C. D. Dampier-Whetham, *Cambridge Readings in the Literature of Science* (Cambridge, 1928), p. 188.

7. *Op. cit.*

the only choice, we had been guided right. But there remains yet another. We may, that is to say, attempt to determine the direction in which scientific method is *aimed,* and endeavor to define science in terms of its ambition rather than in terms of its accomplishment. We may safely hazard the assumption that the reach of science has as yet exceeded its grasp, that it has tried to do more than it has succeeded in doing. We may accordingly venture on the further assumption that it may do more in the future than it has done in the past, provided of course that we do not take too narrow a view of the future. So it appears that we must judge science not entirely by its method nor by its results but by its aims.

We have been seeking an answer to the question: what does science try to do? Some hint of the answer may be uncovered by taking a closer look at scientific method. Scientific method has long been thought to be identical with the logical process of induction, as with Bacon, or, more mystically, identical with intuition, as with Poincaré. Some basis for these identifications occurs in one of the steps of scientific method, which does contain the jump from the sense particulars of common experience to the universal laws which are independent of experience. But surely this is not the whole of scientific method. At either end of this process of induction, deduction is to be found. For it must be noted that the right inductions or "intuitions" do not occur to just anybody, but only to men who are seeking them, and more especially to men who have had some training in the field. Thomas Hunt Morgan, for instance, a scientist who works exclusively in the field of genetics, is not likely to put forward a brilliant hypothesis belonging in the field of astrophysics. Long and careful study of the previous work in a given science usually precedes scientific discovery. Thus deduction serves as a basis for induction. Again, the generalizations or laws which are reached by induction are tested against the empirical data, and if found to be not invalid, are used as a basis for deductions. Thus scientific laws are, as Peirce has pointed out, not merely the summaries of known facts but the finders of new ones. Deduction as well as induction can be a process of discovery.

We have noted, then, that induction is not the whole of scientific method, but that induction is both preceded and followed by deduction. What does this mean? Does it mean that logic and scientific method are one and the same? Not quite. Scientific method is logic plus the empirical sanction. The abstractions or laws of logic, when tested against the run of experience and found to be *not in*validated, are given the status of scientific laws. I say "not invalidated" advisedly, since the empirical test is a negative one; it contradicts and thus disallows some hypotheses, but cannot prove the validity of any. It tells us when so-called scientific laws are not laws but it does not, and indeed cannot, tell us when they are. Thus there is no known way to place the truth of a scientific law forever beyond doubt. That is, nevertheless, the aim of science. To discover laws which are as far as possible beyond doubt is the aim of every science, and this goal is one which is approached always more and more closely. That science whose laws are the least in doubt, and which seems to be approaching the nearest to eternal laws in its formulations, is the best science.

We have found out through scientific method something of what science tries to do. It tries to abstract from actuality to the independent conditions according to which actuality is made possible. That is to say, science endeavors to discover the "laws of nature." This is a definition which, so far, every scientific man would probably be willing to accept. But what does "nature" mean in this sense? In this last question we have posed the problem concerning which there is little agreement. But, proceeding on the basis of the examination we have just made into method, I believe that we are forced to accept Hartmann's definition, and say with him that " 'Nature' is only an expression for the totality of eternal laws not made by man."[8] Science, then, tries to discover the totality of eternal laws not made by man.

Surely we have come a long way from the subjective definitions of science which we examined at the start of our inquiry. Ac-

---

8. Nicolai Hartmann, *Ethics* (London, 1932), I, 203.

cording to these definitions, science was first equated with what the scientist thinks, then more objectively with what he does, and lastly with the method he follows. These were all rejected. For we found that science must be defined in terms of what the scientific method *seeks*. Science, then, may be defined as a certain means of striving toward the attainment of a certain end. The means is that of empiricism or scientific method: a series of inductions and deductions, starting from the level of common sense experience, and reaching to ever higher and higher abstractive levels, while the particulars of sense experience are constantly being sampled in order to make sure that they are not contradicted by the laws of the higher levels. The end is that of the discovery of the "totality of eternal laws." It is this means and this end which make up what we understand by science.

The scientist himself is always inclined to neglect the aim of science and to concentrate on the method. This is the preference of practice, and for practice there seems to be no difficulty that can arise from it. It is the rule of thumb of the scientist's laboratory routine. However, that harm can arise from this kind of guiding principle is made evident from a survey of present day science in America. Led by such men as Professors Bridgman and Lenzen, the attitude of positivism has come to prevail very widely among men of science in America. The spread of this philosophy has had disastrous effects, as Bernard Jaffe points out. When Mr. Jaffe made a trip to over thirty scientific laboratories in the United States he found a very amazing fact. With all the money that is given for scientific research by endowed foundations and rich individuals in this country, Jaffe was able to discover not a single instance of theoretical scientific work in progress. He says:

> The most significant impression I got was the change in the type of research gradually emerging in this country. The United States has kept pace with and even forged ahead of her European contemporaries in the fields of invention and applied science. American men of science have shown extraordinary ingenuity in building new tools with which to apply the fruits of abstract science. . . . Yet in the realm of pure science

... the United States ... lagged behind the leading European nations. We look in vain for a Newton, a Darwin, an Einstein, or a Planck.[9]

The point is significant. Surely the men he has named represent science at its very highest; yet with all our scientific endeavors we have not one to be compared with them.

The history of science reveals a sharply increasing desire on the part of scientists to speculate on the theory of science. The abstract and philosophical question of what science is in itself has begun to be a matter of much concern to the scientists, and the infinite variety of their conclusions in the matter leads us to the conviction that regardless of which theory of science proves to be right, most of them must be wrong. There is the danger that the course of science will be led astray by the speculations, or avowed abrogation of speculation, of the scientists themselves. For this reason, it is well to know, and for the scientist, to bear in mind, what the aim of science is. The definition of science as well as of scientific method must be kept constantly before the scientists.

In the beginning of this chapter, we used our disagreement with the opinions of some scientists as the starting point for discussion. I propose to close, therefore, by presenting some corroboration among the writings of the scientists for the position here set forth. I have said that the scientists do not agree among themselves in the matter of abstract definition. This is perfectly true. I am, however, able to call to my defense three of the greatest and most respected scientists of the day: Albert Einstein and Max Planck, the physicists, and Alexis Carrel, the biologist.

Einstein is fully cognizant of the fact that science does not depend upon the subject, that the subject who does the investigating merely discovers and does not "create" scientific laws. He says that "The belief in an external world independent of the perceiving subject is the basis of all natural science."[10] This would seem to make the subject matter of science the objective world

---

9. Bernard Jaffe, *Outposts of Science*, pp. xxi ff.
10. Albert Einstein, *The World as I See It* (New York, 1934), p. 60.

of phenomena perceived by the subject, the data of sense experience. But not at all. Carrel tells us that this is not the subject matter of science, either. He says that

> From the things encountered in the material world, whether atoms or stars, rocks or clouds, steel or water, certain qualities, such as weight and spatial dimensions, have been abstracted. These abstractions, and not the concrete facts, are the matter of scientific reasoning. The observation of objects constitutes only a lower form of science, the descriptive form. Descriptive science classifies phenomena. But the unchanging relations between variable quantities—that is, the natural laws, only appear when science becomes more abstract.[11]

But if the subject matter of science is not the subject of knowledge, which Einstein has discarded, nor the object of knowledge, which Carrel has discarded, then what in heaven's name can it be? To this question we are given the same reply by both men. It is the independent laws, which come to the subject through the object of knowledge but remain forever and always independent of the knowledge process. "In a certain sense," says Einstein, "I hold it true that pure thought can grasp reality, as the ancients dreamed."[12] And Carrel formulates the same conception in an even more precise fashion. He tells us that "For modern scientists, as for Plato, Ideas are the sole reality."[13] The same conviction is expressed by Max Planck, who understands very well that science is searching for eternal law.

> From the fact that in studying the happenings of nature we strive to eliminate the contingent and accidental and to come finally to what is essential and necessary, it is clear that we always look for the basic thing behind the dependent thing, for what is absolute behind what is relative, for the reality behind the appearance and for what abides behind what is transitory.[14]

Thus we see in the convictions of three of our leading scientists the confirmation of our own position. These quotations are of-

---

11. Alexis Carrel, *Man the Unknown* (New York, 1935), p. 1.
12. Einstein, *op. cit.*, p. 37.
13. Carrel, *op. cit.*, p. 236.
14. Max Planck, *Where is Science Going?* (London, 1933), p. 198.

fered by way of illustration rather than as proof. It is probable that were all scientists equally conscious of their profoundest beliefs they would support the same views. In a religious sense, surely every great scientist must understand that in being a scientist he is serving a cause whose ultimate purpose and fulfillment lies beyond him, that science is in no way a subjective and personal affair but rather an effort toward an end in the course of which the subject is to some extent sacrificed; that, in short, men exist for science and not science for men. And with the attainment of this understanding, definition can go no further.

X

The Relation of Logic to Experiment

THE EFFORT AT CLARIFICATION of scientific problems introduces cosmological implications. The confinement of speculation to the minutiae of science is inconsistent with the larger interests at stake. This is a fact which the modern positivists are loath to admit. Earlier philosophers of science have been occupied with the questions raised by empiricism; logical positivists are preoccupied with their own occupation. The advance in the understanding of science on the part of the various positivistic schools, let us say from Mach to Bridgman, has consisted in a gradual reduction to absurdity. At the other extreme, dogmatic idealists in effect dismiss science through superficial sublation by deeming it an intuitively created contribution to human culture. But despite the fact that the relation of logic to experiment has been effectively derived by such careful scholarship as that of Burtt in his *Metaphysical Foundations of Modern Physical Science* and has been sufficiently set forth by such brilliant and original thinkers as Peirce, the two aspects of scientific method still remain in the opinion of most persons mysteriously opposed.

Although science received its start from metaphysics, its nominalism from the medieval controversies of Berengar, Roscellinus, Occam, and others, it has seemed to progress by means of a program calling for the active encouragement of applied empiricism and for the strict prohibition against philosophical speculation. Needless to say, philosophy cannot be dismissed this easily, and the adoption of such an attitude is in effect the adoption of a philosophy: namely, that of nominalism. Without wishing to attribute any geographical or chronological location to ideas, it may be pointed out that the British philosophers of the seventeenth and eighteenth centuries concerned themselves with the the dilemma of nominalism, brought about through the attempt to find for experimentation some frankly realistic justification which did not seem to be forthcoming. Meanwhile on the continent the older tradition of systematic metaphysics was being maintained without any attention to the new requisite of empiricism, and was no less nominalistic. British empiricism, to which was added the radical empiricism of the Vienna school, and continental rationalism, have come down to us as the alternate positions thought possible to assume in the face of the given state of knowledge.

But such a dichotomy is indefensible, as will be made plain by an examination of scientific method itself. The apparent solution of difficulties of scientific method has been the leading aim of all modern philosophy, which has vacillated from one extreme view to another without coming to anything acceptable. Scientific method, however, is not difficult to grasp. It consists chiefly of two main steps: (a) From an examination of the conditions of actuality an explanatory hypothesis is inductively formed. The hypothesis is then checked against actuality for allowance or disproof. That is, if the facts of actuality do not disprove the hypothesis (and a single instance can effectively do this) it is assumed to be allowed. Allowance only means—not effectively disproved. Proof is never forthcoming, since any future instance of actuality, occurring against enormous probable odds, may constitute a disproof. The checking of hypotheses by the facts of actuality for allowance or disproof is the role played by experimentation in scientific method.

After the first step has been successfully accomplished, there is yet another to be taken. (b) The hypothesis must be reconciled with the given body of existing knowledge in the science in which it occurs; that is, it must be found logically consistent.

This step consists in the deduction of the hypothesis from the established principles and laws of the science. If it is found to form with them a unified and self-consistent system, it is assumed to have become worthy of being considered under the status of law. A law is not an eternal truth but an approach to eternal truth, since any scientific law is capable of being subsumed by some more general formulation. It enjoys the truistic state of being eternally valid only to the extent to which it continues to hold true. Nevertheless, the aim of all science is the discovery of the widest and most inclusive laws which are the least altered by the changing context of actuality, and which are thus least susceptible to revision.

It should be evident from the foregoing that experiment and logic, far from being contradictory, are the two necessary parts of scientific method; without either, method cannot justify its appellation of scientific. That this assertion is denied by uncompromising philosophers who see in experimentation only a threat to the authority of reason, as well as by uncompromising empiricists who see in logic only the uncontrolled dogmatizing of the scholastics, does not in any way change the situation. For illustration we have only to point to the illustrious examples set by the great scientists of the past and present. The occasional writings of Copernicus, Galileo, Boyle, Lavoisier, Newton, and Einstein evince a thorough comprehension of the dual function of scientific method. They have all understood that the laws of logic can never be violated if the results of experimentation are to have any validity, but that, on the other hand, theories of speculation will have to be carefully tested against actuality if they are not themselves to become ridiculously mythological. They have understood that the appeal to actual fact is necessary in the interests of an inquiry into the nature of existence, in order that the most universal principles of that existence should be made known. What happens does so because it is possible, but mere possibility of happening can never become an event. To achieve actuality, possibilities must be twisted and distorted into a spatiotemporal framework within the reach of experience.

The controversy between the defenders of logic and those of experiment can be settled by an appeal to scientific method, which shows them each to be essential parts of an integral process. The epochal systematizers of science have dipped into the conditions of actuality, fully comprehending that they would find there hints and confirmation of conditions that are independent of actuality. The scientific temper does not admit of the distinction between logic and experiment except as parts of a whole. Its greatest exemplars have neither been idle speculators nor "pencil scientists" exclusively, but have deftly employed both requirements to the advance of true science.

Part V
The Revival in Semantics

XI

How to Read a Word

THERE HAS BEEN MUCH controversy lately brought on by a renewed interest in an old subject. Speculative rhetoric has been renamed semantics and around it have clustered many ancient difficulties in modern dress. Vast differences between the viewpoints involved are revealing themselves. Since the systematic presentations of Whitehead and Russell, on the one hand, and of Carnap, Brouwer and their followers, on the other, showed what the realists and the positivists have been thinking about the fundamental problems of semantics, the discussion has from time to time flared up again, and borderline schools have claimed the attention of a popular as well as a technical audience. It now appears, for instance, that the reading of a book[1] requires the limited realism of Aristotelianism petrified into the Neo-Thomist philosophy. In opposition to this contention, it has been maintained that the reading of a page[2] necessitates the holding of the positivist philosophy with a particular slant, namely with special emphasis on the commission of the erstwhile fallacy of psychologism as a valid method of investigation. We may now enter this tragic-comic arena with a return to an old position but (as we may hope) with the fresh approach made possible by calling attention to some implicit but neglected aspects. This third position is that

---

1. Mortimer J. Adler, *How To Read A Book*, New York, 1940.
2. I. A. Richards, *How To Read A Page*, New York, 1942.

of metaphysical realism, which promises only to suggest certain factors which enable us to learn how to read a word.

The clarification of the problems of semantics requires an understanding of the philosophy of language in its more general features. The confusion between the various schools reaches down into the metaphysical fields of investigation involved in the attempt to ascertain the reference of language. A fundamental variety of the confusion is that between psychological and epistemological reference. Still more fundamental, perhaps, is another confusion, namely, that between epistemological and ontological reference. A comparison between the three types of reference—ontological, epistemological, and psychological—will carry us a long way toward comprehending the distinctions between them.

We may begin with the ontological, and as we reach the other two we shall note the diminishing objectivity and compulsion of verbal reference. This difference will be easier to follow if we discuss each in connection with the status of a word.

Ontologically, a word is a thing having being and perhaps also existence. Its being is that of a sign which indicates its object or referent. Such reference may be actually known to something or someone, or may contain the potentiality of knowledge by means of an unoccupied perspective. The effect of the reference of a word is exerted in two directions: in the effect of its object upon it, and in the effect of this relation upon a knower.[3] In the ontological context, however, the being of the word does not depend upon its knowledge relations. Its being does not depend upon its actual effect, either, but only upon its power of affection whether exercised or not. Only in epistemology are we free to assume the perspective on a word as possessed by a knower, and only in the ontological aspect of symbolism the perspective possessed by a referent of any kind. We must rather consider the word independently, for assuredly it is a valid entity in a world of other entities, an entity having internal and external relations and intrinsic and extrinsic elections. The symbolism of the word

---

3. For the direct and indirect reference of the first effect, see further below.

is not a mark on paper nor a part of the grammar, syntax, or vocabulary of a particular language nor even an intended meaning. It is a possible (or actual) sign.

Epistemologically, the word is no longer so stand-offish. We can approach it somewhat closer since we are considering it in the knowledge relation. What can be asked now is, how does a word give us knowledge? In the knowledge process, a word stands for an object to a knower in a certain function. The word is still a sign, but this time it is a sign pointing to something, a vector indicative of an aspect of something, *for* somebody. The word "shoe" consists of the four letters s-h-o-e in that order, and stands for some objects in their function of acting as an outer covering for the human foot, to any persons standing in the perspective furnished by the understanding (to that extent) of the English language. Obviously, shoes may have other functions; for instance, they may be weapons when thrown at cats. And the word "shoe" would be meaningless to persons (or things) who do not comprehend it as part of the English language. The word, any word, is a symbol. It stands for something to a knower who may be possible but not actual (since what is must at one time have been possible but not actual). Thus the actual knower cannot be deemed essential to the reference of the word. In the knowledge process, then, we are still considering the word as central, only this time in its knowledge capacity instead of in its being capacity. The function in which it stands may be any aspect of anything, so that abstractions as well as concretions may act as the function in which the referent is held by its symbol.

Psychologically, we are still closer to the word—now as close as we can get in our status of human beings. This time it is the effect of the word on the knower who apprehends the meaning which is to be taken as central. It is clear that in all psychological considerations we must depart from the strict semantical or rhetorical point of view. It is no longer the meaning of the word with which we are directly and chiefly concerned, but the effect of the meaning of the word on the psychological person. Perhaps this ought to be stated also in another way; the psychological person as he receives or is affected by the meaning of a word is of most importance. The word directs the hearer (or reader or thinker) to the perception of a vague image of its object and a more precise concept of its idea or universal. Here we have stepped out of the philosophy of language, into which category (despite what the positivists may suppose) the investigations of semantics belong, into the perspective of the psychology of language. Since men do think, and moreover can only think in terms of words, the role which words play in the complex psychological processes is an important and vital one. But the confusion of the word as it acts through knowledge on a psychological person, with the word as it exists for epistemology in the relation of the external world to a knower, serves no useful purposes of clarification.

Modern schools, including the various types of positivists and the Neo-Thomists, tend to confine their attention to the bearing which human beings have on meaning. This is anthropocentrism with a vengeance. We have seen above that words have their epistemological and psychological aspects, but we have noticed it only in the bearing which meaning has on the knowledge of words and on the thoughts about them. The modern emphasis is the reverse of this one, and concerns itself with the bearing which the knowledge of words and the thoughts about them have on meaning. The realistic emphasis is the one we shall assume, and we shall in what follows undertake to consider the relations of a word to the thing beyond it from the point of view of the word itself rather than from that of the problems of knowledge and of the mind. First in the consideration of the reference of the word is the object involved in such reference. To what does a word refer (a) directly and (b) indirectly?

(a) The direct reference of a word is not an actual object but rather a possible one, or in other words a universal or value. By universal here is meant an idea which is independent of actuality, a function between possible objects. By value is meant that which has the power to affect or to be affected, anything, in short, which has being. To utter the word "soap," let us say, is to refer to no particular cake of soap but merely to soap in general, which any cake can exemplify adequately if not perfectly.

It is often contended that the universal or general word does not refer to the universal or the general but to a particular image in the mind of the person making the utterance. This cannot be argued here, however, since it is a psychological problem, and we have agreed for the purposes of this investigation to abandon the psychological realm altogether. The question is what does the word refer to ontologically, not what do we as thinkers refer it to epistemologically or psychologically. It may be remarked in passing, however, that the presence of an image would not dispense with generality. The particularity or specificity of an image is a function of its clarity and conciseness. Memories of particular things which we have sensed involve specific features which sometimes may be almost photographic in their faithfulness of reproduction or representation. But the kind of image which is involved in the reference of the universal or general idea is quite different. It is extremely vague, and this vagueness is not its fault but its virtue; the vagueness furnishes the necessary degree of generality; for a vague image may refer to any actual thing answering to the name of the universal, and refers to one no more than to another. Vagueness insures that the reference of the image shall be sufficiently general and non-actual despite the fact that the image itself is an actual thing. The image which occurs to me when I think of soap in general no more resembles Lifebuoy than it does Octagon, though it plainly refers to an idea which both Lifebuoy and Octagon exemplify and illustrate.

A word is the arbitrary symbol standing for an idea. It can take almost innumerable forms. Thus for example the word, "boat," according to English dictionaries, refers to a small open vessel usually propelled by oars, sails or motor. But this meaning of boat does not require the English boat sound but is just as well served by sounds employed in other languages, as for instance, *bateau, batello, schiff, barco, scapha*. It can readily be admitted, of course, that the meaning involved varies somewhat from language to language, without in the least denying that there is a constant of meaning which is the same for all languages. For it is the meaning for which we require a sign and not the thing or even the sound. The direct reference of every word is the meaning to which it refers: the value or universal which stands in the fixed order of possible objects.

(b) The indirect reference of a word is the actual thing which illustrates the object of the direct reference. Any actual thing can be designated by a word, but in the process the designation is indirect, since it has to be mediated by reference to the universal or value. If this were not so, communication would be impossible, for we would not know what actual thing was being indicated in the reference. Suppose, for example, that once again someone refers to soap, this time in the sentence, "Bring me that cake of soap," while seated in a room in which there are a number of objects but only one cake of soap. Unless there were present in the minds of both speaker and hearer a knowledge of the value and function of "soap" in general, how would it be known exactly what was wanted? Only by the fact that, with some knowledge of soap, the particular cake of soap indicated would appeal to the hearer as being the closest thing in the room to an exemplification of "soap"ishness. There is no actual which is not to some extent general, just as there is none which is not to some extent unique. Therefore the actual requires mediation in its representation by a general. The word which refers to it always does so by means of an indirect relation through the general.

Words refer directly to abstract values and universals, and indirectly to actual things. The triangle of reference should read:

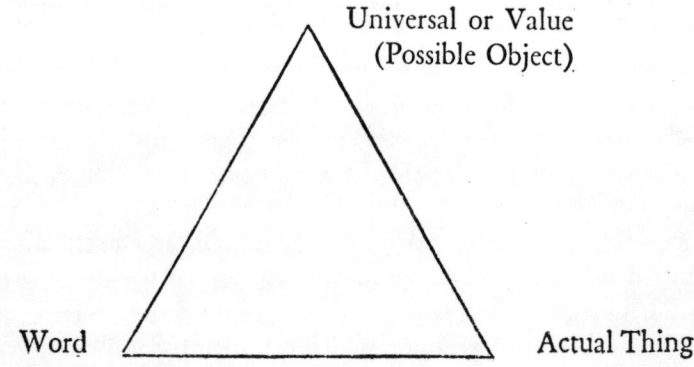

Roughly, we may speak of direct reference as reference and indirect reference as correspondence. In this sense the base line of the triangle marks a correspondence and the sides references. However, both the modes of being—possibility or the value-universal order—and actuality or the historical order are always being referred to in every reference of the word. The value or universal, soap, always implies some actual (or possible) experience with a cake of soap. The actual, *this* cake of soap, always implies some possible (or actual) experience with the abstract idea (or value) of soap. It is not going too far to state that in every enunciation of a word both its direct reference to the value-universal order and its indirect reference in actuality are always involved. Since actuality or existence is an exemplification of the value-universal order of being and a partial exemplification at that, it will be sufficient for our purposes if we concentrate upon the reference of words in the order of being rather than in that of existence. For in the order of being there are various levels of abstraction which will have to be examined in their relation to word-reference. But before we can do this, it will be necessary to explain first what is meant by value.

It is one of the metaphysical facts which few philosophies have ever denied that everything actual is in a constant condition of action-reaction with everything else actual. Now, those things which are not definitely self-contradictory are either in actual action-reaction or are possible of it. The possibility of action-reaction is what is meant in this chapter by value. The use or attraction which one thing has for another, the power of being, as Plato called it, the natural election as it was known to Bacon, is value. Value words, then, will mean those words which refer to possible value. Let us take as an example of a value word the word "green," whereby "green" is meant not any particular green but green in general, yet not the general function of green but the value, the possible feeling of green which anyone standing in the proper perspective could apprehend. This is an instance of the affective aspect of possibility, of the value-logic order of being. To recognize the generality and non-specificness of value is merely to admit that two instances of a specific value, say some quality like "sweet," contain significant elements of identity.

But there is in addition an analytical, functional, and relational aspect also, consisting of universals. By logic in this chapter is meant all forms of the whole-part relation of inclusion, employed in the sense in which both inclusion and implication are special cases. Thus universality and relationality are examples of logic. Universals are the abstract ideas of which values are the affective feelings. Universals will be known here as logic words. Logic words, then, will mean those words which refer to possible functions or relations. Let us take as an example of a logic word the word "green," where by "green" this time is meant the color which in the spectrum is intermediate between blue and yellow and which yields a certain wave-length. Unfortunately, language does not yet distinguish in single words between value and logic, so that the understanding of which meaning of the same word is implied must always be inferred from context. Thus when we say, "Green is preferable because it is so soft," we are not referring to the same meaning of green as we are when we say, "There is no green in the cadmium spectrum."

All possibility is independent of actuality absolutely. There are no degrees of independence, in the sense that one thing is less possible or more possible than another. Possibility is not probability which is likelihood; and it is not potentiality which is possibility in the actual thing. It is that ubiquitous and eternal realm of being upon which all actual existence as partial and selective depends. Value words and logic words are constituents of the order of being and as such are indistinguishable and equally independent of existence. Nevertheless, we can range them in importance, taking as our criterion their constituency in being. All logic is analytical, and since everything that does not come under the category of value must come under that of logic, in the ontological sense in which it has been defined, then what can logic be analytical of if not of value? All relations are ultimately relations of affective aspects, even though mediately they may be relations of relations.

Thus value words exist at the first level of abstraction and logic words at the second. The hierarchy is not a simple one, however, since each may be subdivided. Let us designate value words by the letter A and logic words by B. Then A_1 will be broader value words and A_2 will be narrower ones. The terms broader and narrower are employed here in their relative and not in their absolute meaning. Thus what is narrower in one context may be broader in another. In order to show this as well as to illustrate the particular-general relation of value words, it will be necessary to take three levels of generality of values. Let us take "color" as an example of A_1 and "green" as an example of A_2. Though both "color" and "green" are considered now as values, it is obvious that "color" is a more general value than "green" since "green" is a "color" and there are more "colors" than "green." Similarly, "quality" is a kind of value and "color" is a "quality," and there are more "qualities" than "color"; there are, for example, sounds, smells, tastes, and perhaps others which we lack the organs to detect. Values may be A_1 or A_2 according as they are considered in relation to a greater or a lesser value. Thus "color" is a more general value in relation to "green" but a more particular value in relation to "quality."

All logic words are abstractions from value words. Thus value must have had the relations which logic abstracts in order to make such abstraction feasible. Let us agree that logic words are represented by B, more general logic words by B_1 and more particular ones by B_2. As in the case of value, B_1 and B_2 are relative and not absolute, in the sense that what is B in relation to B_1 may be B_1 in relation to B_2. "Number" is particular in relation to "class," which is more general; but the same word, "number," is general in relation to "four," which is more particular. If we are considering B_2 in relation to B_1, then it is absolutely more particular. There are more "classes" than "number," and more "numbers" than "four." It should be noted, however, that the relation is not arbitrary once established.

The abstraction of logic words from value words makes them abstract, it does not make them mental. Logical relations, represented in language by logic words, are nevertheless parts of the non-linguistic world. The objective reference of the words are the relations which they name and indicate. This is an ontological situation, to which, for the special purposes of ontology, the situation involving our knowledge of it is subordinate. Relations are closer to the content of which they are analytic elements than they are to us. Logic, in other words, is an abstraction from objective and independent value, not from minds. Viewed ontologically the knowledge relation is a special type of relation, namely the relation to a knower. But there are more relations in the world than there are relations known, hence unlimited numbers of cases of the being of words as constituents of the world are more important than those restricted cases where they are known to minds.

Value and logic belong to the order of being. But the order of actuality, the historical order of events, is also represented in language. In addition to value words and logic words, there are fact words. By a fact word is meant a word which describes an actual. These are subdivided into specific references and names. Specific references employ either value words or logic words combined with some indicative word, such as the demonstrative pronoun, "this," as in the example, "this horse," where an animal of the species is present and, let us suppose, pointed out. Of course, "this," employed as a pronoun is in itself general, as is the word "horse"; but taken together as indicating an actual horse they become a fact word. Facts are more often represented by sentences than by single words. Specific references usually require two words to indicate unique particularity. When we wish to refer to a single actual thing as such, we usually designate it by a name. Names are fact words coined as such; they represent actual persons or things chiefly because they were invented for the purpose. An example of a name is Hester or Rover or Hilltop. Names are frequently general but that is not their intent. Hester is intended to designate a specific and partly unique woman; Rover, this dog and not any other; Hilltop, a house occupied by Hester and her dog and not any other. It is not easy to discover a name, or even a combination of names, which has not been employed by someone else at another time or place for a similar purpose. Thus we may know another Hester, but it is assumed that there is only one Hester St. John Tinkleberry. It is hoped that in so far as her name is general, it is the generality of a class having only one member. Nothing actual can be named absolutely, for the simple reason that nothing actual is absolutely actual. The difficulty experienced in finding absolutely unique and specific names has a metaphysical import. It is the actual nexus of values and relations that we are naming, and this part survives into definiteness.

The confusions between value words, logic words, and fact words are the sources of many misunderstandings, both metaphysical and practical. Perhaps the commonest confusion is that which exists between value words and logic words, a confusion which has already been mentioned in this chapter as arising from the failure of language to make the necessary sharp distinctions. Every general term is employed now in its value meaning and now in its logic meaning. Thus, as we have seen, "green" may be employed objectively to refer to a value or a relation, subjectively to refer to a feeling or a concept. It may indicate the value which "green" has in itself or the feeling I get from it when I see it (value); or it may indicate the wave length which its analysis yields or the idea which occurs to me when I think about it (logic). Since often the same verbal expression must stand for the two references of the term, confusions between value meaning and logic meaning are the commonest kind.

Since the content of actuality is value, the confusion between value and fact is an easy one to fall into. We may be referring to an actual exemplification of a value and not generally to the value, and yet, since it is the value itself which we must name, it is often mistakenly supposed that we are referring to the generality of the value. What do we think about when we taste an oyster? Is it *this* oyster, or *oyster*? Of course, we are tasting *this* oyster, but since we have tasted oysters before and know that to some extent all of them have a taste in common, it must follow that we identify the taste of this oyster with the others we have tasted. The difficulties between value and fact are more conceptual than verbal.

The third and last source of confusion between words and their references is that which occurs between logic words and fact words. To specify a relation is to assert that it holds of a given situation, but when we assert the relation of the situation it is sometimes difficult to understand where the emphasis is to be placed: on the relation or on the situation in which it occurs. For instance, when we say that "The decimal system is founded on the use of ten," we mean a different emphasis than we do when we say that "Ten is the lucky number at this roulette wheel," or when we say that "John dislikes all ten of his cousins." The difference is no doubt a subtle one here, and the reference is more difficult to be sure about than it is in the case of the other two types of confusion which have been discussed, but its understanding is all the more important.

In indicating confusions, we have been led back into a consideration of epistemological and psychological aspects. The reference of a word is ontological, but its confusions are epistemological and psychological. We have brought in other aspects here only with a view to emphasizing the ontological.

In the ontological analysis we learned that every word has both a direct and an indirect reference. Directly, a word refers to a universal; indirectly, to an actual thing. Value words are abstractions from actuality to possibility; logic words are abstractions from value. Many confusions arise from mistaking value words for logic words and for fact words, and logic words for fact words.

XII

Russell's Infidelity to Realism

A Reply to Bertrand Russell's Introduction to the Second Edition of The Principles of Mathematics

THE DECISION TO REPRINT *The Principles of Mathematics* after thirty-four years was a most fortunate one. The work has had a tremendous influence and should be available to all interested students of the subject. Here is a landmark in the history of thought which many persons have heard about but never seen, and now the new edition will place it before the public again. The importance of *The Principles* rests to some extent upon two of its points: it is the first comprehensive treatise on symbolic logic to be written in English; and it gives to that system of logic a realistic interpretation. It is with the second point chiefly that these remarks are concerned. Symbolic logic as a discipline is here to stay whatever its philosophical interpretation, but the interpretation itself is still a doubtful question. Of course, the metaphysical interpretation of symbolic logic is not strictly a problem of logic but lies on the borderline between logic and metaphysics. In all probability, it belongs to metaphysics, more particularly to the metaphysics of logic. But it is a most important topic for all that, and moreover constitutes a field in which much yet remains to be done.

Are the foundations of symbolic logic realistic or nominalistic? A reading of *The Principles* should be sufficient to convince any sceptical person of the explanatory usefulness of the realistic philosophy. The assumption that relations are real and non-mental if not true has at least a pragmatic value; and since the criteria of truth cannot be anything except self-consistency and range of applicability, realism must to a large extent be true. That must have been also Russell's opinion when he wrote *The Principles*. Since then he has altered his position sharply, for now in the new Introduction he challenges the validity of the philosophy underlying the work. He says:

Broadly speaking, I still think this book is in the right where it disagrees with what had been previously held, but where it agrees with older theories it is apt to be wrong. The changes in philosophy which seem to me to be called for are partly due to the technical advances of mathematical logic. . . . Broadly, the result is an outlook which is less Platonic, or less realist in the mediaeval sense of the word. How far it is possible to go in the direction of nominalism remains, to my mind, an unsolved question.[1]

The present chapter takes issue with Russell on his new thesis, and is thus in the position of making out a case for an old book in order to defend it against the new rejection by its own author. In other words, the old Russell is to be defended against the new Russell.

Perhaps the simplest method of accomplishing this purpose would be to set forth all the arguments which have ever been advanced by anyone in favor of the truth of realism, and to refute all the arguments which have ever been used against it. But to attempt to defend realism in such a fashion would mean to become embroiled in a controversy which is most likely endless. There is another alternative. Russell puts forward certain specific and clear-cut objections to the validity of his former position. The simplest way would seem to be to show that these objections are groundless arguments, to demonstrate that his present reasons for acceding to the invalidity of his old work are themselves invalid. This will be the method adopted; and we shall take the arguments one by one in the order in which they are introduced.

The first attack upon realism consists in questioning the ex-

---

[1]. Bertrand Russell, *The Principles of Mathematics*, 2nd. ed., p. xiv. All references, unless otherwise stated, will be to this work.

istence of logical constants. Russell asks, "Are there logical constants?" By logical constants is meant such expressions as "or," "and," "if-then," "1," "2," and so on. Russell says that "when we analyze the propositions in the written expression of which such symbols occur, we find that they have no constitutents corresponding to the expressions in question."[2] One way in which the refutation of an opponent's arguments can be made to seem the most effective is first to overstate his position for him. This way, his position appears to be self-evidently untenable and is ripe for ridicule. Where possible, Russell has done this for himself by describing realism in a manner in which it is certain he himself never accepted it even when as a realist he wrote down *The Principles*. Selecting as typical of the logical constants the term "or" he says, "not even the most ardent Platonist would suppose that the perfect 'or' is laid up in heaven, and that the 'or's' here on earth are imperfect copies of the celestial archtype."[3] Do there exist any longer realists who would be willing to accept such a description of their belief? To confine the realistic position to such an extreme version would be equivalent to asserting of all nominalists that they are admitted solipsists, which is very far from being the case. Even Russell has asserted that the question of how far it is possible to go in the direction of nominalism is as yet an unsolved one. Much the same defense might be given for realism.

We can accept a modified realism without asserting the existence of a realm of essence, or heaven, in which perfect actual things are stored in order to cast the shadows which we mistake for them. Certainly there is no perfect "or" laid up in heaven, but this does not establish nominalism or deny a modified realism. From the position of modified realism, the logical constant "or" is logical because it can be neither successfully contradicted nor shown to involve self-contradiction, and a constant because it involves a constant relationship. The relation "or" is that of alternativity, which is a logical possibility, an unchanging rela-

---

2. *Ibid.*, p. ix.
3. *Ibid.*, p. ix.

tionship which actual things *may* have (but do not have to have) and which has being (since it *can* exist) regardless of whether it exists at any special place and date or not. Thus the reply to Russell on this point must be as follows. The logical constant "or" is a symbol which occurs in some propositions. When it occurs in true propositions, and sometimes when it occurs in partly true propositions, "or" has an objective constituent, the constituent corresponding to the expression in question being the relation of alternativity.

Russell next argues that the theory of descriptions, as it is called in symbolic logic, dispenses with the actual particulars which do service as the constituents of some logical terms. For instance, he says that in "Scott is the author of Waverley" there is no constituent corresponding to "the author of Waverley." The argument consists in an analysis of the proposition; and the analysis reduces the proposition to the following. "The propositional function 'x *wrote Waverley* is equivalent to x *is Scott*' is true for all values of x."[4] Russell is correct in his assertion that this does away with the realm of Being of Meinong, in which the golden mountain and the round square have a place. The theory of descriptions does "avoid this and other difficulties," but does it refute realism? The evidence here would seem to be quite to the contrary. The task performed by the theory of descriptions is the elimination of all *specified* actual particulars as the constituents of terms in propositions, and the substitution of propositional functions. Now propositional functions are relations, possibilities which can be specified by actual particulars. These relations or possibilities certainly exist. The relation between the x who wrote Waverley and the x who is Scott—one of equivalence—is "true for all values of x," which is to say the relation can be assigned constituents by assigning specific values for x but holds whether or not specific values be assigned for x.

The theory of descriptions not only refutes the realm of essence but also happily points out the enormously wide gulf which yawns between realm-of-essence realism and modified realism, a

---
4. *Ibid.*, p. x.

gulf as wide as that between realism and nominalism. We do not have any actual golden mountains and round squares; hence the assertion of Meinong that they must exist in a realm of being is equivalent to the assertion not of realism but of crypto-materialism, which is a form of nominalism. Nothing exists really except actual physical particulars, or so asserts nominalism. But golden mountains and round squares *are* actual physical particulars: they are *remote* actual physical particulars, or so asserts crypto-materialism. The refutation of such contentions, accomplished logically by the theory of descriptions, argues for rather than against a modified realism, since it asserts that real existence means possibility of actualization, expressed in propositional functions.

Much the same argument as that employed above can be used to refute Russell's reasons for the abolition of classes. The cardinal numbers, Russell would persuade us, can be made to disappear in a cloud of propositional functions, and he accordingly performs the trick.[5] The numbers 1 and 2 are resolved into invariant relations holding between other invariant relations. The question is, have the numbers "entirely disappeared"? As numbers they have, because numbers are not and never were anything more than relations. Russell in his analysis has revealed their true nature; but he has not caused the relations which they essentially represent to disappear, nor has he given one argument in refutation of realism thereby. Any argument to show that specified things are not independent things but rather things dependent upon invariant relations which they exemplify can hardly be said to be an argument *against* realism. What are invariant relations, what are propositional functions, if not possibilities susceptible of actualization but never necessarily demanding it in order to show their being?

The fact is that Russell has not "dissolved" any numbers nor made them "disappear." He has merely shown them to be invariant relations between variables. This is very far from having disposed of their realistic character. Russell often talks about

---
5. *Ibid.*, p. x.

logic and mathematics as though he had never heard of any realism except the extreme realism which supposes that the Platonic Ideas are laid up forever in a heavenly realm of essence. Even Plato did not always believe this but sometimes argued for a status of possibility for unactualized as well as for actualized universals. Invariant relations, then, are what *can happen* to variables, and numbers are real possibilities as are all invariant relations which are non-contradictory.

Russell continues his argument against logical constants by carrying it over to cover "points of space, instants of time, and particles of matter, substituting for them logical constructions composed of events."[6] The substitution was made following Dr. Whitehead's suggestion. Russell is appearing to present many arguments whereas he is only presenting one. This one is the repeated assertion that since logical constants prove to be relations they are not fixed in the sense we once thought they were. They are not fixed because they have no constant reference; hence realism is untenable. The argument is no more valid in the case of physical relations than it was in the strictly logical field. Space, time, and matter have been resolved into relations varying from frame of reference to frame of reference, but invariant given the frame. The important point to bear in mind is that they are relations instead of actual things, relations which can be exemplified by the actual things to which they refer but not requiring actual things or any specific reference in order to be. This is an argument in favor of realism, and decidedly not one against it.

Russell is taking for granted throughout his argument concerning the disappearance of logical constants a confusion between two distinct meanings of reference. There is (1) the reference of a symbol to its logical possibility, and there is (2) the reference of a logical possibility to its actual exemplification. Russell refers to them both by the same expression, "having a constituent," which is a source of unutterable confusion. In order to show what we mean let us give an example. (1) The letters a-u-t-o-m-o-

---

6. *Ibid.*, p. xi.

b-i-l-e form a symbol, namely "automobile," which may refer to the possibility of constructing a horseless carriage propelled by an internal combustion engine, assuming that there already were or were not any, as in the sentence, "Let us build an automobile." (2) The letters a-u-t-o-m-o-b-i-l-e form a symbol, namely "automobile," which may refer to an actual physical object, assuming that there was at least one, as in the sentence, "This automobile runs well." The unfounded assumption that the refutation of the validity of meaning (2) also does away with the validity of meaning (1) accounts for most of the error responsible for Russell's change of viewpoint.

But perhaps there is more hidden beneath the surface of Russell's argument than we have been able thus for to grasp. A further quotation proves this to be the case. Russell goes on to say that "none of the raw material of the world has smooth logical properties, but whatever appears to have such properties is constructed artificially in order to have them."[7] This is only another way of saying that whenever there appears to be a one-to-one correspondence between logic and actuality it must have been faked. The argument runs that since logic is ideal and actuality is not, logic cannot refer to anything actual. There is an assumption here which will not bear examination. Why cannot the part refer to the whole, the limited to the unlimited, the example to its exemplar, the actual to the ideal? Let us suppose that the fastest airplane would be one which could fly an infinite number of miles in zero seconds, yet we have to admit that, although no airplane flies that fast and probably none ever will, the airplane which flies four hundred miles per hour is nearer to the ideal than one which flies only one hundred and fifty miles per hour. The equivalence to four of two and two is tautological because that is what we mean by two and that is what we mean by four; yet this knowledge helps us to manipulate everything from apples to madonnas.

None of the raw material of the world needs to have smooth logical properties in order to refer to logic as long as it is admissi-

---

7. *Ibid.*, p. xi.

ble for a cat to look at a king. Russell's charge that logic is an artificial construction, since nothing actual is ideal, also assumes the confusion that we have pointed out above in the example of the automobile, the confusion between two distinct levels of reference. Because Whitehead has persuaded Russell to substitute "logical constructions composed of events" for particles of space, time, and matter, Russell feels compelled to the further conclusion that logic is linguistic. This is the nominalistic view; the realist would say that language is logical. But then realism depends upon a careful segregation of the two levels of reference. Smooth logical properties are characteristic both of the tautologies of logic in language and thought, and of the possibilities to which they refer. Actuality exemplifies partially this logical possibility. For the raw material of the world to have smooth logical properties, there would have to be an identity between actuality and possibility, and this would be a signal that everything had happened that could happen. Until then, it is as much a requirement of actuality as it is of logic that the ideal contain more than the actual world.

It would appear that we have wandered a long way from our original point but such is not the case. Having changed over from "points of space, instants of time, and particles of matter" to "logical constructions composed of events," Russell holds Whitehead responsible for his change from the realistic to the nominalistic interpretation of symbolic logic. But a careful inspection of Whitehead's own subsequent writings shows that what Whitehead was endeavoring to do was to change Russell over from a "substance" to a "relations" philosophy. In *Process and Reality* Whitehead himself still finds "eternal objects" (i.e., universals) consistent with the adoption of events. Whitehead's "events" upon analysis reveal themselves to consist of invariant relations, even the Platonic *receptacle* of simple spatiotemporal location having gone by the board.

The statement, "Time consists of instants," is shown by Russell to be false by means of an interpretation of time in terms of comparatively contemporary events. But the argument about the time statement is much the same as that we have given above concerning the cardinal numbers (p. 273). To demonstrate that an entity is analyzable into a process in terms of propositional functions does not invalidate its logically constant nature as an entity. A logical constant should only be expected to be *logically* constant, *not* actually constant as well. Time is actually composed of instants, as anyone who has actually tried to live by the clock can testify. Yet these instants resolve themselves, like all other actual things, into logical events, entities consisting of relations.

Russell's adversion from the view that realism is a valid metaphysical basis for symbolic logic rests chiefly upon the interpretation of the status of logical constants. Logical constants seem to Russell to disappear between actual things (the reference of language) on the one hand, and the formal properties of language itself on the other.[8] Thus by arbitrary definition of terms he has managed to argue himself out of realism. For language itself is merely a shorthand method of formulating and communicating the apprehension of ideas, and not anything in itself. It is safe to assert that everything in language refers beyond itself. Russell himself maintains that "it seems rash to hold that any word is meaningless."[9] Russell's error is the same one that we have pointed out above, and consists in assuming that there is only one level of reference, a situation which automatically precludes realism. The seeds of this confusion were already contained in *The Principles,* where Russell assigned the distinction between intension and extension to psychology.[10]

Language has two kinds of reference: tautological propositions refer to possible things, whereas propositions about matters of fact refer to actual things. There is a third classification, and one that contains the greatest number of propositions: hypotheses, of which we do not know the exact reference, if any. Hypothetical

---

8. *Ibid.,* p. xi. The first sentence of the last paragraph reads, "Logical constants, if we are able to say anything definite about them, must be treated as part of the language, not as part of what the language speaks about."
9. *Ibid.,* p. 71.
10. *Ibid.,* p. 69.

propositions may be false, and therefore not propositions in the true sense at all, or they may belong to tautologies or matters of fact. Thus the distinction between hypotheses and the other two kinds of propositions is a matter of ignorance (psychological), but the difference between tautologies and matters of fact, or between intension and extension, is a genuine objective difference. Russell's error lies in the supposition that tautological propositions are exhausted by the language in which they are expressed and do not refer to anything objective. Thus he disproves realism by first assuming its denial. Logical constants, like all other logical terms, are part of what language expresses, expressed as part of the language. So long as tautological propositions are valid and have a reference, logical constants are emphatically *not* confined to the choice between referring to actual things and being merely verbal (i.e., having no reference at all).

"No proposition of logic," Russell goes on to say, "can mention any particular object." And he proceeds to show that the well known syllogism involving the mortality of Socrates is a special case of a wider and more abstract formulation. The point taken here seems to be quite correct: logic is ideal, and if actual things could be mentioned in ideal propositions, it would infer that actual things were ideal. There are, however, two dangerous fallacies lying in wait upon the outskirts of this argument. One is the conclusion that if logic is ideal and actuality is not, logic can have no reference to actuality at all. This would make of logic a kind of harmless but useless exercise or game, having no application to the real world. The point is that the Socrates syllogism is an *application* of logic. Logic, like mathematics, is ideal and does not refer to any specific actual thing, but it may be applied to any and all actual things. As a proposition in mathematics $2 + 2 = 4$ does not refer to shoes or ships or sealing wax, cabbages or kings, but it may refer to any one of them. The fact is that the abstract syllogism does not apply to Socrates but the form of the argument expressed in the syllogism does not have to be a valid syllogism. The mortality of Socrates is contingent upon the agreement of the mortality of all men with established fact. When taken as so applying, the syllogism is an actual proposition and not a tautological one.

What Russell seems to be arguing against in this passage is the absoluteness of ideal possibles occurring as such in actuality. The dilemma is this. If actual things are made ideal, then logic does not seem to be a discipline akin to mathematics and independent of actuality. But if actual things have nothing logical about them, then ideal disciplines such as logic and mathematics belong to a remote realm of essence and bestow their reality only upon a world superior to our actual world. Thus in protecting realism from the errors of extreme realism, Russell falls into the extreme opposite to nominalism. Logic in the form of "if-then" propositions is not stating anything about logical constants (by which Russell sometimes seems to mean ideal actuals). Neither Socrates nor mortality is asserted in the Socrates syllogism, but (granted the postulates) merely an invariant relation between them.

The question of contradictions is the final argument which Russell launches against his old position.[11] These are chiefly three: the mathematical, the logical, and the linguistic, and Russell offers an example of each.[12] It will be necessary, therefore, to confine our remarks to a few words about each of these specific contradictions as they are set forth in the Introduction.

Burali-Forti's contradiction rests on the assumption that **N** is the greatest of ordinals. But the number of all ordinals from **O** to **N** is **N** + 1, which is greater than **N**. Does the solution of this contradiction lie in the simple fact that **O** is not an ordinal number at all? Zero may be a cardinal but not an ordinal number. A symbol defined by "nothing" is perhaps required for the ordinal corresponding to the cardinal, zero. For zero is not nothing; it represents the absence of *some*thing; namely, the cardinal number before one. Zero enumerates but does not order.

The second contradiction may be stated in Russell's words:

---

11. *Ibid.*, p. xii.
12. *Ibid.*, p. xiii f.

We know from elementary arithmetic that the number of combinations of n things any number at a time is 2^n, i.e., that a class of N terms has 2^n sub-classes. We can prove that this proposition remains true when n is infinite. And Cantor proved that 2^n is always greater than n. Hence there can be no greater cardinal. Yet one would have supposed that the class containing everything would have the greatest possible number of terms. Since, however, the number of classes of things exceeds the number of things, clearly classes of things are not things.[13]

The key to this contradiction lies in the theory of subclasses. Russell's proof that "classes of things are not things" rests on the argument that the last and most inclusive class is not a thing. But if there are subclasses there may be subclasses of subclasses and so on, so that classes form a hierarchical series of inclusiveness, and everything may be a class to the things below and a thing only to the classes above. This would make every class a thing to the classes above (except the last class which would have no classes above it to make it a thing), and would make every thing a class to the things below (except the first thing, i.e., the actual unique thing, which would have no things below it to make it a class). Then there would be first (i.e., actual unique) things that were not a class, and there would be a last class that was not a thing. But all other classes of things would be things.

The third contradiction is linguistic, and, as Russell himself suggests, following Ramsey, linguistic contradictions can be solved by broad linguistic considerations, and lead to the so-called theory of types. The theory of types is a more detailed formula for which de Morgan's "universe of discourse" has already warned us we should have need. But even the theory of types must be applied judiciously. For instance, Russell wants to apply it to show that classes of things are not things. What should be asserted is that classes are not things in their relation to things but are things in their relation to more inclusive classes. He is correct, however, in asserting that the relations of a thing are not the relations of the class of which that thing is a member.

---

13. *Ibid.*, p. xiii.

The fundamental realism of Russell hardly needs to be insisted upon at the last. Russell, as his own remarks betray, is a realist. However, it may be illuminating to show by chapter and verse what a profound realist he was, and perhaps still is. Let us run through *The Principles* for examples of realism. We shall not take the main categories of the work as evidence (although many of them are) but rather be on the lookout for more subtle remarks, on the grounds that the presence of realism in the assumptions will betray itself more clearly in observations and turns of thought, which could only have been implied by an unacknowledged though none the less real and effective fundamentally realistic viewpoint, than it would in more candid expressions.

The symbolic representativeness of words is the first indication we come across in our search. Russell said, *"Words* all have meaning, in the simple sense that they are symbols which stand for something other than themselves."[14] Surely, Russell does not mean here that words always refer to *actual* objects. The inference clearly is that the reference of *some* words, at least, is to possible objects. Another instance is the wholly realistic "distinction between a class containing only one member, and the one member which it contains."[15] The necessity for the viability of such a distinction is highly indicative of a fundamental position. In the same direction is the warning to beware of the extremely narrow limits of the doctrine that analysis is falsification. The whole may be more than its parts, he pointed out, but they are real parts. And while analysis cannot give us the whole truth, it can give us truth.[16] "Where the mind can distinguish elements, there must *be* different elements to distinguish; though, alas! there are often different elements which the mind does not distinguish."[17] But just as analytic elements are real so are the synthetic wholes, or complexities. "All complexity is . . . real in the sense that it has no dependence upon the mind, but only upon the nature of the

---

14. *Ibid.*, p. 47.
15. *Ibid.*, p. 130.
16. *Ibid.*, p. 141.
17. *Ibid.*, p. 466.

object."[18] Since the "complexities" referred to are not only meant to be those of actual objects, possible organizations alone can be intended.

". . . the whole denial of the ultimate reality of relations" is "rejected by the logic advocated by the present work."[19] These are plain words, and the feeling is unavoidable that Russell meant them. Order is reducible neither to psychology nor to Omnipotence itself.[20] Relations, and not terms, are necessary to order.[21] In a brilliant anticipation of modern macroscopic physics, Russell even went so far as to indicate the relational analysis of matter. Since "the only relevant function of a material point is to establish a correlation between all moments of time and some points of space,"[22] it follows that "we may replace a material point by a many-one relation."[23] The coupling of such a denial of actuality with the rejection of psychology already mentioned leaves nothing but the reality of a realm of possibility to be intended. This interpretation is confirmed by the assertion that "though a term may cease to exist, it cannot cease to be; it is still an entity, which can be counted as *one,* and concerning which some propositions are true and others false."[24]

As if in support of such a realistic thesis, Russell goes even farther than this in *The Principles,* in a definition of being. He says,

Being is that which belongs to every conceivable term, to every possible object of thought—in short to everything that can possibly occur in any proposition, true or false, and to all such propositions themselves. Being belongs to whatever can be counted. . . . Numbers, the Homeric gods, relations, chimeras and four-dimensional spaces all have being, for if they were not entities of a kind, we could make no propositions about them. Thus being is a general attribute of everything, and to mention anything is to show that it is.[25]

---

18. *Ibid.*
19. *Ibid.*, p. 166.
20. *Ibid.*, p. 242.
21. *Ibid.*
22. *Ibid.*, p. 468.
23. *Ibid.*
24. *Ibid.*, p. 471.
25. *Ibid.*, p. 449.

The entities of mathematics have being and truth, since "mathematics is throughout indifferent to the question whether its entities exist,"[26] and "what can be mathematically demonstrated is true."[27] Furthermore, propositions that are true are immutably true: "there seems to be no true proposition of which there is any sense in saying that it might have been false. One might as well say that redness might have been a taste and not a colour. What is true, is true; what is false, is false; and concerning fundamentals, there is nothing more to be said."[28] But a true proposition is one which makes an assertion about that to which it refers. There is no difference between a true proposition and an asserted proposition.[29] Thus mathematically demonstrated propositions are likewise assertions. But pure mathematics, such as geometry, is likewise "indifferent to the question whether there exist (in the strict sense) such entities as its premisses define."[30] What else could such non-existential propositions, as those of geometry, assert, except a realm of possibility, of potential being? Since mathematics is "merely a complication" of logic, the primitive ideas of mathematics being those of logic,[31] logic must share the non-existential reference which has been asserted by mathematics.

As a realist (and there can be little doubt that Russell was a realist when he wrote *The Principles*) he was opposed to the earlier positivists, particularly Mach and Lotze. In the course of his opposition, it is clearly revealed that some of the doctrines of these modern nominalists, the logical positivists, are alien to his position in *The Principles,* since positivism in certain respects remains what it was.

For instance, against Mach's argument that the actual world being only what we find it, "any argument that the rotation of the earth could be inferred *if* there were no heavenly bodies is futile. This argument contains the very essence of empiricism, in

---

26. *Ibid.*, p. 458.
27. *Ibid.*, p. 338.
28. *Ibid.*, p. 454.
29. *Ibid.*, p. 504.
30. *Ibid.*, p. 372.
31. *Ibid.*, p. 429.

a sense in which empiricism is radically opposed to the philosophy advocated in the present work."[32] The philosophy advocated is "in all its chief features" derived from G. E. Moore,[33] and the G. E. Moore of 1902 was certainly a realist. Russell did in fact see quite clearly what the issue was. "The logical basis of the argument [i.e., the one stated above concerning the rotation of the earth] is that all propositions are essentially concerned with actual existents, not with entities which may or may not exist."[34] And on this argument, Russell had already stated his own position definitively, as we have seen.

The fate of Lotze in Russell's work is no better than that of Mach. Mach had confined reality to actuality; Lotze, so far as Russell was concerned, repeated the same error in other terms, for after Leibniz, he had defined being as activity.[35] Russell refutes this definition by showing that if activity alone were real, only valid propositions would have being, since these and these alone would refer to active objects. But since false propositions which have no reference still have being, "being belongs to valid and invalid propositions alike."[36] Again, the Kantianism of supposing that propositions which are true are so because the mind cannot help but believe them, is an error due to the failure to make the "fundamental distinction between an idea and its object."[37] "Whatever can be thought of has being, and its being is a precondition, not a result, of its being thought of."[38] Thus he has in his refutation of Lotze rejected nominalism on two scores. He has rejected that objective form of nominalism which consists in holding that actuality alone is real, and he has rejected that subjective form which consists in holding that what the mind knows is real in virtue of being known.

Even now, although he has gone a little way with the logical

---

32. *Ibid.*, p. 492.
33. *Ibid.*, p. xviii.
34. *Ibid.*, p. 493.
35. *Ibid.*, p. 450.
36. *Ibid.*
37. *Ibid.*
38. *Ibid.*, p. 451.

positivists, he finds himself unable to go the whole way.[39] He is unable, for example, to accept the wholly linguistic interpretation of logic as that doctrine is advanced by Carnap. In rejecting Carnap's two logical languages as being too arbitrary, Russell says that "all propositions which are true in virtue of their form ought to be included in any adequate logic."[40] Indeed, the premises of the realism which we have just succeeded in tracing in a number of passages from *The Principles* are in direct contradiction with the whole set of basic tenets set forth by the modern school of logical positivists. For instance, against the notion that complexity as well as analytical elements are real,[41] Carnap maintains that the question of reality concerns the parts of a system but cannot concern the system itself.[42] Carnap admits for the logical positivists a following of empiricism,[43] that same brand of empiricism which Russell has explicitly rejected.[44] As for Bridgman, he seems guilty of an extreme case of the same error which afflicted Lotze, and thus would have to fall under the same ban of the Russell who wrote *The Principles*. Lotze made being into activity;[45] Bridgman narrows activity down to a matter of only certain activity, namely operations.[46] Lotze's second point: the Kantian view that those propositions are true which the mind cannot help but believe,[47] seems also to be held by Bridgman, who maintains that "our thinking mechanism essentially colours any picture that we can form of nature."[48] And finally, the Russell who derived his philosophy "in all its chief features" from the metaphysical realism of the early G. E. Moore[49] could hardly agree with the view of Wittgenstein that "philosophical matters are

---

39. *Ibid.*, p. xii, second paragraph.
40. *Ibid.*, p. xii.
41. P. 281, above.
42. Rudolf Carnap, *Philosophy and Logical Syntax*, p. 20.
43. Rudolf Carnap, *The Unity of Science*, pp. 27-28.
44. P. 284, above.
45. *Ibid*.
46. P. W. Bridgman, *The Logic of Modern Physics*, p. 5.
47. This page.
48. Bridgman, *op. cit.*, p. xi.
49. P. 284, above.

not false but senseless,"[50] or with Carnap that metaphysics is expressive but not assertive,[51] and that metaphysics is equivalent only to mud.[52] It is questionable whether any man who had understood realism so deeply and embraced it so wholeheartedly could ever change his position, no matter how much he wanted to. Despite Russell's rejection of realism and avowal of nominalism, he is not a nominalist but a realist, and it is the apparently insuperable logical difficulties standing in the path of a realistic interpretation of symbolic logic which shake his faith. In other words, he has not changed his early philosophy; he has merely become uncertain about the prospects of defending it.

This situation presents quite another kind of problem. We no longer have to pursue specifically logical answers to paradoxes; we merely have to convince Russell that there are some difficulties with *any* metaphysical interpretation of symbolic logic. Whether these difficulties can be ironed out by an appeal to symbolic logic itself, as Russell suggests,[53] is debatable. It is not easy to see how an empirical fact can conclusively choose its own metaphysical interpretation. Relativity theory in physics seems to demonstrate for the materialists that all is material; it seems to the realists to show that all is resolvable into relations; and it seems to be an argument that the subjectivists can advance in favor of their own mentalism; and so on. Metaphysics is assuredly a world situation, and while not arbitrary, it is at least broader than any limited empirical situation and thus not determinable in terms of the limited situation. If a metaphysical interpretation had no necessary implications to situations other than the one whose metaphysical nature was being investigated, it is likely that each situation would suggest its own. But metaphysics represents a system of universal implications in which non-contradiction is one of the essential features. Hence where one empirical fact "seems to suggest" one broad interpretation and another another, we must

---

50. Wittgenstein, *Tractatus Logico-Philosophicus*, 4.003.
51. Carnap, *Philosophy and Logical Syntax*, p. 29.
52. *Ibid.*, p. 96.
53. *The Principles of Mathematics*, p. xiv.

conclude that at least one of the empirical facts is giving misleading suggestions.

Russell finds himself, before he has done, driven back to an immutable if as yet unknown truth. He is unwilling to accept the veiled subjectivism of the logical positivists' linguistic interpretation of logical truth. Axioms are not arbitrary, as Carnap would have them; they "either do, or do not, have the characteristics of formal truth. . . ."[54] To discover whether they do or do not have these characteristics may be a difficult task indefinitely prolonged; but when we have admitted that the question is not arbitrary we have already admitted that there is such a thing as absolute truth, the knowledge of which we seek to approximate in our limited formulations.

---

54. *Ibid.*, p. xii.

XIII

Toward the Metaphysics of Symbolic Logic

THE IMPLICATIONS OF SYMBOLIC logic in the field of metaphysics have hardly been explored. Researches, in some ways the most remarkable since the time of Aristotle, have been responsible for the confinement of the labors of logicians to the exploration and extension of the newly discovered territory. This course of procedure is just as correct as any other, since the order of discovery of the elements of a system has no necessary reference to the proper order of the elements in the system. Some dim but provocative outlines of such a system must be discerned by means of attention to the relations between its few known elements before the system itself begins to suggest the existence of further elements. Perhaps the only adequate texts are those setting forth topics so long established that there is no important ground which has not been agreed upon thoroughly by experts. In such fields alone is the summary by a final synthesis made possible. But this cannot be done in pioneer studies, and symbolic logic is fairly recent. Much of its subject-matter is the scene for tireless controversy. Fortunately, the path-finding zeal of the experimental logicians has not yet been abated; and until it slackens somewhat, all efforts at tracing the relation of the new logic to metaphysics are bound to be assigned to a second place in importance. However, as Whitehead pertinently remarks, "the reformation of Logic has an essential reference to Metaphysics. For Logic prescribes the shapes of metaphysical thought."[1] Notwithstanding the condi-

---

1. Foreword to Quine, *A System of Logistic*.

tions, it does appear too early to venture upon some tentative speculations concerning the metaphysics which symbolic logic calls forth. For symbolic logic has assumptions, a method, and conclusions which are susceptible to philosophical analysis.

Simultaneous with the historical development of symbolic logic there has sprung up a school of philosophy calling itself logical positivism. This philosophy, with certain exceptions of interpretation,[2] is completely nominalistic, and rightly finds its roots in the positivism of Mach. But things which develop together do not necessarily belong together. There is no reason to accept the proposition, which seems to have slipped in among the assumptions of so many contemporary philosophers, that because logical positivism has developed along with symbolic logic, symbolic logic must be positivistic. Indeed here and there are to be noted philosophers who are fully aware of this error. Professor Pepper has pointed out in an important paper,[3] the insupportable position of positivism, and W. V. Quine has argued in an address[4] to the effect that the principles of positivism do not check with those of modern logic, and there have been others.

However, it is not the purpose of this chapter to add to an already considerable list of refutations of logical positivism in its claims as the foundations of symbolic logic. Besides exposing what symbolic logic is not, we need also to demonstrate what it is. The arguments will take for granted the cogency of the anti-positivist attack, and proceed from there to set forth some suggestions concerning the true metaphysical basis of symbolic logic. That basis seems to be the philosophy of realism. By realism here is meant the theory that the natural world with all its logical structure and affective value is real, and objective to and independent of the cognitional processes whose function is not to create but to appre-

---

2. Prof. Moritz Schlick was a realist, as his version of logical positivism reveals. See, for instance, his paper on "Meaning and Verification" in *The Philosophical Review*, XLV (1936), especially pp. 344, 346, 349.

3. Stephen C. Pepper, "A Criticism of a Positivistic Theory of Mind," in *The Nature of Mind*, University of California Publications in Philosophy, Vol. XIX.

4. "Is Logic a Matter of Words?" Read before the Eastern Division of the American Philosophical Association, Princeton University, December 1937.

hend as actual such a real world. Let us see, then, to what extent symbolic logic is conformable with the realistic philosophy, with the understanding that this effort is intended to be exploratory and tentative and not in any sense final.

I

Logic, as that study of which pure mathematics is a branch, is well defined as the science of types of order, or, in other words, as the science of system; and it is concerned with all entities and processes whatsoever. The attempt to walk through a brick wall is as good an example of the law of contradiction, the genetic inheritance of acquired characters as good an example of transitivity, as any mental operation could possibly afford. Logic is by no means restricted to the operations of the mind, though it certainly includes these operations in its perfect generality. It seems useless to remonstrate here with those who insist upon the exclusively mental function of logic. This contention eventually leads to the position of solipsism, as Bridgman has lately discovered,[5] and solipsism simply cannot be refuted. The solipsist is what he is, and we as his creatures can have nothing to say about it that will influence him in any way.

Those who recognize the absurdity of his position are immediately involved in the acceptance of a further proposition, which can be set forth somewhat as follows. The origins of experienced sensations are experimental facts of psychology. Whether peripherally or centrally aroused, sensations are objects of awareness. In other words, they are objective to the mind. Awareness is frequently compelled to sensations which it would willingly avoid, e.g., acute pain. Furthermore, sensations do not depend so much upon conscious selectivity as they do upon stimulation. Thus at least the referents of sensation, i.e., the stimuli, are not only objective but independent. Now these are the conditions of experienced sensations; but the proposition in question devolves upon the status of thoughts. Do thoughts rest upon the same set of conditions?

---
5. *The Nature of Physical Theory* (Princeton, 1936), p. 14.

We have already said that logic deals with things as well as with thoughts. If this is true, then not only experienced sensations but also logical relations are known directly as objective. The latter proposition can be seen to be thoroughly consistent with the generality of logic. But also like sensations, relations are more than objective; they are independent. Symbolic logic represents over Aristotelian logic the increasing recognition of this situation. Aristotelian logic is a system of classification based on the metaphysics of substance. Symbolic logic by contrast is a system of abstraction based on the metaphysics of relations. Much the same transition has been effected in physics, in the change from Newtonian to modern formulations. Einstein's discovery that spatiotemporal relations are relative to frames of reference, but absolute given the frame, which is true for the relativity theory, and Planck's discovery that underneath the microscopic level of entities further reduction is possible to the emission of energy in fixed amounts, called erg-seconds, which is true for the quantum theory, have together overthrown the classic notion of substance. The older logic depends upon predicates which are nothing more than crude forms of simple classification and substances to which subjective attributes can be assigned. The newer logic depends upon the importance of relations which are held to be objective things in the world.

Conclusive evidence for this assertion is implicit in the entire treatment of symbolic logic. Logic is always primarily concerned with relations, and is concerned with relata only to the extent to which these are required in order to indicate relations. There is no attribution of predicates but instead membership in a class, and membership in a class is given the realistic definition of, for instance, "falling under a concept,"[6] or inclusion within a given notion. Again, it is the implicative relation of $p \supset q$ rather than the separate and distinctive facts of p and of q which interests the symbolic logician. And as his propositions become more abstract and involved, the same relata or symbols appearing over and over again in the same assertion, as in the following

---

6. Susanne K. Langer, *An Introduction to Symbolic Logic* (London, 1927), p. 117.

one selected at random from the *Principia Mathematica*:[7]

$$r :\cdot p \supset q \cdot \supset \cdot p \supset r : \supset : p \cdot \supset \cdot q \supset r$$

it becomes even plainer that what occupies his attention exclusively is the relations and not the relata, which have by now lost all identification except as subordinate elements. The terms of the relation are suffered merely so that the relation may be considered.

Thus the independence of objective stimuli which exist for experienced sensations are paralleled by the independence of objective stimuli which exist for experienced logical relations (thoughts). Neither set can be confined to the objectives of actuality, though actuality furnishes the occasions for their effects. Thus they are independent of both the subject and the object of knowledge.

With the understanding that logical relations reach the knowing subject through the object of knowledge but exist independent of both subject and object, we come to the end of the explanatory usefulness of epistemology for the theory of symbolic logic. The realistic epistemology is not concerned with the question of how ontology comes to be, but only with the much narrower question of how it comes to be known. Logical relations are not subjective creations produced by knowing but ontological properties of the world. Thus it becomes plainly impossible to rest any ontological deductions upon an epistemological basis. We must rather, accepting the whole of symbolic logic as an independent system, look within this system for implications of ontological import.

II

In the language of symbolic logic, it can be asserted that $p \supset q$. Here p and q represent variables and are not, strictly speaking, propositions. They are what are termed propositional functions, and must remain incomplete until some specific value is assigned to them. From this it is plain that symbolic logic is not concerned with anything actual. Specification renders propositional func-

---

7. I, 108.

tions into propositions; but it is primarily with propositional functions that symbolic logic deals, and with the mode of their extensional specificity. Symbolic logic is primarily concerned with possible types of order. This is exemplified by such of its categories as intensional classes, propositional functions, possibility ($\diamond$),[8] and also by the effort to eliminate definite descriptions, and so on.

There would not be any purpose served by abstract studies did they not have some possible evidential bearing on actuality. They are engaged with the logical order of possibility, and not directly with actuality, yet these studies concern themselves with the logical order only to the end that they may understand and control actuality. Symbolic logic fulfills this requirement in the most realistic manner. It is concerned with possibility, and with the relation between possibility and actuality. Intension and propositional function belong to the logical order of possibility; extension and specific value belong to the historical order of actuality. The intensions of a given class are not subject to change or time, whereas the extensions are always susceptible to both change and time.

Symbolic logic is thus not limited to the rigors of absolutism and its inexorable logical order but is also concerned with actuality in so far as actuality is exemplificatory of the universal and unchanging conditions of the possibilities of types of order. In short, it is concerned not only with the logical order but also with the relation between that order and actuality; e.g., it is concerned not only with propositional functions but also with the manner in which these can be rendered by the assignment of specific values into completed propositions. Another recognition of this necessity to mediate in terms of the world of reaction consists in the distinction made by symbolic logic between "formal" and "material" implication. Formal implication holds as between possibles; material implications as between actual things. Further, "specific propositions" are statements of fact, whereas all statements having the status of hypothesis or law are termed "gen-

---

8. C. I. Lewis and C. H. Langford, *Symbolic Logic* (New York, 1932), p. 153.

eral propositions." Law is equivalent to absolute generality, while hypothesis is equivalent to lesser generality. It is unfortunate that symbolic logic has as yet no method for indicating the established degree of generality of a proposition. There is already a universal class but there is as yet no way of indicating the hierarchy of subclasses other than by symbolic inclusion with dots and brackets; but doubtless this will come.

The distinction between uncompromising logical rigor and mediated and compromising logical application is well brought out throughout the newer logical systems. Class and class membership are taken as all-important, and the relation of class member to the class to which it belongs is that of exemplification of a general notion. It is distinctly not that of part to whole as substances.[9] To conceive of the relation of class member to class as that of part to whole renders the class itself exhaustive and actual, which it emphatically is not. We must not allow the old nominalistic presuppositions which had crept into the older logic to vitiate the newer as well. A class is not an affair of aggregation but of generality, and the confusion of the two renders symbolic logic insusceptible of valid interpretation. This is avoidable if we always recall when we should that the class calculus deals with relations and not with parts and wholes.

The advantages of symbolic logic over Aristotelian logic are enormous. Classification is an elementary form of abstraction only, and it can never get much further than it got with Aristotle. The change from a basis of substance to one of relation offers the possibility of a better understanding of the relations of classes to their members. It allows for greater abstraction, and thus, also, for a greater generality. At the same time, the philosophy underlying logic itself is rendered more accessible. The shift from an understanding of parts and wholes as substances to one of their relations is contained in the distinction, to be kept very clear, between the logical order and its application to actuality. A glance at some principal class divisions will suffice to illustrate the acceptance of the foregoing two orders throughout symbolic logic.

---

9. Langer, *op. cit.*, p. 113-14.

That class which has no members is defined as the null-class. A null-class member is identical with another null-class member only with regard to one property; namely, with respect to the absence of members. Now there is nothing necessary about this property; it can be lost or acquired. Moreover, members, when, as and if they occur, would not be identical. Neither the class of phoenixes nor the class of dodos has any members—a fact which marks both subclasses as members of the greater null-class. But actual phoenixes, if they should ever occur, and actual dodos, if they should ever occur again, would not be identical.

There is an unanalyzed confusion in the present understanding of the null-class. To be eligible for null-class membership it is only necessary to have no members, but the absence of members may be due to different kinds of conditions. First, it may be due to the fact that the items in question have for the moment gone out of actuality. There are no well-oiled chariots because there is no current use for them; at present, therefore, the class of well-oiled chariots is a subclass member of the null-class. Secondly, however, the absence of membership may be due to the fact that the item in question contains an inherent contradiction. There are no round squares, and this class, too, is a subclass member of the null-class. It is easy to see that well-oiled chariots and round squares, supposedly identifiable, are far from being so. They differ as to their possibilities of actualization. There are no well-oiled chariots because there is no present use for them; but there are no round squares because there cannot be any, "round square" being a contradiction in terms. Symbolic logic fails to distinguish[10] between those classes which have no members and are non-contradictory, i.e., a well-oiled chariot, and those classes which also have no members but are contradictory, i.e., a round square. Both kinds of classes confuse the issue when they are considered identical subclass members of the one null-class.

There seem to be here two dangerous pitfalls confronting the metaphysics of logic. For, first of all, serious error lurks in the supposition that subclass members of the null-class are not as

---

10. But cf. C. I. Lewis' system of strict implication.

real as members of other classes having positive extension. By "real" here is meant having objective and independent existence. This fallacy has long been familiar to philosophy as nominalism, or the disbelief in the reality of universals. The danger is avoided by recognizing that no ontological distinction is conferred upon a class-member according to whether it falls in or out of the null-class.

The second error is contained in the fallacy of idealism, that universals alone are real. It has also been called crypto-materialism, since it leads to the consideration of universals as divided in possibility, themselves real, actual things possessing perfection. This danger is avoided by recognizing that all members of the null-class are undifferentiated and must remain so until taken out of that class by differentiation, that is, by means of the acquisition of members.

The point can perhaps be made clearer by analyzing a proposition. Ordinarily in symbolic logic, such a statement as, for example, "Centaurs feed on grass," would be said to be false as an existential proposition.[11] This cannot be proved. If there be nothing contradictory in the nature of "centaur," reference to exploration may at any time disclose the presence of centaurs.[12] For all we know, they may very well feed on grass. What can be proved is simply that at the moment centaurs are members of the null-class, which is a different and more limited contention. There are no actual centaurs known, since none have ever been experienced or, at least, are not experienced. Yet for all we know, centaurs have not been but could be experienced. Actuality should be defined not by what has been or is experienced but by what can be experienced. If tomorrow centaurs should become actual through the capability of being experienced, then they would have to be transferred out of the null-class. The proposition, "Centaurs feed on grass," would then be susceptible of allowance by empirical verification.

---

11. A. P. Ushenko, *The Theory of Logic* (New York, 1936), p. 82.
12. The strong probability of its non-existence is quite another matter. Logic at the level under discussion has no traffic with probabilities.

The confusion between so-called "verbal" (i.e., logically possible) and "general" (i.e., actually verifiable) propositions could be avoided by stating all propositions in the form of the propositional functions of logical analysis, specifiable as hypothetical propositions, viz., "If centaurs exist, they must feed on grass." Thus, "If centaurs exist, and if when centaurs exist they must feed on grass, then centaurs feed on grass." Logically possible (i.e., "verbal") propositions are disprovable or allowable by actuality. By definition they are not subject to empirical proof at all.

Next in importance to the null-class for our purpose is the unit-class. The unit-class is defined as a class which has one and only one member, and it differs from other classes in that together with the class it denies it represents infinite unity. Spoon and non-spoon exhaust existence. There are as many unit-classes as there are individuals. The notion of a unit-class as a class having only one member is a highly realistic notion. It represents the essential recognition of the relation, "membership in a class," and is in this regard indifferent to the distinction between one and many among class members. The further condition of the unit-class, that there shall be no more than one member, gives the highest specificity possible to a universal. But highly specific universal and actual things are still kept apart. The unit-class is thus that class having one extended member, such that all members of that class are identical with that member. This is a true instance of identity.

The unit-class is the class of all members having extension. What should be obvious, therefore, is that it constitutes a reaffirmation of the Law of Excluded Middle. Despite the fashionable modern challenge to this Law, symbolic logic assumes its validity, and indeed reaffirms the entire basic position of Aristotelian logic. The latter has in recent years been severely called into question because of the observed fact that the absolutistic and uncompromising nature of its formulation is seldom fulfilled in actuality. Contradictions are actual facts; and in everyone's experience excluded middles abound,

All of which is perfectly true, yet the traditional logic is not upset thereby. Aristotle has through the centuries earned the name of opponent to Plato, and since Plato has been known as a realist, Aristotle has come to be accepted as anti-realistic. Yet the laws of Aristotelian logic are read with an uncompromising severity of application which savors of extreme realism. It has been thought that every instance of practical interpretation of the abstraction formulations of Aristotelian logic must be occasions which are either wholly true or wholly false. The discovery that actuality does not answer to such rigid requirements has been a bitter one for the understanding of syllogistic logic. Whatever laws do not conform to the partial and approximative facts of actuality are deemed false.

But as opposed to the modern interpretation, which gets its start in the mathematical law of probability, we may call upon the support of symbolic logic. If the same kind of distinction which is found in symbolic logic is made throughout all logical formulations, namely, the distinction between the intension and extension of a class (i.e., between possibility and actuality), then the Aristotelian formulations will be seen to be true of actuality exactly to the extent to which the exemplifications of actuality approximate to the truth of the logical order. Or, to rephrase this statement in the language of symbolic logic, absolute and ideal formulations are true exactly to the extent to which the extension of classes approaches the intension. It is rigorously true that no middle term exists between spoon and non-spoon. To the extent to which actual spoons (the extensions of the class, spoon) approach the definition of spoon (its intension), actuality approaches logic.

Thus the truth of Aristotelian logic is affirmed and not denied by symbolic logic. The non-spoonishness of objects in the universe to which the qualification of non-spoon may be applied (e.g., myself, this tree) contains this attribute in the deepest sense, since negative attributes are not mental things only, but objective and independent. This is readily evidenced by one implication of symbolic logic: that the negative of a given class together with that class exhaust the infinite universe. So long as no substance, in the classic sense of that which can exist by itself, can be said to exist, the negative attribution is meaningful and real.

Of all classes other than the null- and unit-classes it is true that the relation between a class and its members is one of position in a system. A subclass, or even an extensional member of a class (taken not merely as actual but as actual *and therefore also as possible*), is in a wider system itself a class having members or possibly null. One criterion of class membership is that "a class shall be of type at least one higher than any of its members, but at most one higher than some member (if it has any members)."[13] The ordered series of class-member-class requires systematic definition.

III

The fact that the new symbolic logic does not contradict but merely subordinates the older Aristotelian logic is highly indicative of the essential nature of logic itself. Thus in physics Newtonian mechanics was not discarded but became subordinated to the wider truth of relativity. Like the progress of natural science, logic advances by making available for analysis wider circles of inclusiveness, ever seeking wider systems which will subsume the traditional systems yet include much more. The understanding that truth is independent, and moreover, that independent truths necessarily belong to a system which is discoverable, forms part of the realistic metaphysics. Peirce has said that systems are not only the summaries but also the finders of facts. But without the realistic understanding of deduction and inductions as *directions* within a framework, logicians are led astray. There is a good illustration of this in the fact that symbolic logicians have not brought out the relative properties of implication and deducibility in such a way as to make clear the relation of the one to the other as well as the difference between them.

Implication and deducibility are often said not to be the same;

---

13. Barkley Rosser, *J. Symb. Log.*, Vol. I (1936), p. 38. See also the discussion of the principle of the extended infinite on p. 37.

but of what does the difference consist? Consider on our principles that in the relation $p \quad q$, q must be an element lower than p. By this is meant that q must be a part of p, and discoverable by the method of analysis. Thus the condition essential for deducibility is the relation of part to whole. Its direction is *downward* from a given organization to the analytic elements of that organization.

But for implication the requirements are somewhat different. It is no longer essential that q be part of p. In fact, q may be part of p, or p part of q, or neither may be true, and there can still be implication. In implication both p and q are parts of a wider system, and indeed this is its only essential condition. It is necessary merely that p and q be parts of a system wider than either p or q or both. The direction of implication is *outward* from one element in a system to another element in that same system. The organization chosen for analysis is, so to speak, a synthesis which is not present. Implication is a far more comprehensive affair than deducibility. The thesis maintained by modern logicians that implication does not demand any relation between p and q except their mutual truth or falsity, is true in the widest sense that all truths form a system. This is observable in the so-called paradoxes of material implication:

$$(p,q) : p. \supset .q \supset p$$

and

$$(p,q) : \sim p. \supset .p \supset q$$

Ushenko's example of implication, "If friction generates heat, then Lincoln was assassinated," is, as he says,[14] a true implication, but both propositions as truths form parts of a system which is deductive albeit enormously wide and largely unknown.

Given a sufficient knowledge of intermediate steps, the deducibility of any given true proposition from any other true proposition systematically one step lower could be demonstrated.

---

14. *The Theory of Logic*, p. 48.

The deducibility of a proposition q from a proposition p is only possible when

$$(\exists p) \ .p . p \supset q$$

That is, where there is both truth-value and implication, then there is the deducibility of q from p. But without mutual truth (or mutual falsity) there is no implication. The requirements for implication are more than the logicians suspect; those for deducibility less.

In this connection the problem of the proper interpretation and validity of the axiom of reducibility arises. The explanation in the light of the foregoing discussion would seem to be somewhat as follows. If implication is primitive to deducibility, the additional factor of truth-value being required, then it can be asserted that identity itself is not identifiable with implication. $A = A$ is not an implication. Every proposition is identical with its own truth, but no proposition implies its own truth. Every proposition is identical with its own truth, and while a proposition may imply the assertion of its own truth, no proposition *ipso facto* does imply its own truth. The notion of assertion is commonly acknowledged to be primitive to the system of symbolic logic, since "nothing can be said about it in the language of the system." It is in such unsuspected places as this that we must look for uncontrolled assumptions. There is nothing more fundamental than informal unassumed premises. In symbolic logic the notion of truth is given no symbol. But nevertheless it is present throughout, having entered with the notation of assertion ($\vdash$). The hidden postulate of a wide system to which all foreground assertions on specific topics are referable needs candid acknowledgment in the metaphysics of symbolic logic. The understanding of the internal relations of symbolic logic serves to throw light upon its metaphysics, but in every study there is also a certain stage of advancement at which the beginnings of an understanding of the metaphysics would in turn facilitate further development.

There is something truly wonderful and almost miraculous about those disciplines which, like physical science and mathematics, are highly abstractive and value-free. They are able to return to the common level of concrete fact with an enormous power of applicability. The understanding that truths form a system has in symbolic logic led to the search for the widest system. The *Principia Mathematica* of Whitehead and Russell endeavors to allow for the deducibility of syllogistic logic. The last chapter of Quine's *A System of Logistic*[15] endeavors to allow for the "deducibility of the system of *Principia Mathematica.*" In this way logic, like all other sciences, supplants the waverings of the dialectic of actuality by offering a more consistent advance from system to wider system to still wider system, subordinating but retaining at each step the truths of the lesser system.

---

15. Chap. XVIII.

Part VI
The Revival in Psychology

XIV

The Logic of Psychoanalysis

THE APPEARANCE OF A NEW series of introductory lectures on psychoanalysis by Sigmund Freud[1] furnishes as good an occasion as any to estimate the extent of the truth this newcomer among the sciences contains. The theory and practice of psychoanalysis have enjoyed an enormous popular success. Starting with the efforts of a single doctor, and within the lifetime of one generation, psychoanalysis has spread from Vienna to all quarters of the Western world. While the more conservative endorsement of the universities has not yet been obtained, the popularity of private disciples and in turn of their disciples, and the success of private clinics, point to positive results achieved and to converts gained in increasingly large numbers. Some of the terms of psychoanalysis have almost passed into popular language, and it is not uncommon to hear reference to such concepts as "introvert," "repression," "castration complex," etc. The amateur interpretation of dreams is frequently attempted. From a superficial point of view there seems every reason to believe that psychoanalysis is here to stay, that it is a new but valid science, and that the objections of the traditional psychologists are utterly without foundation.

There are some signs, however, that all is not well within the psychoanalytic camp. One of these is the failure of agreement

---

[1]. *New Introductory Lectures on Psycho-analysis,* trans. by W. J. H. Sprott, New York, 1933.

among the psychoanalysts themselves. There is no suspension of opinion over undemonstrated hypothesis, such as is found within the ranks of the physicists, but absolute differences arising from opposed dogmas. Moreover, Freud has followers who are at war over the question of the interpretation of his doctrine. The fact that these differences take the form they do immediately suggests a failure of agreement on the method whereby such differences can be settled.

Aside from this factional quarrel and its importance, however, there is one more development which it is fair to say might in any case have been expected. I refer to the fact that, popularly speaking, psychoanalysis is losing its hold on the general imagination. Psychoanalytic concepts are no longer terms to conjure with, and as Professor Joad has pointed out in a recent article,[2] psychoanalysis is definitely in retreat. Psychoanalysis, the most fashionable form of psychology, has been replaced as the current intellectual chic type by Marxism, and psychoanalysis has fallen back upon the support of its more serious advocates. There is a journal in New York devoted exclusively to intellectual interests which offers an amusing illustration of this tendency. Formerly its pages were given over to psychoanalytical articles of every description; within the last few years it has altered its policy and now prints only essays on Marxism! Thus the fog of popular enthusiasm is rapidly clearing away, and the claims of psychoanalysis stand out at last bare and open to the sharp attack of critical analysis. It is the purpose of this chapter, then, to offer briefly such an analysis, and to discover what, if any, is the worth of the new psychology.

Primary among the claims of psychoanalysis is that to the status of science. That psychoanalysis is the "mental science" has been asserted time and again by psychoanalysts. Freud goes so far as to claim that "there are only two sciences—psychology, pure and applied, and natural science."[3] Thus it is clear that psychoanalysis sets itself up as a science. I submit, however, that the

---

2. "Psychology in Retreat," *The New Statesman and Nation*, June 29, 1935.
3. *Op. cit.*, p. 245.

method of psychoanalysis is not the method of science, and that the scientific claims of psychoanalysis are specious and false. In order to demonstrate the dissimilarity of the method of psychoanalysis from that of science, it will be necessary to explain, as succinctly as possible, just what constitutes scientific method.

The method of science, unlike most contemporary procedures, is essentially realistic. The term, realistic, is intended here in its medieval sense, as denoting the real independence of ideas, an independence which extends to the mind as well as to the external world. Scientific method begins with induction and passes to experimentation and then to deduction. That is to say, hypotheses are formed more or less by means of insight, which insight is most common to persons who have acquired some training and facility in the given field. The validity of these hypotheses is tested by experimentation. The empirical test is of course always a negative one; from it can be learned whether a given hypothesis is disproved by the facts of actuality but never whether it is proved. If the empirical test does not disprove the hypothesis, it is then elevated to the status of a law. From the law, new facts can be deduced.

Scientific laws, as Peirce saw, are not only the summaries of old facts but also the finders of new ones. Laws are in no sense to be considered as either statistical summaries or as absolute truths; extreme views of this sort on either side err. Scientific laws are approximations of universal truths and are true in so far as, and *only* in so far as, they succeed to such approximation. But their failure to attain a one-to-one correspondence with absolute truths in no wise means that they are either unreal, fictitious, or false. They are as real as anything in existence, there being no differences in regard to the reality of existents, and they are just as true as their approximation of absolute truth indicates. It is an important observation that the laws of physics, and of much of biology, are abstracted at high levels. That is, they are abstractions of abstractions, or even abstractions three or more times removed. We shall refer to this fact in our comparison of scientific method with the method of psychoanalysis.

When we turn to psychoanalysis, we learn that it is not realistic but on the contrary nominalistic. By nominalism is meant the belief in the sole reality of physical particulars. This view splits existence into an objective world (real) and a subjective world (unreal). Some philosophers have thought, however, that if this objective physical world is alone real there can be no way for the unreal mind to know it, and that therefore speculation concerning it was sure to prove fruitless. They confined their investigations accordingly to the closed subjective world which, if unreal, is at least all that can be known. To this latter class belong the psychoanalytic psychologists. They are interested in the individual in so far as he responds to the stimuli which start either subjectively or objectively, and accept the dichotomy of mental and physical as an unexamined postulate, a primitive notion.

Freud explains that the "mental personality" is divided into the ego, the super-ego, and the id, corresponding to consciousness, conscience, and the unconscious, and we learn that the poor ego has three tyrants which are "the external world, the super-ego, and the id."[4] It is the "mental personality" which Freudian psychoanalysis is exclusively interested in, and this mental personality is conceived as utterly independent of and isolated from the external physical world. The external world, as is clear from the above quotation, is differentiated sharply from the id. Freud constantly employs such terms as "the mental underworld," "depth psychology," "the dark psyche," etc., and seems to feel that he is dealing with evil and irrational forces, which are by nature opposed to the good and rational forces of the external world, and which are only held in check by the rational laws and customs of society and by the censor.

The fact that realism is a valid metaphysical position and nominalism an invalid one, would seem not only to disprove the scientific claims of psychoanalysis but also to negate the benefits of the whole study. This is equal to the assertion that if a metaphysical theory is false, all that is founded on it is false.

---

4. *Ibid.*, p. 108.

The logic of this latter assertion cannot be denied; but the exception arises from the analysis of the validity of the logic employed in laying the foundations. In so far as assertions are nominalistic they are false, and this is by definition, but it would be vain to make the claim that all nominalists are thoroughly consistent. It is an obviously true though paradoxical fact that no nominalist can be inconsistent without stepping over into the realistic realm. Now, no nominalist can be consistent, and therefore false, forever, and thus when he fails to be consistent with the falsity of his metaphysical theory, he errs on the side of—truth. Thus to assert that because psychoanalysis is founded upon the false metaphysical theory of nominalism, all the discoveries of psychoanalysis must be false is to accuse psychoanalysis of a self-consistency and a perfection of logic which no study undertaken by mortal man has ever had. We cannot let our logical analysis rest upon the demonstration that psychoanalytic theory is nominalistic; we must make a further examination in order to determine what is particularly false and why, and what caused the error and finally what, if anything, may be saved.

Let us then turn next to a consideration of some of the entities of psychoanalysis. One of the critics of psychoanalysis, Professor Joad, has accused that study of an unjustified dogmatism and a bewildering change.[5] To this charge, one of the most ardent and uncritical of the English psychoanalysts, Dr. Ernest Jones, replied[6] by pointing out the contradiction contained in the double accusation. But the contradiction is an apparent one only. Since the entities of psychoanalysis have no logical or scientific standing, not being defensible by reason, those which remain appear to have the unjustified fixity of dogmas, and those which swiftly change appear to be equally unjustifiably fickle. In physics, some entities often remain for centuries while others have a life lasting less than a year. But the permanence and change of physical entities always rests upon something rational. Entities are neither kept nor abandoned in physical science without reason. In psycho-

---

5. Joad, *op. cit.*
6. In the following issue of *The New Statesman and Nation*, July 6, 1935.

analysis, on the other hand, it is never easy to determine just what the reasons are which account for the retention or dismissal of entities, and figures in what Joad calls the Freudian drama act as though they obey only some inner artistic compulsion of their own.

It is generally true that the entities of psychoanalysis are abstracted at the level of enlightened common sense and not at the high abstractive levels at which the entities of physics, for example, are found. The *censor,* the *oral type,* the *introvert,* these are all more comparable to the common sense entities of economics, such as *supply, demand,* the *economic man,* than to physical and chemical entities such as *valency,* the *electron,* etc. Many entities of psychoanalysis which seem new and strange to the uninitiated are merely old ideas dressed up in new terms and given unusual importance. Thus for instance, the *ego* stands for the old conception of consciousness, the *super-ego* for the "still small voice of conscience," and the *id* for the unconscious. But there is nothing "scientific" about these new names, although they do give the study an added technical aura which it would not enjoy upon the employment of the old-fashioned ones. Certainly there is no particularly keen insight involved in giving fresh names to old ideas. Moreover, there is a looseness about the construction of the psychoanalytical terminology which argues badly for the kind of thinking which goes on behind it. We are told, for instance, that the id is "the character of being foreign to the ego,"[7] and later on that "the ego is after all only a part of the id."[8] In other words, the ego turns out to be part of that which is defined by being foreign to it!

There is a further confusion, and one of a much worse sort, in the opposition, which goes unacknowledged, between the sexual types and the triune mental personality. Human beings are divided among oral, anal, and urethral types, and on this view the physical would seem to be the cause of the mental. But the emphasis which is laid on the so-called mental personality and

---
7. Freud, *op. cit.,* p. 102.
8. *Ibid.,* p. 107.

the struggles and compromises which take place between the ego, the super-ego and the id, would seem to indicate an intense subjectivism. Even applying the term science to psychoanalysis, in the popular way in which it is used outside the physical sciences, viz., as any study which is very exact, would be out of keeping; for there is nothing very exact about a system which can reveal such obvious confusions and contradictions as those set forth above.

In the kind of highly "scientific" and "empirical" experimentation which is now in vogue among the psychoanalysts, we may clearly see how anxious Freudian psychoanalysis is to be a science, and yet how far the frank imitation of the procedure of physics has led them from that goal. An experiment is made, let us say, with children. Certain toys are presented to them for play; the interpretation of their reaction to these objects will constitute the results of the experiment. The experiment was suggested, of course, by some preconceived hypothesis of the psychoanalyst, who wishes to have his hypothesis either rejected or allowed (which is demonstration, for there is no such thing as empirical confirmation in scientific method) by appeal to empirical fact.

So far, so good; the experiment is being conducted on the proper scientific lines. But what is the result? Some of the children react to the toys in the predicted manner, to that extent allowing the psychoanalytic hypothesis in question. But others of the children do not give the expected reaction; they are indifferent, and after glancing at the toys, walk out of the room in which the experiment is being conducted. How is this reaction interpreted by the psychoanalyst? As a denial of his hypothesis? Not at all. He does not for one moment allow it to interfere with the success of his experiment. The expected reaction of the children was that of "aggression." The failure of certain children to manifest this aggression is interpreted as "inhibited aggression!" Thus the stage was set before the players appeared, but not after the way of the controlled conditions of scientific method. Experiments are conducted in science in order to deny or allow hypotheses; but if an experiment is to be conducted in such a manner that any possible results can be read as allowance, then why conduct the experiment in the first place?

Can we honestly say that such a method of discovery is in any way scientific? Can we say that it involves empirical demonstration? Empirical demonstration is a slippery affair, and unless logic is implicitly present to check the steps and the necessity of the inferences which are drawn, empirical demonstration must mean nothing. Exactness calls for strict adherence to the laws of logic, and this applies as well to empiricism as to anything else in existence. It may fairly be objected, of course, that I have erroneously imagined what the method of Freud must be, and then, taking that method as authoritative, that I have proceeded to attack it as loose and unscientific, an attack which can have no validity as directed against the true method of the psychoanalysts. There is something to be said for this objection. However, I feel that my description of Freud's scientific method must be true. One fact in support of my hypothesis can seriously be offered. This is that throughout Freud's work and the work of other psychoanalysts of prominence it is always possible to detect the historical fallacy. By the historical fallacy is meant the definition of an entity in terms of its origins, the explanation of what a thing is by the description of how it came to be what it is. Now the ahistorical character of science is one of the most notable things about it. Science is wholly concerned with logic and never with history. Science is not concerned with how things have been but with how they must be; its laws are laws of possibility. The inverse square law of gravitation is not the history of fallen objects; it asserts that *if* an object is dropped it must fall to the ground at the accelerated rate of 32 feet per second. We can see, then, that the distinction between science and psychoanalysis is the devotion of psychoanalysis to history.

The historical fallacy is one of the most common in modern thought. Everywhere is found the tendency to deprecate achievements of the present by tracing them to their humble origins. The tensor calculus is nothing of importance, since it may be traced back to savages counting on the fingers of one hand. Christianity is not to be taken seriously since it began with primitive prayers for rain. But as has been shown time and again, the demonstration of the comparative worthlessness of the origins of a thing do not account for the value of that thing. The tensor calculus can accomplish much which would be impossible to a savage equipped with only five digits. Christianity is a vastly more complicated and explanatory affair than prayers for rain could ever be. The historical description always proves to be misleading and insufficient when offered as a definition, and is to be severely distrusted wherever it is met.

This historical fallacy is found, perhaps, in its worst and most virulent form in Freudian psychoanalytic theory. Freud always explains psychic states, neuroses and psychoses, by tracing them to their historical or (since it is the same thing), psychological origins, on the fond assumption that this is the causal method of physical science. But causality in physics is always conceived atemporally; cause and effect in no wise depend upon the temporal sequence but represent a logical nexus. In psychoanalysis, however, historical derivation pure and simple substitutes for what in physics is causality. By arbitrarily taking sex as the causal center of the psychic personality, Freud drives everything back to the sex urge. Then by means of the historical fallacy he drives the sex urge back to its origins in childhood, and some urges are even pushed further, as far as pre-natal influences. Thus the earliest sexual recollections of childhood become of the utmost importance as revealing impressions that are determinative for the adult life. The logic of this movement is superb; once given the premises the conclusions are gathered with the utmost indifference to credibility. The causative factors of the adult situation are driven back and back and become more and more coherent, until the *reductio ad absurdum* of the whole movement is made plain and we approach the ultimate *fons et origo* of human existence, which proves to be infantile anal-erotic sensations. It is, then, infantile anal-erotic sensations which must be held accountable for all activities. This ignores other physical causes, other mental causes (accepting for the moment the nominalistic mental-physical dichotomy of psychoanalysis); it ignores the ideas which are grasped by minds, and it ignores the environment in which the body becomes involved. Nothing remains but infantile anal-erotism, which we as adults are of course powerless to influence in ourselves, since we cannot call back childhood and erase early impressions. The absurdity of such a theory does not require dwelling upon.

We may throw some light upon the problems and difficulties of Freudian psychoanalysis by considerations of a more general nature. It will be interesting to return to Aristotle's psychological conceptions in order to make a comparison. Aristotle distinguishes[9] between the *psyche* and the *nous*. The psyche is the organization of the human organism, and the nous is the mind or consciousness. The nous is merely one part of the psyche, and the psyche is generally more important than the nous as being independent of it, whereas the nous stands to the psyche in the relation of dependence. The distinction drawn by Aristotle is important. Modern usage in psychology tends to dispense with the questions of organization, and the term, psyche, has come to stand for what in Aristotle's terminology is the nous. The modern psyche is the mind or consciousness, and the conception of the organization of the organism has ceased to be employed. This is a very grave omission. It makes the dualistic error of nominalism possible, and it robs psychology of much explanatory value, leading to contradictions and confusions galore. It has forced Freud and the psychoanalysts to split up the psyche (Aristotle's nous) into three divisions, in order to account for the disparateness of mental phenomena. Using the Aristotelian distinction, we may perhaps place the unconscious with the psyche or organization, and keep the conscious for the nous. The super-ego does not belong with these categories, being merely conscience, or the awareness of prevailing customs and morals. This is clearer and more logical. It gives psychology a rational basis and a greater explanatory worth.

---

9. In the *De Anima*.

The business of science is frequently misunderstood by the psychoanalysts, for all their protestations of scientific practice. Science is expected to offer explanations of existence and not to invoke mystery. This is possible only by attempting to explain everything which has a mental existence, and is assuredly not possible by the invocation of deep and irrational forces, and the appeal to the dark psyche of mystery. Now, obviously, to call everything mental is to leave the problem of differentiae unexplained. Even if we accept the mental-physical dualism, the number of distinctions made within the mental category by psychoanalysts is small compared to the number of distinctions which must be made within the physical category. Thus to view all existence through a limited number of mental categories, such as those offered by psychoanalysis, is to beg the question of most of the distinctions which seem to be necessary in the totality of phenomena. This is to make necessary the frequent invocation of mystery, and the reference to the ineffableness of the psyche as the end product of psychoanalytic explanation. It is the kind of impasse which all the irrational, mystery cults get us into; it is typical of nominalism. How much better and clearer is the realistic interpretation of the mental category. On the realistic view, that which is known is not affected by being known. The relation of being-known is only one of a number of relations and not a necessary one. Thus the mind is merely an orientation toward, and a certain perspective on, a world of relations-to-be-known.

The psychoanalytic conception of mentality is not as startlingly new as it first appears to be. The voluntaristic sources of some of Freud's conceptions are well known. Psychoanalysis has merely remodelled and renamed the old categories of the faculty psychology on a voluntaristic basis. We have the same number of disparate instincts, uncorrelated and unrelated. The sex instinct or libido, the "drives," are certainly voluntaristic and completely irrational. Dr. Wexberg has remarked that in psychoanalysis the subject is missing. This is partly true. In place of the subject there is the triune mental category: ego, super-ego, and id, but as

I have already shown above, these are so loosely defined and manipulated, that attempts to weld them together into a single subject usually prove to be conflicting and contradictory. Moreover, the problem of what the mind or consciousness is, is usually dodged. Unification of the subject usually consists in trying to bring the items of the mental life: the ego, the super-ego and the id, together under a fourth category, the personality. But this is done on the old atomistic fallacy of trying to build up to synthesis with the elements of analysis. The subject consists in the differing and conflicting items of ego, super-ego, and id, brought together as a single mental conception by utilizing a fourth and more binding conception—personality.[10] It is impossible to build up to synthesis with merely the elements of analysis: something is always found to be missing. In the case of psychoanalysis, the missing something is brought in under the name of personality, which is merely a term to cover ignorance of the missing synthesis. But this atomistic fallacy always crops up in studies which start with nominalistic presuppositions, as psychoanalysis assuredly does.

It is instructive to note that psychology has run much the same course as has biology, and has met with exactly the same failure in its attempt to supplement the shortcomings of mechanism. First there was the old association psychology, which corresponded to mechanism in biology. The associationists ascribed all psychological happenings to atomic sensations, which were connected with their corresponding behavior patterns by laws of association. This left no accounting for the purposiveness of human nature. The psychology of Freud attempted to remedy this defect. Psychoanalytic psychology corresponds roughly to vitalism in biology. Freud has continued the old faculty or "association" psychology, but has made over the atomic and instinctual elements into something more purposive. But this new substitute, Freudian psychology, merely hides the old defect by supplying sets of sex-urges to provide the necessary teleology. Psycho-

---

10. See Paul Schilder, "Personality in the Light of Psychoanalysis," *The Psychoanalytic Review*, January, 1935.

analysis thus fails to satisfy the scientific demands, which were much more closely met by the old school of psychology, and fails as well to offer an acceptable teleological psychology.

The extremely negative criticism which I have been setting forth might lead the reader to believe that the whole study and practice of psychoanalysis has gone for nothing. This is simply not true, nor is it what I have been trying to say in this chapter. On the theoretical side, psychoanalysis has accomplished much by discovering and emphasizing certain functions and processes which were hardly known before, or if they were known at least overlooked. The calling of attention to the importance of the sexual side of man's nature in his total constitution is the contribution of Freud, just as the focusing of attention on the important part played by the economic side of man's nature in his total constitution is the contribution of Karl Marx. These are the most importunate, but not the most important, aspects of the human being, and certainly we must not overemphasize them to the submergence of everything else. But on the other hand, what is most important can be thoroughly understood only if we understand and study the satisfaction of that which is most importunate.

On the practical side, quite a large pragmatic argument can be adduced in defense of psychoanalysis. Although much harm has undoubtedly resulted from the fact that the practice of psychoanalysis came to be the fashion, and has therefore been followed by many self-made neurotics who are cursed with much idleness, the astonishing cures effected by psychoanalysis in cases of neuroses and psychoses call for further discussion of what such success is due to.

This clinical success seems to be due to two factors: (1) The claims of psychoanalysis to the status of science, and the fact that science has taken the place of religion as the discoverer of the real in the popular imagination, give the practitioner of psychoanalysis all the faith he requires, a faith which is comparable only to the Catholic confessional and to special Catholic cures, such as the one at Lourdes. Thus on the sufferer's side there is complete acceptance and acquiescence, always a primary requirement, and a help even in the practice of medicine. (2) On the practitioner's side it is important to remember that, although what he does is done in the name of irrational mysteries, the practice of psychoanalysis is an affair strictly answerable to logic. The neurotic or psychotic suffers from what may be described as a false logical nexus, the association of ideas which have no justification for belonging together. The psychoanalyst calmly explains, frequently giving the reasons, why the elements of the false logical nexus must be dissociated. What he is unable to do, obviously, is to reassociate the ideas in their correct order. For this latter service it is necessary to begin with a complete metaphysics, a cosmology in terms of which all ideas can be judged true or false. This the psychoanalyst, being an irrationalist, is not equipped for, and his study, claiming to be a science, avoids metaphysics rather than offers it.

But the need for a metaphysics remains, and metaphysics is only made possible by the change from an implicit nominalism, such as now prevails in psychoanalysis, to an explicit realism. Such a change in basic presupposition could only confirm the present desire of psychology to be a science, but would make it possible to be a true science. The subject matter of psychoanalysis would have to be taken into account, but despite the importance of the psychoanalytic subject-matter and the logicality of much of its practice, it may be necessary to abandon most (if not all) of what has been done thus far, and to make an entirely fresh start.

We may conclude by noting that psychoanalysis as at present constituted is not a science. It frankly imitates the science of physics, but whereas physics is nominalistic in theory and realistic in practice, psychoanalysis is nominalistic throughout. Psychoanalysis accepts the sole reality of physical particulars and proceeds to erect unreal mental entities and processes. These mental entities and processes it names without explaining, as though to name a process were to explain enough. The entities and processes of psychoanalysis are irrational and unscientific, and therefore for science appear unduly dogmatic and fickle. One method by which imposters always manage to make themselves feel at home is to join in the fight on the common enemy, and so it is amusing to listen as Dr. Freud does battle[11] with what is usually considered (mistakenly enough) to be the common enemy of science: religion. The new physicists understand a little more, for although they fail to reconcile their science with their religion, they yet see the necessity of retaining both.

In psychoanalysis, scientific method is completely misunderstood, and inductions made at the level of enlightened common sense are taken for both the highly abstractive inductions and the experimentation of physical science. The result is an inchoate and unjustified division of mentality into three separate entities, improperly defined and contradictory. The attempt to reassemble these entities back into the conception of a unified mentality under the fourth term of personality, reveals the kind of confused thinking which takes place in psychoanalysis. Most certainly cures have been effected, and the whole of psychoanalytic theory and practice has not gone for nothing. But it may prove necessary to abandon most of what has been done in favor of a fresh start, in order to establish what has been heretofore covered by the theory and practice of psychoanalysis on a sound and more permanent and rational scientific basis. Before any branch of psychology can be a science, that is to say, before any branch of psychology can achieve results on which later investigators can build by starting from each other's work, as in physics, and not by merely departing from each other's work, as in psychoanalysis, it will be necessary to comprehend scientific method, and to apply it in the most thoroughgoing manner. In this way, and only in this way, can a unanimity of agreement be reached in psychoanalysis, comparable to that which now prevails in the natural sciences.

---

11. *Op. cit.*, pp. 219 ff.

XV

Individual Psychology and the Ethics of Peirce

IT IS THE PURPOSE of this chapter to show the relation of Peirce's logical ethics to Adler's ethical psychology. Peirce's work preceded Adler's, and it is highly improbable that Adler has been influenced in any direct way by the writings of Peirce. The relation between the two systems is a logical rather than a historical one.

In an earlier chapter we have set forth the essence of Peirce's ethics. Starting from an analysis of the mathematical theory of probability, Peirce sought to show that that individual is illogical who confines his interests to any finite thing or event. To limit one's loyalty to a given person or collection of persons is to suffer contradiction, since we have good reason to suppose that every actual organization is finite and that none can survive forever. Each person, each group, each civilization, comes to its end sooner or later; and to pin eternal faith to something that cannot possibly be eternal is obviously fatal.

Thus what started out as a logical point concludes as the first principle of all ethics, which is that to be logical one cannot be selfish, either in terms of himself or of any limited group with which he may conceive of identifying himself. He must instead identify his interests with those of an unlimited community, an infinite community, transcending all times and spaces, extending back into the past as well as forward into the future, a community consisting of all living persons as well as of those yet unborn, though not confined to human beings, either, but reaching, in Peirce's words, beyond "all geological epochs, beyond all bounds."

Another way to formulate Peirce's principle would be to say that man is a finite part of the infinite whole, from which he is only quasi-separated and to which he must some day return. If, then, he is part of the great whole and independent only as fiction, he must act ethically in a way that would benefit not his independent and discrete self but the whole of which he is a part. It is this whole, this totality of existence, that is the entity to which he owes his ethical allegiance. He must identify his interests with an unlimited community.

This community, however, is seen from the perspective possible to any part of the whole as an ascending organizational series of parts. From the point of view of the individual, society appears as the next upward step in inclusiveness of existence. Therefore the individual must identify his interests with those of society. But this society or community is not an end but the means to a further end, and thus must appear as a community, an *unlimited* community to which man ethically aspires and is loyal.

So much for Peirce; now let us turn to Adler.

Of all the psychoanalytic schools which have in some way derived from the work of Freud and his followers, the school of individual psychology of Alfred Adler presents itself as the most realistic. By "realistic" here is intended the medieval scholastic meaning of the term: what is real is objective and independent of the knowledge process. The psychological problems of the Adlerian school are the problems of the individual in an objectively real and independent environment. A large part of this environment is constituted of society. "The tasks which are presented to an individual," says Adler, "as well as the means of their performance, are conceived and formulated within the framework of society. Only within this framework is psychology possible at all. Anything that we estimate as valuable, good, right, and normal, we estimate simply in so far as it is 'virtue' from the point of view of an ideal society."

The words might very well be those of Peirce. Both Adler and Peirce deal with individual man at the level of meaning; both ignore as too limited the immediate society or social group in which the individual finds himself immersed; both are led to the doctrine of an ideal and infinite society as the criterion of ethical notions and moral acts; and finally both point the necessity of previsioning logic, ethics, and theology, as forming an integral unity of theory to govern practice.

Although Peirce has shown the logical skeleton on which ethics rests better than has Adler, in one sense Adler may be said to have carried the formulation one step farther than did Peirce. Peirce was concerned directly with ethics, and therefore the implications for practice which are present in his doctrine were left for others to explore. Adler is a psychologist, and has understood his subject correctly as the study of the apprehension of value. Therefore in his version of the ethical doctrine the participation of the individual is set forth as being more dynamic, purposive, and responsive, than in Peirce's. Apparently, the reconciliation of this conception of the self-determination of the individual with the realistic understanding of the individual as reacting to external stimulation, is the central problem with which Adler has always been struggling.

Such a reconciliation is contained by implication in the writings of Peirce, for despite Peirce's manifest and indeed admitted antipathy to psychology, his ethics are enormously fruitful in suggestions for psychological investigation, and his hints toward the establishment of a realistic psychology are capable of doing more to provide that science with a firm metaphysical footing than the works of any other philosopher. Psychology is the science which has suffered most from the errors consequent upon the implicit acceptance of the nominalistic philosophy. It is because Peirce saw the main issue of philosophy as the struggle of realism against nominalism and laid the basis for a realistic philosophy consistent with science and scientific method that he was able to provide a realistic outline of psychology.

His work in this direction lies close to that of Adler, who has, somewhat more intuitively, arrived at the same realistic psychology. But the fact that the identical ethical and psychological conclusions have been arrived at from two entirely different avenues of approach can only serve to strengthen the mutual positions, and moreover, to indicate the existence of some genuine underlying truths. For this reason it has seemed worth while to show the doctrines that Peirce and Adler hold in common.

Index

(*See also* Index of Names, p. 331)

Absolute humanism, 18
Absolutes, necessity for, 96
Action and understanding, 98
Actual entities, 61; as feeling subjects, 73
Actuality, and possibility, 118 ff.; as limited, 97; value as content of, 267
Adler and Peirce, 322
American men of letters, slow recognition of, 31
Appearance and reality, 118
Archaism, 190 f.
Aristotelian and symbolic logic, 294
Aristotle's attack on Platonic theory of ideas, 111
Arithmetic contradiction, 280
Astronomical systems, 123
Authority, appeal to, 11
Availability of heroes, 197

Barbarization in art, 199
Being, abstractness of, 113; and existence, 5; confused with knowledge, 89; described, 5, 282
Breakdown of civilizations, 167, 184 f.
Burali-Forti's contradiction, 279

Cause-and-effect, as undemonstrable, 17
Cell-theory of all actuality, 66
Censor, 310
Chain of being, 101 ff.; craving for, 130; failures of, 130 ff.; fruitfulness of, 129 ff.; shortcomings of, 125 ff.; temporalizing of, 122
Challenge-and-response, 180 f.
Change, reflexive argument against, 96
Charm versus force, 188 f.
Christianity, achievement of, 206
Church vs. science, 225
Civilization, future of, 210; indeterminism of, 211
Civilized epics, 198
Class membership, as place in system, 299
Classes, "abolition" of, 273
Classics, rediscovery of, 13
Common sense, as primitive judgments, 21; philosophy of, 20; school, as precursor of modern realism, 21
Conceptualism, 8
Consequences and time categories, 143
Continuity, discussed, 104 f.; principle of, 101
Correspondence, 227
Cosmic purpose, as push or pull, 132
Cosmogony, modern, 160 f.
Cosmological, categories, Whitehead's and Spinoza's compared, 77; contradictions in organic philosophy, 56
Cosmology, of nominalism, 15; of seventeenth century empiricists, 56; of *Timaeus,* 56; of Whitehead, 76

INDEX

Creative minority, 182
Critical common-sensism, 22
Cryptic and ostensive ontologies, 89
Culture, as philosophy in practice, 13

Deducibility, 301; and implication, 299 f.
Definition, absence of in Toynbee, 177
Democracy and industrialism, 207
Detachment, 191 f.
Determinism of history in Toynbee, 171
Discontinuity, privation and inequality, 121
Disintegration of civilizations, 167, 186 f.
Dominant minorities, 168

Ego, 308
Eighteenth-century biology, 125
Emphasis on practice, 236
Empiricism, 13; as anti-rational, 14
Epic poetry, 196 f.
Epistemological, contradictions in organic philosophy, 55; realism, 6, 22
Epistemology, and ontology, 90; and organic philosophy, 54; modern, 16
Essence and existence, 116
Eternal objects, 57 f.; criticism of, 59 f.
Etherialization, 182
Ethics, first principle of, 320; of Peirce, 41 f.; of pragmatism, 40; of unlimited community, 321
Europe as source of theory, 235
European philosophy as nominalistic, 16
Evil, problem of, 107
Existence, and being, 5; and essence, 116; as seeking fullness, 119; described, 5; imperfections of, 120; problem of as required by being, 133
Experience, and inquiry, 87; opposed to subjective idealism, 86; philosophy of, 85 ff.; universality of, 87
Experiment, and logic, 253
Experimental study of nature, 13
Extension and intension, 298
External proletariat, 168

Extreme empiricism, fallacy of, 228

Fact, testimony of, 21; value and logic words, as distinguished, 267
Fallacies of historicism, 27
First principle of ethics, 320
Firstness, 34
Fisher's "population of possibilities," 141
Folk epics, 197
Fossils, as organized, 124
Futurism, 190 f.

Genesis, of civilizations, 165 f., 179 f.; stimulated by challenges, 166
Gentleness and violence, 190
God, as irrational ground of rationality, 134; natures of, 79
God's will, 120
Gradation, discussed, 106 f.
Greece, 154
Greek, knowledge, still of value, 162; psychology, 159 f.; world, as theatre of ideas, 4
Greeks, and psychology, 156, 159; modern view of, 153
Growth of civilizations, 166 f., 181 f.

Historical fallacy, 312 f.
History, and human nature, 215; of a theory, a series of misunderstandings, 45
Human nature, and history, 215; as absolute, 18; as starting-point, 20
Hypothesis, 227; role of, 144; testing of, 228

Id, 308
Idea, in James's philosophy, 139; of The Good, 117
Idealism, and realism, 108 f.; confused with realism, 8; Dewey's attack on, 84; fallacy of, 296, attacked, 116 f.; of church, 10
Ideals and actuality, 279
Ideas as essences in Plato, 100
Implication, 300; and deducibility, 299 f.

INDEX 327

Individual, importance of, 109
Individual psychology, 321 f.; and Peirce's ethics, 322
Induction, 226
Inequality, discontinuity and privation, 121
Infinity, paradoxes of, 105
Inquiry, and experience, 87; confused with metaphysical inquiry, 88; instigation of, 229; theory of, 88
Instrumentalism, objectivity of, 94
Intension and extension, 298
Internal proletariat, 168; as source of civilization, 180
Introvert, 310
Inverse probability, error of, 147

James's method, not that of science, 145 f.; consistent with inverse probability, 147 f.
James's pragmatism, differs from Peirce's, 148 f.

Knowing, problem of, 19
Knowledge, confused with being, 89; of logical relations, 292; relation, as one among many, 91

Language, and myth, 112; limitations of, 112; two kinds of reference of, 277
Levels, of abstraction, 265; of being, as human trap, 134
Life-Force and Monism, 128
Limited rationality, attack on, 123 f.
Linguistic contradiction, 280
Living as inquiry, 88
Logic, 264; and experiment, 253; and particular objects, 278; and relations, 291; and value, in order of being, 266; defined, 290; field of, 291; in human culture, 204 f.; of pragmatism, 38; value and fact words, as distinguished, 267; words, 265; words, as abstraction from value words, 265
Logical atomism of Russell, 23
Logical constants, 277

Logical positivists, 44 f.
Logical positivism, 232; and symbolic logic, 289; doctrines of, 285; Russell's rejection of, 284
Logical properties, as non-actual, 275; relations, knowledge of, 292

Many and One, 113
Marx and Toynbee, 213 f.
Marxism, Toynbee's attack on, 207
Mathematics, entities of, 283
Meaning, in metaphysics, 50; modern views of, 260; of words, in Russell, 281
Mental personality, elements of, 308
Mentality, psychoanalytic conception of, 315
Metaphysical, categories, of Peirce, 34; interpretation, difficulties of, 286; levels, 5
Metaphysics, as postulates for action, 39
Method of science, as realistic, 306; meaning of, 252; preference of scientist for, 247
Method of Toynbee, 173 f.
Modified realism, 271
Monism and Life-Force, 128
Monistic philosophies, 81
Monomaniac philosophers, 85
Myth and language, 112

Names, as fact words, 266
Natural, and revealed theology, 11; law, 226
Nature as eternal law, 246
Nature's grand syllogism, 226
Negative prehension, 69 f.
Neo-Platonic, philosophies, 6; philosophy, 118
Neo-Platonism, 9
Nexus, 67 f.
Nominalism, defined, 7; determines Renaissance culture, 13; doctrine of, 155 f.; importance of, 109; in philosophy, 14; in science, 14; in sixth century, 6; of Kant, 19; of Occam, 12;

origins of, 7; prevalence of, 19; subdivisions of, 9; triumph of, 10
Nominalistic cosmology, 15
Nominalists, as politicians, 155
Non-being, as positive difference, 70
Nous and *psyche,* 314
Null-class, 295

Objectivity, 74
Occam's "Razor," 131, 234
One and Many, 113
One-idead philosophy as overemphasis, 95 f.
Ontological, contradictions in organic philosophy, 55; dualism in Toynbee, 169; principle, 62
Ontology, and epistemology, 90; and semantics, 258; and theology, 79; rise of, 47
Operational definition of science, 242
Operationalism, 233
Optimism in eighteenth century, 104
Oral type, 310
Organic philosophy, and epistemology, 54; and others, 52 f.; inclusiveness of, 75; of Whitehead, 25; origins of, 48; terminology of, 49; theology of, 79
Organism, philosophy of, 46 ff.
Origin of pattern of history in Toynbee, 175
Origins of nominalism, 7
Ostensive, and cryptic ontologies, 89; philosophy of Dewey, inconsistencies of, 93
Otherworldliness, and thisworldliness, 110; in Toynbee's system, 202 f.

Particular objects, and logic, 278
Past, reversion to, 209
Peirce, and Adler, 322; life of, 32 ff.
Peirce's ethics, and individual psychology, 322
Philosophers, and scientists, 223; as monomaniacs, 85; attitudes of, 224
Philosophers in Toynbee, 194 f.
Philosophy, and religion, 195; and science, proper relations of, 237; as cultural development, 94; as profession, 223; as social shock, 81; class origins of, 195 f.; function of, 196; of organism, 46 ff., original notions of, 65; of science, 14, denial of, 236; scope of, 239, task of, 238; of Toynbee, 172
Platonic, Ideas, 118, 119; philosophy, two strains of, 129; theory of ideas, meant seriously, 112; theory of realism, 111
Plenitude, discussed, 102 f.; principle of, 100
Politics, Greek influence on, 158
Positivism, danger of, 234
Possibilities, 264; enforced actualization of, 119
Possibility, 103; and actuality, 118 ff.; in symbolic logic, 293
Postulates, acknowledged in Toynbee's system, 169
Practical consequences, meaning of, 139
Practice, and theory, 235
Pragmatic theory of truth, 138
Pragmatism, and scientific method, 142 f.; as branch of epistemology, 139; as realistic, 37; of James, 39 f., criticized, 40; of Peirce, 36 f.
Predictions, in Toynbee, 210; of Toynbee's system, 206 f.
Prehension, 67
Pre-Socratics, 5
Privation, discontinuity and inequality, 121
Probabilities in science, 230
Probability statistics of Fisher, 141
Process, as ultimate, 74; of disintegration, 167
Protestant Christianity, cultural trend toward, 178
Protestantism, 11
Psyche and *nous,* 314
Psychoanalysis, abstractions of, 310; as fashion, 306; clinical success of, 317; entities of, 309; evaluation of, 318; looseness of method in, 312; metaphysics of, 308; scientific aims of,

INDEX

311; scientific claims of, 306; scientific experiments in, 311; value of, 317
Psychological meaning of word, 259
Psychologistic fallacy, 68
Psychology, and the Greeks, 156, 159; follows biology, 316; of Greeks, 159 f.

Range of historical knowledge, 173
Rational dogmatism, fallacy of, 228
Rationalism and reality, 122 ff.
Reaction, world of, 262
Realism, and idealism, 108 f.; and scientific method, 240; argument against, 274; confused with idealism, 8; description of, 271; distinguished from idealism, 110; first great modern system of, 46; history of English, 22 ff.; in epistemology, 6; Lovejoy's rejection of, 111 f.; modern school of, 26; of Russell, 281, 283; of Schelling, 127 f.; of Schiller, 127 f.; of Spinoza, 15; opposed to idealism and materialism, 92; overstatement of, 271; pioneer of, 3; recurrence of in modern world, 3; secular, 22; subtle balance of, 64; unsolved problems of, 133 ff.
Realism-nominalism controversy, in Peirce, 33
Realist, literary meaning as materialist, 6
Realistic, definition of science, 243; fallacy, and Whitehead, 63
Reality, and rationalism, 122 ff.; and the metaphysical levels, 5; and truth, 140; of external world, 21; of relations, denial of, 281
Reference, of word, indirect, 262; two kinds of, 274
Relations, having being and being known, 6
Religion, and philosophy, 195; as goal of Toynbee's system, 189; as product of disintegration, 188
Religious belief, decline of, 208
Revealed and natural theology, 11
Rise of science, 13

Russell, changes in views of, 269 f.

Sacrament of the Eucharist, 7
Saint, as biological mutation, 185
Scepticism, feigned of Descartes, 15; of Hume, 17
Science, aim of, 244; and philosophy, proper relations of, 237; as antirational, 225; as pursuit of truth, 201; assumptions of, 226; business of, 314; complementary movements in, 228; condemnation of by Toynbee, 208; confused with technology, 200 f.; goal of, 232; Greek influence on, 157; history of, 224 f.; ideal of, 249; marred by its history, 224; philosophy and method, 251; rise of, 13; value of, 205; vs. the Church, 225
Scientific, laws as finders of facts, 307; method, 226 f., 245, and pragmatism compared, 142 f., realism of, 142, summarized, 246; view of philosophy, 241
Scientists, and philosophers, 223
Secondness, 35
Semantics, and ontology, 258
Sensation, validity of, 20 f.
Sensationalist principle, 71
Senses, Reid's trust in, 20
Social progressivism, as Dewey's absolute, 96
Societies, as species, 165
Socrates, issue with Sophists, 154
Solipsism and catatonia, 82
Sophists, issue with Socrates, 154
Species of societies, 165
Specific implication, 292 f.
Spengler, and Toynbee, 214 f.; parochialism of, 216
Subjective, idealism, 17, criticism of, 92; terms and objective processes, 72
Subjectivism of Berkeley, 16 f.
Subjectivist principle, 71
Superego, 308
Supernaturalism in morals of Toynbee, 171
Symbolic and Aristotelian logic, 294

Symbolic logic, as value-free, 302; interpretation of, 276; metaphysics of, 288; subordinates Aristotelian, 299
Sympathetic approach to philosophy, 82
System, of natural law, presumed by science, 231; of Toynbee, as closed, 179, shortcomings of, 198
Systems of knowledge, as closed, 125

Temporalizing of chain of being, 131
Terms of psychoanalysis, 305
Theology, and ontology, 79; of Whitehead, 78
Theory, and practice, 235; of descriptions, 272; of science, increasing interest in, 248; of Toynbee, value of, 217 f.
Thirdness, 35
Thisworldliness and otherworldliness, 110
Three philosophies, in Plato, 4
Time, categories and consequences, 143; left unexplained by chain of being, 130
Toynbee, charm of style, 176 f.
Toynbee, and Marx, 213 f.; and Spengler, 214 f.; and the specialist, 174; and Vico, 212
Transcendental theology, 202
Transcendentalism in theology of Toynbee, 170

Transfiguration, 191 f.
Triangle of reference, 262
True realism, 115
Truth, as matter of consequences, 140; objectivity of, 21; pragmatic theory of, 138

Understanding and action, 98
Unit-class, 297
Unity of universe, 114
Universal, churches, 187 f.; states, 193 f.
Universals, 264; status of, 9
Unlimited community, 42 f., 320
Unmoved Mover, 131, 132
Unsolved problems of realism, 133 ff.

Validity of systems, 123
Value and logic, in order of being, 266
Value, logic, and fact words as distinguished, 267
Value words, 265
Verification, as criterion, 234
Vico and Toynbee, 212
Violence and gentleness, 190

Western civilization, future of, 211
Whitehead, as Platonist, 51
Withdrawal-and-return, 183
Word, as symbol of idea, 261; as universal, 261; meaning of, 258; reference of, 260

Index of Names

Abbot, F. E., 34
Abelard, 8
Adler, Alfred, 320, 321, 323
Albertus Magnus, 9
Alexander of Egypt, 224
Alexander the Great, 197
Alexander, Samuel, 24, 208
Anaximander, 5
Antisthenes, 196
Aquinas, Thomas, 9, 11, 195
Aristotle, 7, 8, 11, 33, 38, 51, 64, 101, 111, 112, 130, 153, 154, 157, 158, 159, 163, 175, 195, 288, 294, 298, 314
Augustine, 9, 54, 120, 191
Averroes, 115
Avicenna, 9, 115, 124, 145

Bach, J. S., 185
Bacon, Francis, 122, 245, 263
Basil Digénis Akrítas, 197
Berengar, 7, 12, 251
Bergson, Henri, 52, 53, 98, 172, 195
Berkeley, Bishop, 16, 17, 75, 76
Boethius, 7
Boole, John, 31
Boyle, Sir Robert, 253
Bridgman, Professor P. W., 233, 242, 243, 244, 247, 251, 285, 290
Brouwer, 257
Burali-Forti, 279
Burtt, E. A., 251

Cantor, George, 280
Carnap, Rudolf, 28, 233, 257, 285, 286, 287
Carrel, Alexis, 248, 249
Cézanne, 199
Champeaux, William of, 8
Cohen, Professor Morris R., 31, 158, 243, 244
Comte, Auguste, 208
Cook, Wilson, 23, 24
Copernicus, 14, 122, 253
Cleomenes, 175
Cusa, Nicolas Cardinal of, 54, 158

Dante, 198
Darwin, 248
de Morgan, Augustus, 280
Derham, William, 116
Descartes, René, 14, 15, 16, 20, 26, 51, 52, 54, 61, 75, 77, 120, 195, 208
Dewey, John, 28, 44, 45, 52, 53, 84, 85, 86, 87, 88, 89, 90, 91, 92, 93, 94, 95, 96, 97, 98
Diogenes, 196
Duns Scotus, 9, 10, 32, 34, 45, 54

Einstein, Albert, 200, 223, 248, 249, 253, 291
Engels, Frederich, 213
Epictetus, 196
Epicurus, 196

331

INDEX OF NAMES

Euclid, 153, 154

Faraday, 200
Fenelon, E., 103
Fisher, R. A., 138, 141, 142, 143, 146, 147
Fosdick, Raymond, 235
Frazer, J. G., 193
Frege, 31
Freud, Sigmund, 305, 306, 308, 312, 313, 314, 315, 316, 317, 319, 321

Galileo, 14, 15, 253
Gautama, 196
Ghandi, 196
God, 88, 117, 128, 129, 131, 133, 134, 192, 205
Goethe, 198, 219
Gracchi, 175
Gregory the VII, 209

Hartmann, Nicolai, 26, 246
Haserot, Francis S., 26, 105
Hegel, 158, 208
Heraclitus, 5, 158
Hicks, G. Dawes, 22
Hook, Sidney, 44, 45
Hume, David, 16, 17, 18, 20, 21, 24, 26, 48, 51, 52, 55, 75
Huxley, Thomas H., 205

Iamblichus, 201
Ikhnaton, 196

Jaeger, Werner, 111, 112
Jaffe, Bernard, 247
James, William, 38, 39, 40, 44, 51, 52, 53, 115, 137, 138, 139, 140, 141, 142, 143, 144, 145, 146, 147, 148, 149, 150
Jastrow, Joseph, 33
Jesus, 50, 193, 205, 206
Joad, Professor C. E. M., 306, 309, 310
Jones, Dr. Ernest, 309
Jordan, E., 26

Kant, Immanuel, 12, 16, 18, 19, 20, 22, 32, 52, 72, 73, 105, 122, 156, 208

Kepler, 14

Laird, John, 25
Lao-Tse, 196
Lavoisier, 253
Leibniz, Gottfried, 17, 20, 75, 104, 284
Lenzen, V. F., 247
Lincoln, Abraham, 183, 300
Linnaeus, 243
Locke, John, 16, 17, 52, 55, 65, 75, 155
Lotze, 283, 284, 285
Lovejoy, Arthur O., 99, 100, 101, 102, 104, 105, 106, 107, 109, 110, 111, 112, 113, 114, 115, 116, 117, 119, 120, 121, 122, 124, 125, 126, 127, 129, 130, 133, 134, 135, 136
Lucretius, 211

Mach, E., 251, 283, 284, 289
Mani Mahavira, 196
Maritain, Jacques, 26
Marx, Karl, 44, 158, 208, 212, 213, 214, 317
Melville, Herman, 31
Milton, 198
Montague, W. P., 26
Moore, G. E., 23, 24, 25, 54, 208, 284, 285
Morgan, Augustus de, 280
Morgan, Thomas Hunt, 245
Moses, 196

Nanak, 196
Napoleon, 183
Newton, Isaac, 15, 52, 200, 230, 231, 248, 253

Occam, William of, 12, 32, 251

Parmenides, 5
Paul, 188
Peirce, Charles S., 17, 22, 31, 32, 33, 34, 35, 36, 37, 38, 39, 40, 41, 42, 43, 44, 45, 51, 113, 115, 137, 149, 150, 226, 245, 251, 299, 307, 320, 321, 322
Pepper, Professor, 289
Planck, 200, 248, 249, 291

INDEX OF NAMES

Plato, 3, 4, 5, 6, 8, 11, 41, 45, 51, 57, 59, 64, 65, 70, 75, 83, 100, 101, 110, 111, 112, 113, 116, 117, 124, 129, 130, 136, 155, 157, 159, 175, 194, 249, 263, 274, 298
Plotinus, 9
Poe, Edgar A., 31
Poincaré, 245
Porphyry of Tyre, 7
Proclus, 201
Pseudo-Dionysius, 115, 119
Pyrrho of Elis, 7
Pythagoras, 153, 157

Quine, W. V., 289, 302

Ramsey, 280
Reid, Thomas, 18, 19, 20, 21, 22, 23, 24, 25, 26, 54
Ritter, C., 111, 112
Robinet, 124
Roosevelt, Franklin D., 208
Roscellinus, 7, 12, 251
Royce, Josiah, 44
Russell, Bertrand, 24, 25, 241, 257, 270, 271, 272, 273, 274, 275, 276, 277, 278, 279, 280, 281, 282, 283, 284, 285, 286, 287, 302
Ruysbroek, Jan van, 11

St. Dominic, 189
St. Francis, 11, 185, 196
Santayana, George, 26, 224
Schelling, 128, 129
Schiller, 126, 127, 132
Scotus Erigena, 129
Sextus Empiricus, 7

Shorey, Paul, 111
Smuts, 172, 176, 195
Socrates, 3, 5, 154, 155, 157, 196, 278, 279
Spengler, Oswald, 200, 212, 214, 215, 216, 217
Speusippus, 8, 112
Spinoza, 15, 20, 75, 77, 78, 80, 81, 104, 107, 108, 116, 117, 196
Spinozism, 117
Stevenson, 120
Stout, G. F., 24

Thales, 153
Thomas, Norman, 208
Thomas Aquinas, 9, 11, 195
Toynbee, Professor Arnold J., 28, 164, 165, 168-182, 184-220

Ushenko, 300

Velasquez, 185, 199
Vico, G., 212, 213
Voltaire, 107, 108

Wexberg, Dr. Irwin, 315
Whitehead, Alfred N., 25, 38, 46-75, 77-81, 83, 97, 112, 120, 124, 128, 130, 134, 208, 239, 257, 274, 276, 288, 302
Whitman, Walt, 31
Wilson, Cook, 23, 24
Wittgenstein, Professor L. von, 242, 243, 244, 285
Wolff, Christian, 17

Xenocrates, 112